PRISONERS
OF THE
PRESENT TENSE

PRISONERS
OF THE
PRESENT TENSE

And the Cult of Laissez-Faire

DEAN EKOLA

authorHOUSE®

AuthorHouse™ LLC
1663 Liberty Drive
Bloomington, IN 47403
www.authorhouse.com
Phone: 1-800-839-8640

Published by AuthorHouse   08/22/2013

ISBN: 978-1-4772-9214-3 (sc)
ISBN: 978-1-4772-9213-6 (hc)
ISBN: 978-1-4772-9212-9 (e)

Library of Congress Control Number: 2012921824

PREFACE

I must admit that structurally this is an odd piece of work. It has a rambling, helter-skelter quality, almost as if it were written by a madman - or someone in the throes of Alzheimer's. As a result, it is not so organized as to make it amenable to a refined table of contents. In fact that is one of my biggest regrets about this book: it lacks the structure expected of a disciplined academic. Nor should that surprise, since I lack such credentials. Nevertheless, I do take satisfaction in the finished product because it is documented extensively and provides insights seldom discussed in our public debates about political economy. I also take a dogged satisfaction in it because its lack of structure is a reflection of the evolutionary process that guided its progress.

Specifically, over the course of the past nine years, this book was revised, corrected and rewritten numerous times as my earlier interpretations were undermined by an ongoing process of inquiry and due diligence. Then several years into this process, the tone and overview of this work were nearly trashed anew by the cataclysmic events of the financial/economic crisis of 2007-09.

This brought on new paths of inquiry, more revised interpretations and another spate of major rewriting. All of this added to the storm-tossed character of this work. Hence on balance, despite its structural faults, I am satisfied that this is a book worth reading because it brings to light numerous forgotten gems of our intellectual heritage highlighting a journey of discovery through one of the most tumultuous periods of our nation's economic history. As to the table of contents, I am providing a very rudimentary one so that the reader may access its extensive index and endnotes with greater ease.

Dean Ekola
June 11, 2013

CONTENTS

Introduction

The power attributed exclusively to the 'rugged individual' in American culture is so exaggerated it ignores the role of social and familial nurture in the creation of a successful culture and successful individuals. This lack of proportion creates a psychologically untenable condition focusing disproportionately on ego, power and acquisition of material wealth. It is untenable because it promotes an unbridled egotism incapable of satisfying the unmet inner needs of the individual. Hence, no achievement is ever great enough to fill the psychological chasm between unsatisfied inner needs and the demands of this arbitrary ideal. Dean Ekola

The final work on this essay is being done in the closing months of the 2012 presidential election campaign. It is a somber time of high unemployment and slow growth brought on by a half-century of chickens - both political and economic - coming home to roost. Unfortunately for the well-being of the nation's future, it is not at all clear that an electoral majority understands the depth of this economic crisis. Many have lost sight of the fact that it started in 2007 and, by the closing months of 2008, developed all of the destructive potential of a full-blown depression. The problem with this lack of clarity, of course, is that if you don't realize the depth of your problem, you are prone to stumble right back into the same old policies that brought you down in the first place.

I started this journey 8 years ago because I could not understand why the Democratic nominee for president in 2004, John Kerrey, lost the election. He understood the fiscal perils of the Bush tax cuts, made an impressive showing in his debates with President George W. Bush and was a decorated combat veteran of the Vietnam War. In short, there was no question in my mind that Kerry was the slam-dunk favorite to win the presidency. His loss was not only a shock, but also a wake-up call that many of my assumptions about American politics were just plain wrong. I especially did not understand the unique manner in which a substantial number of Americans interpret the interrelated subjects of politics, religion and economics.

Their unique interpretation is based, in part, on the assumption that free markets, unfettered by government involvement, create a smoothly functioning economy beneficial to everyone. And these free markets perform their marvelous task without anyone having to consciously steer them. It's amazing. Moreover, for many, this assumption is reinforced by a religious explanation of human existence, based on the biblical account of human creation. This latter wrinkle is even more amazing. It involves nothing less than a belief in the divine creation of the human species and, for many, a time line beginning this process a mere four to six thousand years ago. Equally noteworthy is the fact that, for many, this divine intervention extends to the discovery, colonization and independence of the United States. In short, in the eyes of both the Almighty and many Americans, we are pretty much a chosen people. Naturally, as might be expected with something plucked right out of the divine cupboard, both of these immaculate conceptions share a predisposition toward magical thinking processes.

The economic component of this magical ideology often is referred to as laissez-faire economics, because that is what it was called when one of the first economists, a Frenchman, conjured up the concept and coined the term in the 1700s. It is worth noting, though, this theory initially held that land and agriculture were the only sources of a nation's wealth. Everything else was a distraction and a detriment to these singularly productive pursuits. All that was needed then was for everyone to get out of the way of those who owned and worked the land. Left to their own devices, those in the agricultural sector would produce such bounty that everyone's needs would be met. As our discussion progresses, we will see the significance - and the irony - of this narrowly focused view of economic reality. We will see how the original hero of this antiquated version gets replaced by new heroes. First, farmers get replaced by captains of industry and then, more recently, by entrepreneurs. However, for the moment suffice to say that economic ideas, as with most things, have a way of undergoing enormous changes as they are overrun by the ever-changing tide of circumstance. And one of those big changes today is that our modern iteration of laissez-faire now embraces the entrepreneur as high priest in the cult of this antiquated economic theory.

An important corollary of contemporary laissez-faire is that rational self-interest of free market participants, by itself, is sufficient to keep the economy on course and delivering bountiful results. A natural corollary of this assumption is there is little need for due diligence in gathering the kind of information that is contained in this essay. In fact, there is little need for history. Consequently, as was trumpeted throughout the recent Republican national convention, it does not matter where we have been, it only matters where we are going. After all, to do otherwise only serves to dig up distracting information that detracts from America's essential unity of purpose. And, according to its adherents, such distractions too often play into the hands of those bent on stirring up class warfare and undermining America's special calling as the exceptional nation. To correct these distortions, the following pages will focus on the past as much as necessary to get a clear idea of how we got into our current mess.

Most of us are familiar with the idea of something being a work in progress. In its essence, this phrase acknowledges the reality of changing circumstances and the changes in our perception of that reality. Similarly, at its best, the essence of writing involves the refinement of our perception of that changing reality. Hence, it should come as no surprise that as this work neared completion, I increasingly came to recognize two subjects as elements of bedrock importance in comprehending the intertwined reality of political economy. These two elements are momentum and human capital.

The overriding significance of these two subjects lies in the fact that, while they are critical to an understanding of the economic process, they play no clear role in contemporary mainstream political or economic discussions. One searches in vain through the recent presidential campaign for an explicit mention of economic momentum or a comprehensive discussion of human capital as fixed capital. In short, they are like stealth prime movers. They operate below the surface - unnoticed and unremarked. In this manner they are not unlike the new financial instruments that became trillion dollar wild cards in our economic affairs. The ones Warren Buffet famously baptized as 'financial weapons of mass destruction.' The ones operating out of sight of regulators and financial administrators alike and bringing down enormously destructive forces on all of us because no one was monitoring or regulating them.

The first of these bedrock elements is momentum. While it is a force that crops up occasionally in our descriptions of economic events, it is a force so ubiquitous in our daily lives that we simply do not focus on it - let alone recognize the wide-ranging nature of its impact. As we will discuss in the essay, a big reason we take it for granted can be traced to our evolutionary heritage. In short, the trials of our ancient journey and the physical limitations of our brain forced us to abbreviate our notice of that which does not immediately threaten us. But we may also attribute part of our failure to recognize economic momentum to the incomprehensible magnitude of our economy. At $14 trillion, our gross domestic product (GDP) has grown so vast that it long ago burst the poetic confines of a kitchen-table talk about the family budget.

This is especially true when the analogy must take into account: the predatory dynamics of outsourcing and garden variety greed; the atrophic dynamics of obsolesced human capital and institutional stagnation; the sclerotic impact of costly peak oil on an economy originally built on cheap oil; and an economic conventional wisdom that has failed to sort out the schizoid legacy of Adam Smith. All of these elements - along with numerous others - play key roles in whether our $14 trillion economy ascends, or descends, and the rate at which that movement proceeds. But most important is the recognition that the direction and speed of that movement is an enormously powerful force - given its magnitude - when the elements listed above get seriously out of balance.

The following are a few of those elements that became - and most of which remain - most seriously out of balance: credit default swaps collapsed by the staggering sum of $31.7 trillion between 2007 and 2009; U.S. household net worth lost $16.8 trillion in those same years; and the equity derivatives market - principal funding source for the real estate market - lost $3.2 trillion. Factor in a $7 trillion loss of home equity - as part of the previously cited loss in household net worth - and you begin to get a better idea of just how enormous are the headwinds working against recovery in our $14 trillion economy. These combined losses of $51.7 trillion dwarf our $14 trillion economy by a factor of 369 percent. It would have taken Merlin several lifetimes of alchemy to generate sufficient gold to erase such losses.

The importance of the concept of economic balance was recognized with unique clarity by a presidential commission in the 1920s. As we will see in the following essay, that group anticipated the onset of the Great Depression with its report titled: "Recent Economic Changes in the United States, Volumes 1 and 2." While it is true that it did not literally predict the Great Crash of 1929, which followed its publication by a few months, the report did provide a detailed examination of the dysfunctional elements driving the onset of the depression. It also coined a term - *dynamic equilibrium* - that captured the essence of an advanced economy as a system that either moves up or down in response to the degree it successfully balances the proportional requirements of its main constituent interests. In this manner, the commission broke new ground and recognized the importance of demand to the overall sustainability of the economy. But to our detriment, their appreciation of this critical role, played by balance and demand in the sustainability of our economy, has been swept away by the contemporary belief that supply is all it takes to keep an economy moving forward. Moreover, this long-forgotten commission, consisting of the leading economic thinkers of the period, also broke free of the dominant laissez-faire ideology of the time by asserting a need for public oversight of this process of dynamic equilibrium. And by so doing, it also recognized the Hamiltonian requisite of due diligence. It recognized the reality that automatic doctrines - like supply-side economics or Adam Smith's 'invisible hand' - cannot be counted on as a reliable substitute for economic leadership based on due diligence.

Not having read this report in its entirety, I cannot say for certain if it got down to a level of detail embracing Adam Smith's unique insights into how certain types of labor - those we would call human capital - must be regarded as fixed capital. However, the general thrust of its concept of dynamic equilibrium certainly is compatible with it. And this brings us to a consideration of that second stealth element of bedrock importance to our economic discussion: human capital as fixed capital.

In Adam Smith's world, fixed capital was like seed money. Considered in its traditional agricultural context, a farmer would not consider spending his seed money. Seed money was essential to planting next year's crop and you wouldn't spend that - period. You had to hold that in reserve for its intended purpose. All of this was well understood in the good old days when 95% of the American economy was dependent upon agriculture. People understood that their very survival depended upon their judicious handling of their seed money. But, to our detriment as a self-sustaining society, this sharp focus on the critical importance of seed money got lost as we transitioned through the agro-industrial revolution. On the one hand, the urgency of the concept got buried by the seemingly endless agricultural surpluses spawned by that revolution, while, on the other hand, the productive energies of the nation shifted relentlessly away from seed and the planting of crops. Given the incremental pace of this process, it should not come as a surprise that we failed to recognize that an entirely new fixed capital was replacing seed money. This new fixed capital consisted of those institutions supporting and nurturing human capital on which our new-age bureaucratic industrial economy increasingly depended.

Probably without fully realizing its revolutionary consequences, Adam Smith anticipated this shift in the nature of fixed capital. He did so with his specific views on the "acquired and useful abilities of all the inhabitants or members of society." He regarded these abilities as a "capital fixed and realized, as it were, in his person."* We will discuss this in greater detail in the following essay. But suffice to say for the moment, that Adam Smith laid the foundation for a refined view of the economy in which the educational establishment plays a fundamental role in the wealth creation process. It is the institution that provides human capital - one of the most important fixed capitals of our day.

Our failure to recognize this bedrock role of human capital - and especially government's key role in its creation and maintenance - is not difficult to understand. The traditional view of seed money was something that concerned the individual. The individual farmer was responsible for seeing to it that his family kept an adequate reserve

*The Wealth of Nations, Adam Smith, Penguin Classics, 375 Hudson Street, New York, NY 10014, 1999, page 377.

of seed, or seed money, for next year's crop. But, as the agro-industrial revolution got underway and dramatically increased the need for educational resources, the very small-scale private educational establishment was overtaken in importance by public education. This socialized the educational process for the good and sufficient reason that the need for an education had grown so pervasive that it became a public good, exceeding the resources of both the private education establishment and the individual companies requiring its product.

 The important point is that we never fully absorbed the significance of how the bedrock nature of our ancient fixed capital, seed money, was transformed from an individual responsibility into the social responsibility of public education. This failure of perception also impacts our view of private property. To the degree that we cannot see the role of our public education institutions as an essential source of society's fixed capital, we cannot see how this impacts our view of the gross revenues of society. Instead of viewing these gross revenues as an agglomeration of pots of private property - as is the tendency for most of us - the reality is that a very significant part of those gross revenues consists of society's fixed capital. It is revenue that needs to be reinvested by the public authority responsible for education and research.

In traditional terms, this is society's seed money. It is society's seed money in the same manner that individual entrepreneurs have their own fixed capital requirements. It is society's fixed capital that spells the difference between future productivity increases - or economic stagnation - for the overall economy. It spells the difference between an economy humming along in a state of dynamic equilibrium or one faltering in the grip of unemployment, falling demand and speculative bubbles driven by a lack of genuine investment opportunities. Finally, of course, the means by which this reinvestment takes place is taxation. It is taxation that recovers this fixed capital out of society's gross revenues. It is not a taking - or as some would have it, a theft - of someone's personal property. It is a necessary process of reinvestment, without which the overall economy inflates, stagnates and falters.

The recent Republican National Convention illustrated the depth of our national confusion on these subjects. There was a near total eclipse of historical reference to the origins and causes of our current economic crisis. As we will see, such a blind eye to the past is essential if you wish to avoid an honest discussion of the truly massive deflationary forces undermining our economy before Obama assumed the presidency. Similarly, such a blind eye is essential if you wish to avoid an honest discussion of the actual trajectory of unemployment, falling GDP and growing gross national debt. Hence, one of the main background themes of the convention: it doesn't matter where we've come from, only where we are going.

But that's only part of the story. Aside from these historically uninformed attacks upon Obama's record, most speakers focused the balance of their energy on the role of entrepreneurs. Indeed, one could say that the main theme of the convention was to glorify the role of the entrepreneur - and, in particular, Mitt Romney's role as entrepreneur - as if the economy depended exclusively upon them for the value of its output. This brings us back to the historical context, previously noted, that such a skewed vision of reality resembles the similarly lopsided theories of the original proponents of laissez-faire - with the one exception that the latter regarded agriculture as the sole source of economic value.

It just goes to show that as times change, so do our economic doctrines. Hence, at the time our Founding Fathers were crafting our Declaration of Independence and Constitution, the leading school of laissez-faire was convinced that nothing but agriculture mattered. By way of contrast, today's leading school of laissez-faire holds that only entrepreneurs matter; because - in their view - only an entrepreneur has the keen insights essential to an accurate diagnosis of economic ills. However, as a practical matter, the backward focus of new-age Republican economic theory advocates for economic practices that were appropriate to a rural-based agrarian society - not a new-age techno-urban civilization.

Quite simply, this is the essence of the enormous time-warp that separates the backward focus of new-age Republicans from forward-looking Democrats. The former look back to a time that systemically was more congenial to a laissez-faire view of political economy than the present. But even then, laissez-faire taken to extremes did not work. And as we will see, that is the too-often neglected story of our Constitutional Convention. That is the story of how our Founding Fathers initial attempt at governance failed. It failed due to an excess of laissez-faire in their statecraft. This failure of our *First Confederacy* failed due to a lack of central government authority and power. Of course, this reality does not sit well with all those Tea-Party denizens, running around in their tri-cornered hats. They want to return to the womb of the American Revolution and take another shot at that basket-case of a government.

The reality is that some two centuries of agro-industrial revolution separate us from those simpler times. And within the space of the last half-century, an even more dramatic techno-digital revolution has occurred. These revolutions have generated - and been driven by - the astounding evolution of human capital. This is a form of capital that is wholly dependent on a deliberate program of constant renewal. It not only cannot thrive on a diet of laissez-faire, it cannot survive on a diet of laissez-faire.

This brings us to the title of this work: *Prisoners of the Present Tense and the Cult of Laissez-Faire.* As it suggests, we have neglected our history and embraced a magical doctrine of economics - unburdened by the demands of due diligence. By neglecting our history, we have avoided coming to terms with the reality that we are a hybrid economy. We are a hybrid economy consisting of both private and public components. Indeed, we are a composite socialist-free market economy in that the state does own the public education system and a variety of public research facilities. These state-owned institutions are significant contributors to the wealth-creation process and fit the definition of socialism. But that does not make our entire economy socialist - only those parts long-ago deemed necessary for the production of public goods. Nor does it make the educational sector entirely socialist. Approximately 56 percent of college/university level education was provided by private institutions in 2006-07.[**]

In the past these two parts of our hybrid economy coexisted reasonably well. In fact, we have enjoyed periods when they both flourished in synergistic harmony. It only has been in the recent past that the whole system has eroded to the point of near collapse. Part of the reason for this is our failure to forthrightly acknowledge the socialist sector of our economy, as such, and the essential role it plays in supplying us with human capital. This has enabled those who promote the inherently unsustainable vision of restoring a very limited public sector appropriate to the bygone age of an agrarian economy.

They are enabled, in part, by the generally negative perception of the socialist label and the accepted wisdom that anything socialist is profoundly un-American. They also are enabled by our failure to understand the uniquely pragmatic, uniquely American, manner in which we embraced public education, long before the Europeans, and the role it played in driving our amazingly productive version of the agro-industrial revolution.

[**]A much smaller amount, about 5 percent, of elementary/secondary education was provided by private institutions that year. *The New York Times Almanac 2011*, Ed. by John W. Wright, Penguin Books, 375 Hudson Street, New York, NY 10014, 2010, page 368.

Most ironically, perhaps, is the fact that our new-age free-market economic theory amounts to a rejection of our Puritan heritage of both respect for learning and the economic imperative of safeguarding seed money. The result has been a corruption of our economic common sense and a growing addiction to tax cuts as a magical remedy for anything that ails the economy. It is a corruption that has had a disabling impact on the creation and equitable distribution of human capital. This, in turn, has degraded the dynamic equilibrium of our economy to the point of near collapse and continues to hinder its recovery. Ultimately, it is a corruption that arises - as our Founding Fathers once cautioned - out of the darker side of our nature. It is a corruption that arises out of greed and myopia.

Our Broken Compass
Our current economic crisis is rooted in our failure to
recognize that the foundation of our economy rests upon
a synthesis of public and private resources. Ultimately,
this failure of perception arises out of our uniquely
American predisposition to exaggerate the power and
rights of the individual when viewed in the context of
social forces. This exaggeration naturally promotes the
delusion that our economy will perform in an adequate
manner with inadequate public resources. By the same
token, it makes it easier for those in command of the
private sector to divert resources away from public
infrastructure into private hands. Given the short-term
material advantages that this myopic strategy bestows
upon the private sector, it is more than understandable
that private interests have consistently and strenuously
advocated these policies since not long after the birth of
our independent republic. Our renewed embrace of this
radical and dangerous hypothesis over the course of the
past generation has brought us, once again, to the brink
of ruin. What is more difficult to understand is that this
shell game continues to succeed even though it seriously
damages the interests of the general public.
Dean Ekola

As historians sift through the record of President George W. Bush's administration, his handling of one event will stand out as the most decisive. And for those who lived through it, it will come as no surprise that 9/11/01 is that singular event. However, as the hangover from the Great Recession lingers on, the place of that infamous crime in our conventional wisdom even now is shifting away from its initial role as a battle cry for the War on Terror. Once embraced as the overarching issue for the American agenda and the justification for the wars in Afghanistan and Iraq, that view of 9/11/01 is being eroded by the destructive and costly consequences of the deeply flawed strategy of those wars.[1]

The heavy costs resulting from Bush's flawed war strategy[2] - made worse by his refusal to adequately finance them - contributed to our soaring national debt and the onset of our current economic crisis. Indeed, the depth of this economic crisis, now measured in years and a daunting backlog of millions unemployed, mirrors the implacable character of our decade long wars in Iraq and Afghanistan. But while the rude metrics of common sense suggest a strong linkage between these two wars and our current problems, we must not fall into the trap of mistaking a contributing, albeit significant, factor for an exclusive one.

 We must keep in mind that an economic crisis as deep as our current one cannot be explained entirely by a single cause, nor by the failures of a single administration. Hence, when we view the fiscal improvidence of Bush 2 in the wider context of the past 50 years, we find a wide range of macroeconomic/sociological/ perceptual problems. All of these contributed in their own way to our current difficulties, and all were made worse by our growing predilection for deficit-financed government. This predilection has led us to resort to deficits not only in bad times, as prescribed by John Maynard Keynes, but too often in good times as well - when Keynesian theory called for setting aside surpluses for a rainy day.

A not-so-brief inventory of these problems would include the following:

- ❖ Baby boom household formation starting in the late 1960s;
- ❖ Unfunded costs of the Vietnam War;
- ❖ The collapse of the Bretton Woods international exchange rate system;

- The advent of two-income households;
- Loss of self-sufficiency in energy;
- Failure to adhere to all the key elements of Keynesian policy; i.e., the failure to follow reasonably sensible fiscal policies in paying for current government operations - including wars - in good times with adequate levels of taxation.
- The transformation of our traditional credit markets - once dominated by banks - into a hydra-headed entity operating outside the view of public and regulators alike;[3]
- Erratic Federal Reserve policies arising in part out of the Fed's failure to monitor how the new players in the credit market were expanding the money supply;[4]
- Chickens of the Marshall Plan coming home to roost;
- Increased health care costs arising out of expanded access ushered in by Medicare and Medicaid;
- Stagnation of average hourly wages over the past 40 years;
- Additional health care cost increases arising out of refined technology and medical science;
- Additional health care cost increases arising out of the redistribution of unpaid health care fees for the uninsured;
- Job loss due to technological advances and the outsourcing of our industrial plant;
- The effort to address, after a century of festering delay, massive social damage arising out of our most destructive experiment in social-engineering: America's centuries-long embrace of a race-based system of slave labor;
- The failure to adequately fund education/training costs to prepare our human capital for the challenges of a post-industrial global economy;
- The failure to implement the reforms of our educational establishment necessary for successful outcomes in a post-industrial global economy;
- Unfunded costs of the wars in Iraq and Afghanistan;

❖ Exacerbating the above are two problems that impede our very recognition of how all of the above work together to create a perversely destructive dynamic that metastasizes over time:

1. The perceptual problem of failing to recognize the role of social and human capital as it relates to the success of an economy in the same manner as fixed capital relates to the success of a private business venture;

2. The perceptual problem of failing to understand the fundamental role of momentum as it relates to the enormous mass of a $14 trillion economy, stricken by a financial crisis resulting in wealth destruction of some $51.7 trillion.[5] The staggering scale of this financial maelstrom naturally translated into huge recovery times amounting to not just years - but even a decade or more. But this calculus appears to have eluded a very large sector of the American electorate.

❖ And finally, the impediments - both constitutional and cultural - which stand in the way of addressing these problems with legislative action on the federal level.

Over the years, we not only failed to get a handle on the inflationary/deficit pressures arising from this economic rogue's gallery, but, we also made the situation worse - with few exceptions - by lowering tax rates on a regular basis. As a result, these inflationary dynamics - and our gross federal debt - steadily increased in mass and momentum. The brief respite during the Clinton years was reversed by a return to tax cutting and our costly response to 9/11/01 under Bush 2. From that point on, the combined negative thrust of all of these inflationary/deficit pressures eventually overwhelmed the sustainability bulwarks of our economy. Unfortunately, aside from the amorphous unease expressed in numerous 'wrong-way' polls, we are a long way from glimpsing the significance of but one or two of these rogue dynamics, not to mention achieving an actionable consensus on how to deal with all of them.

For the moment, correcting this failure of perception remains a work scarcely out of the gate. For the moment, our conventional wisdom still struggles against decades of half-baked supply-side economic theories. These are spiked with equal measures of self-indulgent tax-cuts and alarms sounded against our government as the bogeyman of socialism - carelessly defined.[6] As a result of such distractions, our conventional wisdom has lost its way and become a broken compass, promoting what is destructive and castigating what is useful. Thus hobbled it has become worse than useless as a guide through the labyrinth of our present economic crisis.

Perhaps even more difficult for us to comprehend is the enormous momentum of the historical forces driving our current economic stagnation. This is so for a variety of reasons; one of which is that we have managed to unlearn critical lessons of the Great Depression - lessons purchased through bitter experiences not unlike our current ones. This unlearning process has been driven by the hard sell of economic theories appropriate to the early stages of capitalism, but unsupported by contemporary economic reality. Hence, despite their obsolescence, two theories - one from the mid-1700s and the other from the early 1800s - have been dusted off and used to discredit the work of Keynes and other Depression-era economists.

The first of these resurgent theories is Adam Smith's 'invisible hand' and the second is Jean Baptiste Say's maxim that supply single-handedly generates demand. Both of these theories share the intellectual simplicity of self-regulating mechanisms. As such, they free the faithful from the intellectual drudgery of marshalling detailed evidence and weighing its merits. The theory provides the answer. The faithful need only be careful about selecting data supportive of the theory. And as our current American political debate demonstrates, this bankrupt intellectual process resonates powerfully with a large sector of the American electorate.

We will look more closely at these two theories later in our discussion, but for the present, suffice to say both of them were discredited by the depth and length of economic devastation ushered in by the Great Depression. The specific cause of their lost credibility was the collapse of demand that continued to impede full economic recovery until the outbreak of World War II. Since both theories posited an automatic self-correcting function within free market economies, the continued failure of the depression-era economy to self-correct, restore demand and generate jobs for the masses of unemployed laid bare their great error.

Today we are confronted by a notably similar collapse of demand. This collapse of demand will occupy our attention more fully as our discussion proceeds. For the moment, though, it will suffice to note that this collapse of contemporary demand and its similarity to our experiences of the Great Depression is ignored by that well-funded cohort who continually redirect our attention toward supply side issues.

Even more regrettably, this failure of analysis is enabled by the routine failure of the electronic media to notice it, let alone directly confront it. Whether this failure results from journalistic cowardice, incompetence, a profound lack of understanding about our nation's history, or a mixture of all three is difficult to ascertain. However, the unfortunate result is plain to see. The electronic media habitually projects an image of bipartisan neutrality more appropriate to the bygone era in which bipartisanship actually existed. That era no longer exists. It has been supplanted by an era in which a radicalized Republican Party embraces ideological dogma to the complete disregard of scientific evidence, historical fact and verifiable economic data. A truly neutral observer of such cavalier treatment of reality would have to address it as a significant phenomenon worthy of notice. But, unfortunately, the electronic media are not up to the task of confronting this propaganda campaign promoting an alternate reality. With few exceptions, they capitulate in a pitiful pretense of honoring a bygone era of bipartisanship.

A recent example illustrates this point. On NBC's "Meet The Press" program on 10/23/11, Republican presidential candidate Ron Paul, declared that "...finally, we got over the depression by having these draconian [spending and tax] cuts...after WWII." By so saying, he manages to omit entirely the singular role played by the production demands of WWII in overcoming the stagnation of the Great Depression. Similarly, his version omits the federal government's successful role in financing and directing war production, not to mention its support and coordination of a multitude of basic research projects - along with their technological applications. By evading this remarkably successful effort, he also avoids giving credit for the positive role such government sponsored research and development played in the post-war economy. Nor should we fail to mention the federal government's role in creating the G.I. Bill and the powerful role played by it in the recovery of the real estate market, as well as how its role in expanding access for veterans to higher education invigorated the overall economy. Yet the host of Meet The Press, Dick Gregory, failed to challenge any of these, or the following, distortions.

An equally significant distortion is that - contrary to Representative Paul - the high marginal tax rates of the WWII era were not abandoned at the end of the war, but persisted largely intact until they were cut from 91% in 1963 to 77% in 1964. It is true that top marginal tax rates were reduced briefly at the end of WWII from 94% (on income over $200,000) in 1945 to 86.45% (over $200,000) in 1946-47 and to 82.13% (over $400,000)in 1948-49. But to characterize these cuts as draconian loses its credibility when contrasted with today's top marginal rate of 35%.[7] Indeed, to suggest that rates in excess of 80% were the cause of an economic boom suggests that we could raise today's rates substantially without causing economic harm.

These brief reductions in post-WWII rates were reversed in 1951 when they were returned to 91% (over $400,000) and remained at that level until 1964.

In short, Representative Paul's revisions of the historical record ignores many of the most important drivers of the golden age of the American economy - many of which were the product of federally funded and directed programs, both during and after WWII. Rounding out Representative Paul's deceptive version of WWII history is the fact that it dovetails nicely with contemporary efforts to deny any government role in the wealth creation process. This denial flies in the face of the reality that government has played an essential role providing critical nuts and bolts for a technologically refined civilization - nuts and bolts that otherwise would fall through the cracks of a pristine competitive economic model. Public education, basic research and capital intensive, high-risk cutting edge projects are a few of these critically essential nuts and bolts. Specific examples of government contributions to basic research and their technological applications would include such icons of innovation as nuclear energy, jet engines, synthetic materials, semiconductors and the internet.

Equally important is the government's much-maligned role in the income distribution process. While not so much a part of the wealth creation process, it does play a critical role in the damage-control side of the capitalist model. Absent its balancing role in income distribution, the typical capitalist economy concentrates wealth in the few hands ideally situated to seize it by virtue of their combined roles of entrepreneur and gatekeeper of society's wealth. The confusion generated by this combination of functions and the complexity of the modern technocratic economy enables an aggrandizement of the entrepreneur's economic claims. Hence, absent government intervention through its power of taxation, the resulting concentration of wealth in the hands of these gatekeepers grows so far out of proportion to their actual contributions that the demand side of the economy withers - just as we have experienced over the past forty years. And naturally, as demand withers, the economy also withers and either slips into chronic stagnation or eventual collapse. Charts 7, 7a and 7b below provide a detailed look at how income distribution - and demand - has faltered over the periods 1964-2009 and 1972-2009.[8]

The confusion surrounding our income distribution system arises out of the fact that modern products are the culmination of a long train of inputs of material resources and human skills, all of which are the results of substantial investments, both public and private. The public investments for education, infrastructure and high end research are essential to this hybrid wealth creation process because, not only do they usually exceed the resources of most corporations, but even if they did not, they would place any corporations who voluntarily assumed them at a competitive disadvantage. Hence, the shotgun marriage between the private and public sector.

A result of this tension between the public and private sector is the constant effort by the private sector to minimize its funding of the public sector, especially since there is a natural - and necessary - tendency for public sector investment to grow apace with technological refinement and the problems that accompany it. A prominent part of this push-back effort by the private sector has been to mischaracterize the wealth creation process and the wealth it produces as entirely private. One measure of its success has been an increasing acceptance of the self-serving libel that taxation amounts to the theft of any kind of earnings, whether they are from wages, investments or corporate profits.

Such deceptiveness on the part of the private sector is not new. Even Adam Smith, that icon of conservative pundits, cautioned against accepting the word of employers, dealers, merchants and master manufacturers. In his Wealth of Nations, published in 1776, he states:

The proposal of any new law or regulation which comes from this order [of men] ought always to be listened to with great precaution, and ought never to be adopted till after having been long and carefully examined, not only with the most scrupulous, but with the most suspicious attention. It comes from an order of men whose interest is never exactly the same with that of the public, who have generally an interest to deceive and even to oppress the public, and who accordingly have upon many occasions, both deceived and oppressed it.[9]

This quote should be cast in bronze and erected over the entrance to Congress, where perhaps it would inspire more intense scrutiny of lobbyists writing our laws.

Returning to our metaphor of the broken compass, we turn to the proliferation of public opinion polls that find overwhelming majorities of Americans believing the nation is on the wrong track. Significantly though, there is no consistent consensus, grounded in an understanding of our post-WWII economic odyssey, about the exact causes of our errant course or in which direction we ought to turn. Over the past decade, these polls have expressed an ineffable sense that we're going the wrong way - regardless of whom is at the helm and regardless of what direction is characterized as wrong.[10]

Certainly in the period closer to 9/11/01, such polls were influenced by the terror attacks which injected a wild card, focused on national security, into our public debates about the nation's agenda. However, the proposition that this sense of misdirection no longer has much to do with the terror attacks themselves is supported by a NYTimes/CBS News poll of 10/25/11. In this poll, President Barack Obama's handling of the War on Terror earns him a 60% approval rating, while his chances for reelection are placed in some doubt by a lackluster 35% approval rating for his handling of the economy - and a pervasive sense (74% in the same poll) that the nation is on the wrong track. At the same time, public opinion concerning specific government policies to boost the economy reflect utter confusion about what will provide a clear path forward. Hence, on the one hand, we find substantial majority approval in the same poll regarding most of Obama's specific proposals to encourage job growth, while, as mentioned previously, only 35% approve his overall record in promoting job growth.[11]

When we try to uncover what is at the bottom of this sense of collective aimlessness, we run into two problems. The first is scarce recognition of the previously listed problems that have surfaced over the past 50 years. This has resulted in historically uninformed analyses that lead us even deeper into the swamp. The reason for this is relatively simple. Our brave new world is drowning in data. This results from the explosive growth of our scientific disciplines, the refinements of our technology and the impact these have upon our economic systems. This explosive growth of data fills vast silos of information which most individuals, already burdened with their individual concerns, are too distracted to skim even in the most superficial manner - let alone fully comprehend. Hence, it ought not surprise that one of our venerable elder statesmen, Zbigniew Brzezinski, characterized the American public's understanding of world affairs as "abysmal" in his interview, on February 8, 2012, with Jeffrey Brown on PBS NewsHour. He went on to state: "It is ignorant. It is probably the least-informed public about the world among the developed countries in the world." And judging by the superficiality of our current public debate about our economy, the same could be said about our understanding of the economy.

The second problem is the cultural component of this explosive growth of data. This cultural component arises out of the need to effectively manage this huge stock of data, which, in turn, drives the growth of committees and bureaucracy, both in government and private industry. As John K. Galbraith observed some fifty years ago:

It is not to individuals but to organizations that power in the business enterprise and power in the society has passed....[This shift arises from] the circumstance that in modern industry a large number of decisions, and all that are important, draw on information possessed by more than one man.[12]

This paradigm shift from the individual to the group has undermined some of our most prized cultural assumptions about the sovereignty of the individual. This, in turn, has created a new social and economic reality that challenges us, intellectually, at every turn - while simultaneously creating a collective yearning for all of those prized, but marginalized, cultural assumptions about individual sovereignty.

Finally, this paradigm shift in the foundations of our culture is made more challenging by the fact that it attacks the democratic foundations of our government. It does this by undermining our long-cherished mantra about the role of a well-informed citizenry as the bedrock of democracy. If the majority of individuals no longer can hope to master sufficient stocks of data for well-informed political decisions about our economy and social existence, how can those individuals be expected to participate rationally in the democratic process? Such questions inject a spectral pessimism into our collective self-image and, for many, lead to efforts to avoid such disturbing reflections by a redoubled embrace of our ancient verities - carelessly construed. This, of course, is a classic instance of denial. Those who defend this mythic vision of the status quo - otherwise known as the 'Party of NO' - make light of this significant challenge to the democratic process as if ignorance were worthy of celebration. They stigmatize those who try to distill this mass of data for broader consumption as 'pointy-heads,' while simultaneously promoting highly skewed versions of fact that support their ideological views. The result is that we have arrived at the end game of a cultural schism - more than two generations in the making - which pits two versions of reality against each other.

The result of this schism is that we no longer have an accepted body of facts forming the consensual foundations of compromise. And that is precisely what is destroying the viability of our political system.

This is especially disturbing when we consider that such a fundamental schism, resulting in our infamous politics of gridlock, blocks critical investment in maintenance and reform of our civilization. This, in turn, accelerates the downturn of our fortunes and provides grist for even greater conflict down the road. In the meantime, the new gurus of political science - the marketing specialists and hucksters - rule the roost and continue to pollute our political discourse with their highly distorted 20-30 second sound bites.

We also ought to take note of the role of the commercial broadcast media in our collective muddle. For whatever reasons, they have adopted the view of the new political marketing class that the attention span of the public can absorb only the most elemental messages. As a result, they package their news broadcasts in appropriately truncated form, while as a natural consequence, they generally avoid wading into the swampland of our full blown cultural schism. To do otherwise would force them to get into what they must regard as a lengthy, detailed and highly controversial discussion of how the merits, or the lack thereof, are distributed between the two contesting factions of this schism. And, perhaps most importantly - as not just students, but conductors of political polls - they know the commercial dangers implicit in such an effort. The destructive consequence of this situation is that the commercial broadcast media, with few exceptions, have adopted a posture of neutrality toward a situation that cries out for an honest arbiter of facts, not a spineless bystander posing as a neutral observer.

The result has been a volatility in our political life that resembles a ping-pong match. The Democrats won an impressive victory in the midterm elections of 2006. This was followed by their nearly complete control of the presidency and both chambers of Congress in 2008. This was followed by Republican resurgence in the midterm elections of 2010, giving them the opportunity to quash any further legislative initiatives by Obama and the Democrats. It is against this background that we approach the elections of 2012. How it will end is anyone's guess. And that is deeply disturbing given what's at stake. The issue is nothing less than whether we will turn over the affairs of our nation to those who are committed to an alternative-reality vision, or those who see the world as it is. In a bygone era, we would have recognized the inherent dangers in such a choice. Such recognition was then expressed by placing those who see the world as it is in the mainstream, while the alternative-reality camp was dismissed as reactionary.

To better explore the facts that define this choice, we now turn to a series of charts presenting snapshots of our downward spiral into our current economic crisis. The first two of these charts deliberately limit our focus to the last 30 years. The thirty year time line was selected as a good starting point because, typically, that is the outer limit of historical reference for those few mainstream discussions that we regard as ambitious. But, as we will see when we turn to Charts 3 and 4, this 30-year focus severely distorts our perception of historical reality. Despite these limitations, though, Charts 1 and 2 still provide more useful insights than typically are disclosed by our contemporary mainstream discussions.

Chart 1 below, Gross Federal Debt @ Administration 1982-2009, summarizes the federal debt, expressed in billions of dollars, as it is customarily portrayed in terms of both On and Off Budget items. Aside from the soaring trajectory of Gross Federal Debt, the next most conspicuous thing to catch the attention of the lay reader is the use of fiscal rather than chronological years in determining an administration's budgetary responsibilities.

In this system, the first year of an administration's fiscal responsibility begins approximately eight and one-half months after their assumption of office (October 1 of the year they assume office).

Similarly, in the fourth and final year, it then continues nearly one year (or nine months) into the first chronological year of their successor's

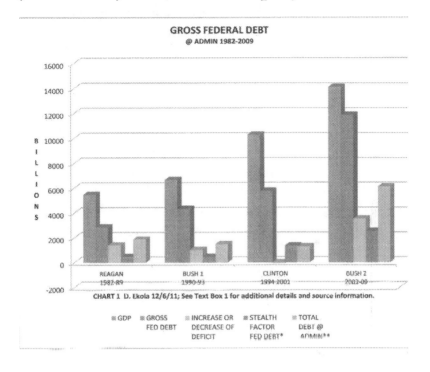

CHART 1 D. Ekola 12/6/11; See Text Box 1 for additional details and source information.

▓ GDP ▓ GROSS
FED DEBT

▓ INCREASE OR
DECREASE OF
DEFICIT

▓ STEALTH
FACTOR
FED DEBT*

▓ TOTAL
DEBT @
ADMIN**

TEXT BOX 1
Companion to Charts 1 & 2

*Stealth Factor of Federal Debt is that part of the Gross Federal Debt of a given administration which exceeds the sum of (1) Gross Federal Debt of preceding administration and (2) the cumulative annual increases (or decreases) of the current/given administration's deficits. In short, it is that part of the debt accumulation process that is, as a practical matter, hidden from public view.

**Total debt is the sum of annual deficits plus Stealth Factor.

SOURCE (Data): Dept of Commerce (BEA); Dept of Treasury; and Office of Management and Budget.

The analysis and interpretation of the data is the work of the author.

administration. Hence, the fiscal term of the Reagan administration ran from October 1, 1981 to September 30, 1989, or as officially rounded off, from 1982-1989, rather than the conventional view of its chronological term from 1981-1988.[13]

As we will see in the following example of the Bush 2 administration, this makes sense given the fact that his outgoing administration spent its last two chronological years, or 2007-08, drafting the budget for the first chronological year (2009) of Barak Obama's incoming administration. This is reflected in the fact that George W. Bush, as is required by statute, sent his Budget for FY 2009 to Congress in the first week of February (February 4, 2008). Obviously, given the considerable amount of time that goes into the preparation of the federal budget, the work involved in drafting this preliminary budget had to take place before that date and therefore extended back into 2007. The impact of the administration of Bush 2 on Obama's, whether for good or ill, was further enhanced by the momentum that naturally accompanies a nearly four trillion dollar operation, which is the approximate size of the budget of the federal government. Finally, it also needs to be noted that these inroads of the fiscal operations of an outgoing administration on an incoming administration are not the result of a contemporary gimmick; these formal practices have their origins in the Budget and Accounting Act of 1921 and the Twentieth Amendment to the U.S. Constitution of 1933.

For the most part, the current field of Republican presidential candidates do not recognize this reality. Presumably this is so because it would blunt their attacks on the Obama administration, based upon statistical data from the transitional fiscal year of 2009. Regrettably, they are not the only ones to ignore the reality of these fiscal year budget practices. Scarcely any journalist in the mainstream media has called them to account for their misrepresentations. But, surprisingly, one contender for the Republican nomination, Herman

Cain, acknowledged this fiscal year hiccup, arising out of the transition from one administration to the next. In a PBS News Hour interview with Judy Woodruff on 10/31/11, he stated: "Well, we got to make sure we're talking apples and apples here. What I'm referring to is in my first year - in the first full fiscal year of my presidency, because remember, when you are sworn in, you inherit a fiscal year." Nevertheless, any damage to the Republican message was mitigated by the facts that Woodruff allowed this gem to slip by unremarked and that the PBS News Hour has comparatively few viewers.

The third thing to catch the reader's attention is the 'stealth factor' in our federal debt. This stealth factor arises out of the discrepancy

---

TEXT BOX 2
The Stealth Factor in Gross Federal Debt

One rationale for this seeming sleight of hand is that it eliminates the 'curse of the mattress' that otherwise would attach to the sequestration of surpluses of these two agencies. Specifically, if these surpluses were not used to neutralize an equivalent part of the federal deficit, it would have the effect of removing these funds from circulation. As a result, it would increase pressure on private capital markets and thereby push interest rates higher. In other words, it would slow the economy proportionally to the amount of currency withdrawn from circulation.

The problem with this approach is that it does not extinguish the amount of federal debt covered by these intergovernmental transfers. It places these debts into a kind of budgetary purgatory where the issue of private refinancing, oftentimes postponed for decades, falls off the grid of consciousness. Another troublesome wrinkle is that not all other programs also funded Off-Budget have their own funding source. Presumably, these just fall off the budgetary grid altogether - until they are returned to the On-Budget category.

---

between the cumulative total of annual budget deficits during a given administration and the increase of the gross federal debt during that administration. It results from an accounting practice, at least as regards Social Security revenues, dating back to 1936. Today's federal budget keeps not only these revenues of the Social Security trust funds and the Post Office - but also accounts of miscellaneous other programs - separate from the main budget. The former are referred to as "Off Budget" items, while those on the main budget are known as "On Budget." The segregation of Social Security and Postal revenues is based in law and, presumably, was adopted as a well-meaning effort to safeguard the revenues of these two agencies. However, there are several problems with this approach.[14]

First, as mentioned, other items that require federal funding also wind up in this special 'Off-Budget' category, expanding its size. George W. Bush resorted to this practice with the costs of the wars in Afghanistan and Iraq.[15] Barak Obama reversed this practice and that naturally contributed to the increase of his administration's budget deficit. Second, whether as a result of accounting sleight-of-hand - or for legitimate reasons of stabilizing the money supply - there has been a long-standing practice of merging these On-Budget and Off-Budget items into a 'Unified' or 'Total Budget.'[16] The budgetary effect of this has been to understate the size of annual federal budget deficits because the surpluses of these two agencies offset a corresponding amount of the annual deficit.

Finally, regardless of their on- or off-budget status, all the elements of these two budgets still are part of the overall national debt and, as a result, are included in the Gross Federal Debt in its annual reckoning. Hence, as stealth debt has increased as part of the Gross National Debt, it has increased the amount of the Gross National Debt flying under the radar screen of the combined total of our annual unified budgets. (A more detailed discussion of the rationale for these accounting practices may be found in Text Box 2 above.)

We now move to Chart 2 below: Federal Debt As % of GDP. At first glance, we are struck by the massive extent of the gross federal debt. All four administrations register at least 50 percent of GDP in this category and Bush 1 and Bush 2 register over 60 and 80 percent, respectively. Beyond that there is a steady decrease of budget deficits for each administration starting with Bush 1, culminating with their complete elimination under Clinton and then soaring back to over 20 percent under Bush 2. A somewhat similar trend line also may be seen for the total debt of these administrations. While these two charts provide far more useful information than we get from mainstream discussions about our national debt, they still deny us critical insights provided by a much longer time frame. This longer

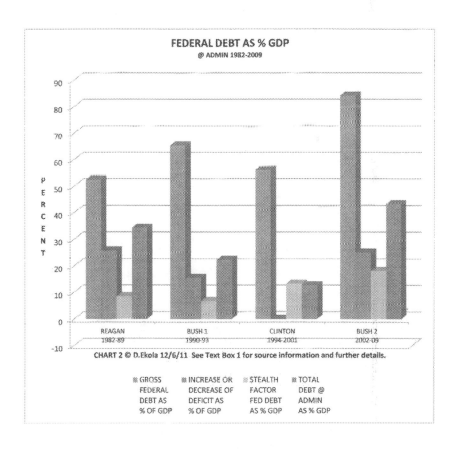

CHART 2 © D.Ekola 12/6/11 See Text Box 1 for source information and further details.

time frame, provided by Charts 3 and 4, will give us a better understanding of the glacial quality of momentum as reflected in the economic fundamentals of fiscal policy.

Charts 3 and 3A below, spanning 64 years instead of the 28 years in Charts 1 and 2, illustrate fundamental shifts in U.S. fiscal policy. These charts begin with the first fiscal year of the Truman administration - in actual terms starting April 12, 1945, but fiscally listed as 1946-53 - and include the terms of Dwight Eisenhower (1954-1961), the combined terms of John Kennedy and Lyndon Johnson (1962-69),

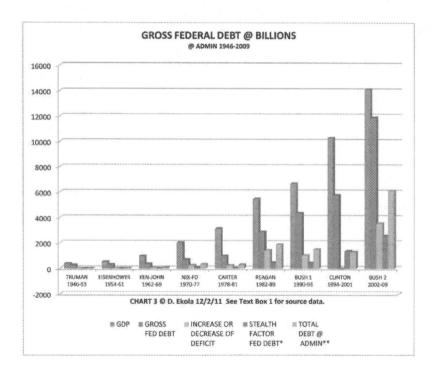

the combined terms of Richard Nixon and Gerald Ford (1970-77), and Jimmy Carter (1978-81), along with those of Reagan, Bush 1, Clinton and Bush 2. Parenthetically, we should note that it was during President Ford's term that fiscal years were adjusted to begin three months later, on October 1, 1976, instead of July 1, 1976.

Chart 3, Gross Federal Debt @ Administration 1946-2009, resembles Chart 1 in revealing a smoothly ascending trajectory of GDP and gross federal debt over their respective time frames. Hence, in the absence of further data we would be drawn to the conclusion that all 9 of these administrations share similar fiscal policies and other significant circumstances.   But we would be wrong.   Chart 3A below illustrates this point.

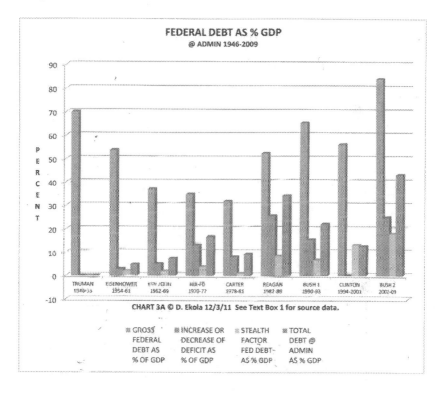

Chart 3A, Federal Debt As % GDP 1946-2009, reveals how these administrations differed dramatically in their handling of fiscal policies. Three fundamentals drive these differences. The first is that gross federal debt steadily decreases during the initial 32 years: quite rapidly from Truman through Kennedy-Johnson and then more gradually during Nixon-Ford and Carter. The second is that gross federal debt then reverses direction and soars upward from Reagan through Bush 2, only slowing perceptibly during Clinton's term.   The third is that, despite Truman's inherited gross federal debt at a staggering 70% of GDP, his administration actually generated next to nothing in terms of increased deficits, stealth factor debt and total debt.

This represents a huge difference in fiscal policy from our current practices, especially when we take into account that the burdens of his administration included not only the legacy debts of the Great Depression and World War II, but also extraordinary expenditures for the Korean War and the Marshall plan. After Truman's administration, though, things begin to change. Subsequent administrations show a steady increase in their accumulated deficits and total incurred debt, ultimately skyrocketing during the administrations of Reagan and Bush 2. The only exceptions are modest reversals for Carter and Bush 1, owing to their abbreviated terms, followed by the conspicuous exception of Clinton's administration. His administration achieved the elimination of its unified budget deficit, resulting largely from its own tax increases along with those implemented by Bush 1.

The most significant insights that result from these four charts are the following: in the post-WW II era there has been a sea-change in U.S. fiscal policy, gradual at first, then growing reckless under Reagan and Bush 2; this produced a staggering amount of gross federal debt before President Barack Obama's first fiscal year started on October 1, 2009; the accumulation of this debt has served to exacerbate the inflationary forces previously cited at the outset of this essay; taken together the growing momentum of these destabilizing dynamics have magnified the swings between recession and inflationary balloons until the economy finally collapsed into a recessionary trench not seen since the Great Depression. And that is why we find ourselves still struggling with what amounts to a depression within a recession for those millions of unemployed and underemployed.

To better illustrate the dynamic of momentum, let's turn to Charts 4, 4A and 5. These charts focus on GDP: Chart 4 on annual growth of GDP during the period 1960-2010; Chart 4A on abstract rates (2%, 3% and 12%) of GDP growth; Chart 5 further refines this focus by zeroing in on quarterly GDP growth during the period 2007-2011.

Chart 4 below portrays a gradually ascendant trajectory of GDP growth during the 1960s which then grows at a rapidly increasing rate starting in the 1970s up until it first falls into negative territory in

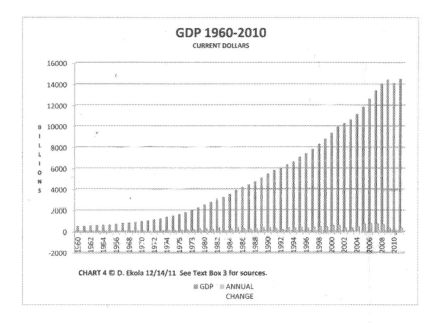

GDP 1960-2010
CURRENT DOLLARS

CHART 4 © D. Ekola 12/14/11 See Text Box 3 for sources.
GDP ANNUAL CHANGE

2009. For much of this period of rapid GDP growth its trajectory approximates a 12 percent rate of growth annually. This can be seen when we compare Chart 4 with Chart 4A below. This 12 percent rate of annual GDP growth contrasts sharply with the 1.9 percent average annual rate of productivity growth for the years 1972-2009.[17] The difference of 10 percent must be attributed to other causes - presumably inflation and population growth.

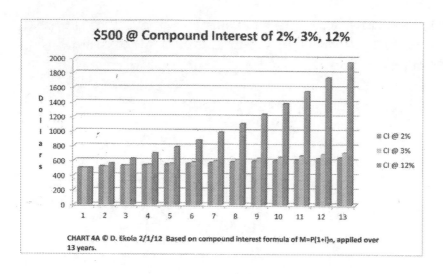

$500 @ Compound Interest of 2%, 3%, 12%

CHART 4A © D. Ekola 2/1/12 Based on compound interest formula of M=P(1+i)n, applied over 13 years.

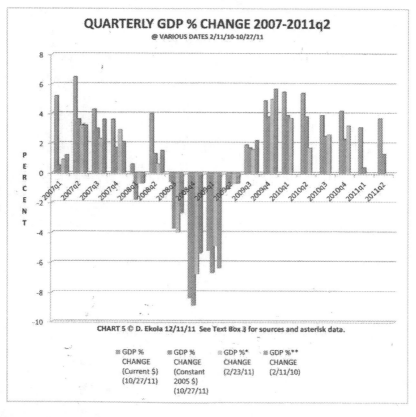

QUARTERLY GDP % CHANGE 2007-2011q2
@ VARIOUS DATES 2/11/10-10/27/11

CHART 5 © D. Ekola 12/11/11 See Text Box 3 for sources and asterisk data.

GDP % CHANGE (Current $) (10/27/11)   GDP % CHANGE (Constant 2005 $) (10/27/11)   GDP %* CHANGE (2/23/11)   GDP %** CHANGE (2/11/10)

When we take a closer look at the apparent fall of GDP into negative territory in 2009, we find that the timing of this fall actually is a misrepresentation. It is a misrepresentation that results from the combined impact of: (1) mathematical averaging inherent in annual GDP data; (2) timing in the sense that the deepest point of the recession hit right in the closing months of 2008 and the opening months of 2009; and (3) on the gradually evolving nature of near term economic data.

First, with regard to mathematical averaging, the annual averages for GDP growth for the years 2008-09 blurs the fact that the deepest point of the recession hit right between those two years - mitigating the 2008 average with the lesser losses of the first three quarters and casting 2009 in a deceptively much worse light. This blurring of the

TEXT BOX 3
Companion to Charts 3a, 3b and 5

SOURCE (Data): Economic Report of the President 2010, Table B-4. Percent changes in real gross domestic product, 1960-2009; Economic Report of the President 2011, Table B-4. Percent changes in real gross domestic product, 1960-2010; Economic Report of the President 2011, Letter of Transmittal, Council of Economic Advisers 2/23/11, page 29; Current-Dollar and "Real" Gross Domestic Product(9/29/11) - bea.gov/national/xls/gdplev.xls.

The following sources are especially helpful in understanding the concept of the gradually evolving nature of near term economic data. "How did the recent GDP revisions change the picture of the 2007-2009 recession and the recovery?" Frequently Asked Questions; Bureau of Economic Analysis (bea.gov/faq/index.cfm?faq_id=1004 [8/5/2011]); "Why has the initial estimate of real GDP for the fourth quarter of 2008 been revised down so much?" Frequently Asked Questions; bea.gov/faq/index.cfm?faq_id=1003 [8/5/2011].

actual course of the recession only comes into focus with the benefit of quarterly data - as shown in Chart 5 above. Second, this lack of clarity is made worse by the fact that preliminary GDP data is just that. It is based on those sources that are available in the short term. More refined data can take as long as two or more years to become available. As a result, GDP data often is subject to significant revision. And in the case of the 2008-09 recession, very substantial revisions were made over the course of the next two and one-half years. These revisions are also shown in Chart 5.

A brief narrative of our collapse into the trench of the Great Recession follows. First, both the threshold and the bottom of the Great Recession may be found squarely in the administration of Bush 2. The decline started in the third quarter of 2007 (2007-q3) and reached negative territory in 2008-q1. This decline was interrupted briefly in 2008-q2, following significant monetary easing by the Federal Reserve in January 2008.[18] But these gains were short-lived. The collapse of Bear Stearns in March 2008 reignited fears of greater financial losses arising out of the subprime mortgage market. These immediately thrust GDP growth back into negative territory in 2008-q3 and from there into the deepest part of the Great Recession in 2008-q4. (We should note at this point that GDP data is collected in the traditional timeframe of chronological years [i.e., 1st quarter is January-March], not fiscal years [i.e., 1st quarter is October-December]).

The second point is that contemporary economic data only comes into focus gradually. This results, in part, from the fact that GDP estimates are based on a variety of data sources, the scheduled collection of which varies, both in terms of how long it takes to report their initial collection, and in their refinement over time. In short, this data collection process is designed to provide a sequence of updates providing greater accuracy over a period of a few years.

The multiple bars in Chart 5 are the medium that illustrates this gradual evolution and refinement of this near term economic data. Specifically, the most significant dynamic represented by these four bars are the growth, or decrease, of GDP as estimated at three different points of time. The first two bars (blue for current dollars and red for constant 2005 dollars), starting on the left of each quarter, portray the growth of GDP as estimated on 10/27/11. The other two bars represent the growth of GDP as estimated on 2/23/11 (green) and 2/11/10 (purple).[19]

The third point is the accuracy of government's assessment of economic trends necessarily suffers in the short term due to the inherent delays in this process of data collection. It is the inevitable result of the complex character of our economy and is not due to a lack of integrity or competence on the part of the bureaucracy. It simply reflects the magnitude of the task of (1) collecting relevant data from our 14 trillion dollar economy and (2) the dynamic of momentum as its upward and downward shifts impact the various sectors of the overall economy.[20] Presumably, the velocity of the deflation, or inflation, of this momentum also varies proportionally with the quantity of leverage - as reflected in its extreme volatility during the highly leveraged period 2007-2009.

The specific numbers for the estimates of 2008-q4 - and the dates on which they were made - are as follows: -5.4% (2/11/10); -6.8% (2/23/11); -8.9% (10/27/11 constant 2005 dollars); and -8.4% (10/27/11 current, or inflated, dollars).[21] But this is not the whole story. To get a better idea of the actual data the Obama administration had in hand at the beginning of their term, we need to turn to the initial, or advance, estimate provided to them as of January 30, 2009. That estimate was substantially lower than all of the above at 3.8%.[22] Most significantly, this was the estimate Obama's economic advisers had in hand when they forecast on 1/9/2009, replete with disclaimers about the tentative character of their forecast, that the rate of unemployment would not exceed 8% if Obama's stimulus act was approved.[23] Nevertheless, in the universe of alternative reality occupied by the extreme right, this estimate is presented as an ironclad promise by Obama himself that come Hell or high water unemployment would not exceed 8% if his Stimulus Act was enacted into law. For those who wish to pursue this point further, you will find a thorough discussion of it in PolitiFact.com of the St Petersburg Times, dated 1/26/2011.[24]

Before moving on, let's go back to 2007, the leading edge of the Great Recession. This year is critical for a thorough understanding of the Great Recession because it marks not only the first signs of persistent decline in GDP, but also the first public revelations of serious misconduct in private financial markets. It also is significant that these revelations coincided with the ongoing profligate handling of the fiscal affairs of the U.S. government, although the importance of this coincidence certainly was not recognized by the conventional wisdom at that time, let alone now.

Although this misconduct was chronicled in numerous articles and analyses during the summer and fall of 2007, we need to go back a little further to include what could be considered one of the seminal documents of the period. That document, "Mortgage Liquidity du Jour: Underestimated No More," dated 3/12/2007, was authored by four research analysts at Credit Suisse: Ivy L. Zelman, Dennis McGill (CFA), Justin Speer and Alan Ratner. Their assessment, aimed at "the recent turmoil in the mortgage market," was enough to cause great anxiety among those with an insider's understanding of the real estate market.[25]

Some of the main points of their assessment were as follows:

We believe that 40% of the market (share of subprime and Alt-A) is at risk of significant fallout from tightening credit and increased regulatory scrutiny. In particular, we believe the most pressing areas of concern should be stated income (49% of originations), high CLTV/piggyback (39%), and interest only/negative amortizing loans (23%). The proliferation of these exotic mortgage products has been disproportionately weighted to former hotbeds such as California, Nevada, Arizona and Florida, which have accounted for the lion share of builder profits.[26]

The report went on to project that these concerns would result in the following reduction of market activity:

Combining the reduction in demand from credit tightening with the excessive level of investor speculation in recent years and the risks of a softening economy/declining consumer confidence yields our total estimated peak-to-trough drop in housing starts of 35-45%. This compares to our previous forecast of a 25% decline as discussed in our September 2006 report titled "Data Masks Grim Reality," and the current 16% decline thus far on a trailing twelve month basis.[27]

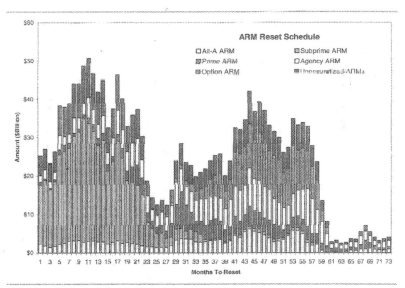

Note: Data as of January 2007.

Source: Credit Suisse Fixed Income U.S. Mortgage Strategy.

Taken together, these two paragraphs were enough to trigger even greater market unease among the cognoscenti, but there was more. The above chart, "Adjustable Rate Mortgage Schedule," disclosed the reset schedule for six different forms of adjustable rate mortgages for the six year period January 2007 to January 2014.[28] Certainly this chart would not immediately capture the attention of market outsiders, if it ever would, nor would it unduly concern those with a purely rationalist view of the economy. After all, in the larger scheme of a $14 trillion economy, just how important is a $50 billion screw-up in a given year? In terms of percentage, it's not even 4 tenths of a percent.

However, for those market insiders who had not drunk the kool-aid of the rational school of economics, they understood the severity of the problem disclosed by this chart. They understood that, not unlike an affrighted herd, once alarmed by revelations of market misconduct, the emotional underpinnings of these highly leveraged financial markets were capable of exerting enormous downward financial leverage. For them, this chart was a wake-up call. It foreshadowed with stunning clarity the depth and duration of the financial crisis the nation was about to enter. It revealed the financial architecture of those forces that would strangle the demand side of the economy for years to come. In hindsight, it provides an insight into the struggling recovery that has impeded job creation for the past several years.

But it would take months for this grim assessment to trickle down through the ranks of the financial markets and into the nation's consciousness. During these subsequent months, the media focused with greater attention on a confusing vocabulary of old and new - albeit uniformly arcane - terms. These described a variety of exotic financial instruments along with the truly hare-brained quality of some of their contents.

For purposes of our discussion, the most significant of these are derivatives, credit default swaps, collateralized debt obligations (CDOs), synthetic CDOs, asset backed securities and financial conduits. Starting with derivatives, these are financial instruments that have evolved over time from their traditional asset-backed form into a larger class that may include non-asset backed, or synthetic, objects of speculation.

Synthetic CDOs are asset backed securities that include non-asset based elements like credit default swaps. But, whether derivatives are traditional or more recent in vintage, they are essentially speculative in nature with a projected value linked to that of some other object of speculation.

Conduits typically are asset-backed securities held off the balance sheet of the lending institution - a maneuver that, on the one hand, eliminates the need for setting aside reserves and, on the other, facilitates increased leverage and greater profits on the upside. Credit default swaps are financial instruments created to allocate risk in purportedly the same manner as an insurance policy. Designed to cover losses arising out of speculative failures, they are non-asset backed. In short, they are not grounded in anything of intrinsic value. Unfortunately, though proffered as a form of insurance against failed bets in the derivatives market, they had neither the reserves nor the regulation of the insurance industry. This miscalculation would play an enormously destructive role in the financial meltdown of 2008.

In his classic study, *The Great Crash of 1929*, John K. Galbraith describes a dynamic nearly identical to our contemporary proliferation of exotic financial instruments. In the 1920s these financial instruments were issued by investment trusts. They came into being because the economy, awash in capital due to the very low tax rates of the 1920s, was not able to put this capital glut to work in traditional investments generating capital goods or consumer products. One of the consequences of this capital glut was an insatiable demand for common stocks exceeding Wall Street's supply. Wall Street naturally saw this as a wonderful opportunity for profitable innovation and turned to what had been the underutilized investment trust.[29]

Originally, the investment trust had been a genuine trust in which "the investor bought an interest in a specified assortment of securities which were then deposited with a trust company."[30] However, over the course of the 1920s the format of this traditional investment trust was transformed radically. It went from a reasonably well-managed trust, backed with substantial assets, into a highly leveraged corporation with very few assets. And, in too many cases, it was little more than a front to skim off as much of the capital glut as possible. As Galbraith observed:

The virtue of the investment trust was that it brought about an almost complete divorce of the volume of corporate securities outstanding from the volume of corporate assets in existence. The former could be twice, thrice, or any multiple of the latter. The volume of underwriting business and of securities available for trading on the exchanges all expanded accordingly....It is hard to imagine an invention better suited to the time or one better designed to eliminate the anxiety about the possible shortage of common stocks.[31]

As noted above, there is a compelling similarity between this headlong rush into wanton speculation in the 1920s and that which occurred in the run-up to the Great Recession. Both were episodes of extreme speculation that developed over a decade of unusually low taxation and unusually high concentration of wealth in the highest income brackets. And just as with the corruption of the investment trust into highly leveraged corporations, so too the contemporary market for financial derivatives underwent an equally great expansion of leverage and risk. In addition, both eras enabled this risk-taking with inept or non-existent regulation.

In the case of the 1920s, the excessive risk-taking of that decade, culminating in the crash of 1929, was the catalyst for the passage of the Glass-Steagall Act in 1933.[32] One of the principal features of this act was that it created a firewall that separated traditional banks, on the one hand, from insurance companies and investment banks. This was designed to protect traditional bank assets from the higher risk activities pursued by investment banks. Consequently, prior to the passage of Glass-Steagall, there neither was much regulation of financial markets, nor was there effective protection of traditional banking assets from the speculative activities of investment banks.

In the case of the Great Recession, the surviving restraints of the Glass-Steagall Act were gutted with the passage of the Gramm-Leach-Bliley Act of 11/4/1999. The removal of this firewall enabled not only a merger of traditional banking with that of investment banking, but also promoted mergers throughout the banking sector. This facilitated further growth of the largest banks into mega-banks that would be 'too-big-to-fail.'[33]

But perhaps most insidiously, this merger activity coincided with several innovations within the investment banking sector. Taken together, these innovations mixed a lack of transparency with an astounding increase of leverage to create a Wall Street version of blind-mans-bluff that came within inches of crashing the entire economy in 2008. One of these innovations, called a financial conduit, is an asset-backed security especially designed to keep the transaction off the books of the host bank. It uses auto loans, credit-card receivable or mortgages as collateral to sell largely short term commercial paper to big investors. The attraction of these conduits is that they offer a somewhat higher return than the most secure investments, while, presumably, still providing an acceptable level of safety.[34]

However, several significant problems spoiled the long-term viability of these conduits. First, they were crafted as short-term financial products; they typically matured within 90 days. Second, the banks who packaged them "often agree[d] to provide funding if a conduit can't resell its commercial paper when it matures."[35] Third, the volatility of these instruments was dramatically increased because this short-term commercial paper often was used "to fund the purchase of long-term assets."[36] Finally, the Achilles' heel of this product was that some of them included subprime mortgage securities. Hence, they shared the unfortunate flaw of many of the innovative financial instruments of this speculative era in that they depended upon an ascendant market for their viability.

An even more significant innovation, measured by both its upside and downside, was the credit default swap. As previously noted, they were insurance against failed bets in the financial market. And not unlike the stocks issued by the investment 'trust' corporations of the 1920s, they were investments generally grounded on next-to-nothing in terms of inherent asset value. Moreover, they were exceedingly hot items in the financial products industry. According to a 2010 ISDA Market Survey, the market for credit default swaps in 2000 was so negligible, they did not warrant an entry. By the following year, the notional value of CDSs was $918.9 billion and by 2007, when it peaked, it reached $62.2 trillion dollars. This compares with the derivatives market for that same year of $10 trillion.[37]

Of course, in Newton's world what goes up, comes down. Consequently, as public revelations of flawed judgment and misconduct in private financial markets mounted during the year 2007, the fundamental building block of a capitalist economy - trust - began to crumble. Trust in the basic competence and honesty of the system was essential for its continued operation. Now that trust was eroding day-by-day with each new report of fraud or miscalculation eroding billions more from the balance sheets of some of the nation's most storied investment houses. Most troubling was that these downward trends were now being reflected in the value of our homes and retirement accounts.

Unfortunately, although the actual extent of some of these losses was so enormous it strains our comprehension, for some reason these losses never showed up in a manner that left a memorable impression on the public mind. Hence, while it is a matter of public record that the market for credit default swaps suffered an enormous loss, it is reasonably certain that not even 1 percent of Americans could tell you that loss amounted to over 50 percent when it fell from $62.2 trillion in 2007 to $30.4 trillion in 2009.[38] Yet that loss occurred and we still struggle with its economic consequences.

The institutional landscape of Wall Street and its correspondent partners bear its scars. Bear Stearns is gone; Lehman Brothers is gone; Merrill Lynch was swallowed by Bank of America; AIG was put on life support by the federal government, as were Fannie Mae and Freddie Mac. And just as foreshadowed by the ARM reset chart of Credit Suisse in 2007, the real estate foreclosures resulting from these failed mortgage resets still cast a shadow on the real estate market and the nation's recovery. Moreover, when we dig down further, we find that the enormous size of all these foreclosures taken together, when correlated with gross federal debt incurred prior to this crisis, simply exceeded the already constrained fiscal capacity of the federal government. Indeed, the total value of lost home equity during the financial crisis is conservatively estimated at $7 trillion by the Federal Reserve.[39]

This explains why neither the administration of Bush 2, nor of Barack Obama, came up with a mortgage rescue plan adequate to the task of restoring a healthy real estate market. It would have taken a rescue program so massive that not even the resources of the federal government - even had it been unimpaired by our enormous gross federal debt - would have been adequate to such a monumental undertaking. But, fiscally impaired as we were - and are - it was out of the question. This also explains why neither administration chose a more aggressive path in dealing with the banking crisis. The banking crisis was precipitated not only by the specter of $7 trillion in compromised mortgages, but by what would become the even more staggering $31.8 trillion in credit default losses in 2009 - augmented by an additional $3.2 trillion loss in equity derivatives.[40] Moreover, the enormity of these losses does not even begin to consider the logistical problems of sorting out the actual ownership of the various fragments of these ultra-refined, sliced-and-diced financial products. The end result was an unprecedented mountain of debt buried so deeply in a black hole of anonymity that the country had neither the resources nor the acumen to resolve it. In short, our devotion to unbridled economic freedom and liberty had unleashed an unregulated new age financial monster so vast and so impenetrable that it exceeded our physical and intellectual powers to tame it.

While there is a certain sense of inevitability about this crisis, that we simply are fated to fall victim to such enormous calamities about once every hundred years, it could just as well be argued that nations periodically lose sight of the economic traditions that really matter and wind up paying the price for their failed judgment. The key, of course, is determining the criteria of well-grounded judgment.

One litmus test of well-grounded judgment was provided by repeal of the Glass-Steagall Act in 1999. A New York Times article from 11/5/1999, the day after its repeal, set forth the main points of this debate.[41] First, unlike today, this was basically a bipartisan debate. The measure passed with overwhelming support. The vote in the Senate was 90 to 8, while the House voted 362 to 57. Both Republicans and Democrats supported it, while a relatively small number of Democrats - and even fewer Republicans - opposed it. Democratic supporters included President Clinton, who signed it into law, along with Senators Charles E. Schumer of New York and Bob Kerrey of Nebraska. Republican opponents included Senator Richard C. Shelby of Alabama, the only Republican Senator to vote against it, along with 5 Republican house members.

The main arguments for the repeal were that de-regulation was the wave of the future and that the U.S. ran the risk of becoming a second-rate financial power if it did not embrace it. This argument was reinforced by the contention, voiced by Senator Kerrey of Nebraska, that: "The concerns that we will have a meltdown like 1929 are dramatically overblown."[42] Both Senators Byron L. Dorgan of North Dakota and Paul Wellstone of Minnesota championed the opposite view, that Congress, as Wellstone put it: "seemed determined to unlearn the lessons from our past mistakes....Glass-Steagall was intended to protect our financial system by insulating commercial banking from other forms of risk. It was one of several stabilizers designed to keep a similar tragedy from recurring. Now Congress is about to repeal that economic stabilizer without putting any comparable safeguard in place."[43]

Another significant theme in this debate was that some provisions in the repeal act (Gramm-Leach-Bliley) were "aimed at discouraging community groups from pressing banks to make more loans to the disadvantaged."[44] Democratic representatives Maxine Waters, of California, and Barney Frank, of Massachusetts, voiced these minority concerns. The very large irony of these concerns was that the repeal of Glass-Steagall shredded any scruples of underwriting caution to the point where anyone, regardless of their blatant lack of financial qualifications, could get a subprime mortgage loan. Indeed, the ensuing corruption of underwriting standards became so widespread that these notoriously toxic subprime mortgages became a key element in the financial meltdown of 2008-09.

But the main point of this pivotal event was that the spirit of the times had embarked upon an enormous change. Not unlike the 1920s, the new spirit of the times conveyed a sense of optimism and the belief that the economy had entered a new age of steadfast growth, sustained in part by the stewardship of Federal Reserve Chairman Alan Greenspan, and, in part, by the collapse of the Soviet Union. Capitalism now reigned supreme - no longer challenged by an ideologically antagonistic super-state. The majority of the country now believed in the unfettered exercise of capitalism. It was time to complete the task of deregulation that had begun in earnest in the 1970s.

Indeed, an indication of the strength of this new faith in unregulated capitalism was revealed in the near collapse of the hedge fund, Long Term Capital Management. The near collapse of this hedge fund was the poster child for most of the extreme risks hidden in the innovative financial securities of the period. The essence of these extreme risks lay in the following: First, the gurus behind these hedge funds were selling the belief that their "computer-oriented trading firms relied on statistical distributions and normal curves, and advertised that they didn't take risks in the market because they understood the probabilities of all the price movements and placed their bets scientifically."[45] Second, the scientific exploitation of these probabilities required enormous sums of money, because the profits on the individual transactions were measured in pennies. Hence, meaningful profits required an enormous number of transactions, which, in turn, required an enormous amount of capital. Third, the funds were able to borrow these enormous sums because they were able to sell bankers, or securities firms, on their belief in the scientific certainty of their probability formulas. Fourth, "They were incorporated in places like the Cayman Islands, and nobody in any financial center, including the Federal Reserve System, knew what they were doing."[46]

Emphasizing the last point, Martin Mayer, in *The Fed*, observed:

The belief here is that the reason why the Federal Reserve Bank of New York engineered the rescue of the Long Term Capital Management hedge fund in September 1998 was fear that the collapse of the fund would have exposed to public view the sloppy performance of the world's great financial institutions - and the careless, trusting supervision that had permitted this overconfident crowd of Ph.D. economists, mathematicians, and gamblers to carry positions in excess of $100 billion, and derivative contracts with nominal values over $1 trillion, on a capital base of less than $2 billion.[47]

The fact that all of these elements were at play in the near collapse of LTCM obviously should have rung alarm bells in the deliberations that preceded the passage of Gramm-Leach-Bliley. But the alarm bells remained muffled, if not completely silent. In fact, just 6 months prior to the passage of G-L-B, the *President's Working Group on Financial Markets on Hedge Funds, Leverage, and the Lessons of Long-Term Capital Management* failed to make any recommendations for substantive legislative changes, aside from one tightly focused upon financial contract netting in the event of bankruptcy. Instead they limited their recommendations to an agenda of coaching suggestions for regulators.[48]

This conservative, business-as-usual tenor of their report was reflected in their ho-hum attitude about the risks to overall financial markets presented by these highly leveraged hedge funds:

Concerns have been expressed about the activities of highly leveraged institutions with respect to their impact on market dynamics generally and vulnerable economies in particular. Such activity can affect markets in some circumstances and for limited periods although, as a number of independent studies that have been undertaken so far have suggested, the activities of highly leveraged institutions do not appear to have played a significant role in precipitating the financial market crises of the past few years.[49]

In addition, in what must be regarded as a risibly inert disposition of the toxic role played by offshore financial havens, the Working Group had this to say: "Regulators should consider stronger incentives to encourage offshore financial centers to comply with international standards."[50]

One of the most significant points, albeit lurking in the debris of this debate, was a revisionist view of the causes of the Great Depression. It is the very questionable notion that the Great Depression arose not out of a breakdown in the dynamic equilibrium of the economy - resulting in both collapse of demand and virulent stock market speculation - but exclusively out of a failure by the Federal Reserve Bank to adequately maintain the monetary supply of the nation. Relying upon this questionable interpretation, supporters of the repeal of Glass-Steagall claimed that "historians and economists have concluded that the Glass-Steagall Act was not the correct response to the banking crisis [of the Great Depression] because it was a failure of the Federal Reserve in carrying out monetary policy, not speculation in the stock market, that caused the collapse of 11,000 banks. If anything, the supporters said, the new law will give financial companies the ability to diversify and therefore reduce their risks."[51]

Whether consciously contrived or not, this attempt to reduce the cause of the Great Depression into a choice between stock market speculation and monetary mismanagement by the Federal Reserve is false. It is false because it leaves out of account the huge role played by creative destruction within the agricultural sector of the economy. This creative destruction was of sufficient magnitude to severely erode overall demand, thereby upsetting the dynamic equilibrium of the economy. With overall economic equilibrium undermined by these structural problems in the agricultural sector, the additional blows of enormous wealth destruction, arising out of stock market speculation and monetary mismanagement by the Federal Reserve, were sufficient to push the economy into economic collapse and a decade of stagnation. We will defer a more detailed consideration of this creative destruction resulting from the agro-industrial revolution of the 19th and early 20th century until later. But suffice to say for the moment, structural failures impairing the demand side of the economy played a very large role in the Great Depression.

With that thought in mind, let's turn to unemployment trends during our contemporary era. We will first look at unemployment as annual percentages for the period 1960-2010, and second, in numerical terms of thousands of jobless by month for the period 2007-2010. Charts 6 and 6a, below, display the former and the latter, respectively.

At first glance, it is difficult to see any rhyme or reason in the peaks and valleys of unemployment that surge within and between the various administrations. What eventually comes to light, though, is the degree to which successor administrations are burdened by the unemployment legacies of their predecessors. For example, it is clear that the Nixon administration suffered an immediate jolt of a two

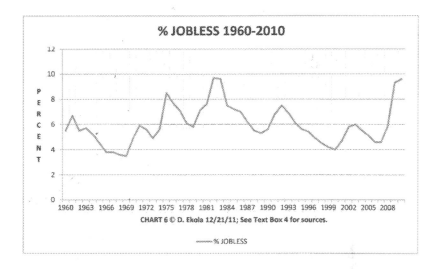

% JOBLESS 1960-2010

CHART 6 © D. Ekola 12/21/11; See Text Box 4 for sources.

———— % JOBLESS

TEXT BOX 4

Companion to Charts 6 and 6a

Economic Report of the President: 2011 Report Spreadsheet Tables;
TABLE B-42. Civilian unemployment rate, 1964-2010.
Bureau of Labor Statistics Data: http://data.bls.gov;pdq/Survey
Output Servlet; Series Id: LNU03000000; Labor force status:
Unemployed.

---

percent increase in unemployment as soon as they assumed office - in
what was the last fiscal year of the Johnson administration. This was
such an abrupt change that common sense indicates we must seek its
origins in the preceding Johnson administration - especially when we
review the list of macroeconomic rogue elements on pages 14-16 for
those having a clear connection to the 1960s.

The most conspicuous would include Lyndon Johnson's aversion to
tax increases summed up in his mantra that the country was so rich
that it could afford both 'Guns and Butter' - that it could afford both
the escalating costs of the Vietnam War and his new Great Society
programs. Johnson's aversion was reinforced by the political reality

that grass roots America shared it. At that point in time, while economists, bankers and big business could still understand the need for a tax increase when the economy overheated, Congress understood that voters did not share that view. As a result, by the time President Johnson belatedly recognized the need for a surtax to cool down the inflationary spiral, Congress was still opposed to it and refused to act.[52]

So just as sure as a stitch in time saves nine, the failure to stitch in a timely manner compounded the damage. In this case, the damage resulting from inadequate revenues was made worse by the coincidental erosion and ultimate collapse of a critical part of the Bretton Woods international monetary system. One of the principal objectives of the Bretton Woods agreement, originating out of the economic rubble of WWII, was to create a stable system of exchange rates for currencies of the member states and provide for their adjustment when the need arose. Unfortunately, this adjustment mechanism broke down when the lynchpin of the system, the United States, became a debtor nation in terms of its international balance of payments. This transition was driven by a number of factors, but perhaps the most significant, in terms of being something the U.S. could control, was the inflation generated by its fiscal improvidence.

The process works like this. Wars tend to have an inflationary impact under the best of circumstances because a significant part of a nation's wealth is expended in pursuit of destruction - and destruction, by definition, does not generate further short-term economic activity. In short, wars do not have a self-sustaining economic component. In fact, they have an inherent inflationary component in that the producers of the implements of war and the warriors who fight them receive compensation lacking a complementary production of consumer goods. In short, their wages generate demand in excess of the supply to satisfy it. That is the reason increased taxation is important for price stability in times of war. Tax increases are essential to curb excess demand created by war.

These basic inflationary dynamics of war were accentuated by the fixed exchange rates of the Bretton Woods system. Deficit financing of the costs of the Vietnam War and Great Society programs resulted in inflation and a weakened dollar beyond what would have resulted from a properly funded war. This had the perverse effect of making foreign goods cheaper - and U.S. goods more expensive - in the U.S. Hence, while, on the one hand, the initial stages of this perverse process resulted in an overheated economy in which unemployment dropped to very low levels in the mid-1960s, on the other, the encroachment of attractively priced foreign goods into the U.S. market gradually took their toll. Demand for domestically produced goods fell and unemployment started to rise. By the time Nixon assumed office in January 1969, unemployment was surging upward with a vengeance. This marked the beginning of the decade of stagflation, the decade of recession accompanied by both inflation and unnaturally high unemployment.[53] All of this can be traced in the fluctuations of unemployment in Chart 6 above.

At the same time, as the dollar weakened further, foreign governments availed themselves of the provision of the Bretton Woods agreement that allowed them to purchase gold from the U.S. at the bargain basement price of $35.00 an ounce. This resulted in the seldom-referenced moment of U.S. economic ignominy - the moment when President Nixon unilaterally suspended the exchange rate system of the Bretton Woods agreement in August 1971.[54]

It is significant that one seldom hears mention of the Bretton Woods agreement these days. The failure to do so probably arises, in part, out of the complexity of the topic and, in part, due to a loss of U.S. prestige arising out of unilaterally suspending a critical part of the agreement. Having said that, the complexity of the agreements fundamentals - and a principal cause of the ultimate demise of its exchange rate provisions - may be summed up as follows: the Bretton Woods agreement attempted to mediate and stabilize international financial and commercial transactions arising out of a diverse hodge-podge of nationally based economies. Augmenting this challenge was that it unfolded in a period of ascendant economic values, while simultaneously bound within the confines of a rigid system of fixed exchange rates. The foundation of this fixed exchange rate system was the U.S. dollar, pegged to a rigidly established price of $35.00 for an ounce of gold.[55]

Further complicating this scenario were the substantial differences in breadth and depth of the respective international obligations assumed by them. Two of the most significant examples involved the U.S. First, the U.S. assumed a hugely disparate burden in its peace-keeping and military role around the world. Second, the U.S. also shouldered the burden of assisting European economies overcome the devastation of WWII by means of funding the Marshall Plan. Both of these burdens had a profound impact on U.S. monetary relationships with its economic partners for two reasons. First, both contributed to a further drain on the U.S. treasury and an amplification of fiscal imbalance in the U.S. budget. Second, while the source of these burdens lay outside the narrow scope of the fixed-exchange-rate terms of the Bretton Woods Agreement, the cost of these burdens undermined the capacity of the U.S. to observe those very terms.

Lurking in the background, though, was an even more profound - and ultimately destabilizing - dynamic. This dynamic consisted of the intertwined U.S. roles, on the one hand, as provider of the defacto international reserve currency in the form of the U.S. dollar, and, on the other, as the financier of last resort of "the recovery of world trade from the aftermath of depression and war."[56] The latter role showed up in the form of "persistent U.S. balance-of-payments deficits."[57] With the passage of time, these naturally contributed to an accumulation of 'Eurodollars' in European central banks. As described by Mayer in *The FED*, those countries most heavily impacted by the accumulation of these Eurodollars suffered an inflationary effect: "European exporters took their dollars to their central banks to exchange for their own currency. This was a problem for the Bundesbank, to take the most frequent end recipient of the dollars, because the marks it had to create to buy the dollars would have an inflationary effect in Germany."[58]

These systemic difficulties were further compounded by the success of the Marshal Plan. The Marshall Plan's success reignited the competitive capacity of Europe. This confronted the U.S. with increased competition at the same time its competitive posture struggled against increasing fiscal burdens of its expanding welfare state, the still mounting costs of the Viet Nam War, continued resistance to tax increases and the costs of its other international obligations. All of these took their toll in a diminished confidence in the value of the U.S. dollar and increased pressures to redeem foreign reserves of U.S. dollars at what had become an unsustainable price for gold at $35.00 per ounce.

When we place all of these elements in their historical context, we can see the fixed exchange rate system of Bretton Woods became a victim of creative destruction in the form of post-WWII economic evolution. The devastation of war, along with the stagnation of depression, gave way to a flourishing international economy and substantial increases in economic values. No fixed rate exchange system could have survived such dramatic changes.

In addition to the rigidities of the system, an equally systemic difficulty lay in what might be called the faulty contrivances of a confederation. After all, the goal of the Bretton Woods agreement was the creation of a multi-national system, designed to regulate and stabilize the competitive arena of international trade and finance. The fault of this system arose out of three inherent weaknesses.

First, it was designed by a confederacy of sovereign nation-states reluctant to surrender their sovereignty; second, the international trade and finance it was intended to regulate was the very arena in which those sovereign states contended for their own advantage; and third, further complicating this scenario was the role of private enterprise - especially in the form of those multinationals holding - and speculating in - large reserves of a variety of international currencies.[59]

In short, it was a system inspired by a structured multi-national vision; but bereft of the force of multi-national law, buttressed by the capacity for change in the form of an empowered executive; and subject to the 'wild-card' centrifugal forces of private enterprise. In that sense, the collapse of the fixed exchange rates of the Bretton Woods agreement could be regarded as the precursor to the contemporary struggles of the European monetary union. Similarly, in the broadest sense, both systems mirror the same fatal flaw as our first attempt at union - the unwillingness of a confederation of sovereign states to surrender their sovereignty to the central government. Without that surrender, the only long-term result could be a half-baked confederation unable to manage its own affairs.

Having said that, however, we should not lose sight of the positive side of this story. Specifically, the Bretton Woods Agreement created an international monetary system that served the immediate purposes of post-WWII recovery very well. Most importantly, its constructive vision of economic renewal avoided the self-destructive myopia of those punitive measures contained in the Versailles Treaty ending WWI.[60] Inspired by that constructive spirit, the United States found the political will to assist those devastated nations achieve renewed self-sustaining prosperity. Especially intriguing, when we consider our contemporary challenges, is the added insight that the funding for that epic economic recovery was found in the deficit margins of monetary, fiscal and trade policy of the western world's one surviving super-state - the United States.

Given our preceding discussion, we can see that the events triggering the collapse of the Bretton Woods exchange rate system played an integral role in the U.S. economic downturn at the outset of the dismal decade of the 1970s. In the same vein, it provides us with two significant insights. First, it focuses our attention on the reality that a series of negative dynamics had overtaken the U.S. economy prior to the loss of our self-sufficiency in oil production in 1970. Hence, it confronts us with the reality that the U.S. economy was in a vulnerable position prior to this loss of our energy independence and the virtual coup de grace of the Arab oil embargo in 1973. Second, it graphically illustrates the transitional impact, or the force of momentum, of a predecessor administration upon its successor.

In the case of the transition from the Kennedy-Johnson administration to the Nixon-Ford, it is clear that the latter had its hands full not only dealing with the fiscal legacy of the former, but also with the evolution of 20 years of post-WWII economic development. Indeed, Nixon's abandonment of the exchange rate mechanism of the Bretton Woods agreement in August 1971 was not the result of forces that arose spontaneously that year - or the year before. It was the result of a lengthy process that combined the numerous dynamics listed above with the fiscal improvidence of the Johnson administration.

As we have already discussed, the latter tardily passed a surtax in July 1968, several years after Federal Reserve Chairman William McChesney Martin, Jr., first noticed the precursors of inflation in March 1965.[61] Similarly, Nixon's actions were foreshadowed by calls for reform of the Bretton Woods agreement as early as December 6, 1968 - a month and a half prior to his inauguration. At that time, an article in Time magazine discussed the urgency of the matter.[62] Finally, as previously noted, there was another tier of forces also contributing to the gestation of the dismal decade. These were rooted more deeply and ranged from the success of the Marshall Plan - upon which the renewed vigor of European economic competition was based - to sea changes in credit markets. The latter were significant because they were one more dynamic that outflanked both the expertise and control of the Federal Reserve.[63]

All of this speaks to the reality of economic momentum as an evolutionary process - gradually unfolding over a period of years and, at times, spanning decades or generations. The reality of this process is reinforced by the trend lines that appear in Chart 6a below, which show the increase and decrease of unemployment, in thousands, for the period July 2007-December 2010. Since this chart details the monthly progress of unemployment data, it is far more jagged than the annual averages presented in Chart 6. However, it does illustrate the overall trend line of the various surges that marked this period. Starting in August 2007, jobless numbers begin to increase as the unemployment rate rises until it briefly re-enters negative territory in November 2007. The unemployment numbers then course upward in waves, occasionally punctuated with precipitous drops, until it reached its high point in January 2009, when more than two million were cast into unemployment that month. [63a]

Of course, just as in the case of Nixon inheriting a very bad hand from the Johnson administration, so to Barak Obama received a very bad hand from President George W. Bush. Such a negative legacy, clearly perceived, naturally harms the political prospects of the Republican Party. Hence, just as naturally, the Republicans have worked diligently to sculpt an alternate vision of reality that avoids history, with minor exceptions, and cherry picks those contemporary statistics that cast President Obama's efforts in the most damaging terms. Rep. Michele Bachmann's response to President Obama's 2011 State of the Union address provides a good example of this tactic. Disingenuously discussing unemployment, she states:

In October 2001, our national unemployment rate was at 5.3 percent. In 2008 it
was at 6.6 percent, But, just eight months after President Obama promised
lower unemployment, that rate spiked to a staggering 10.1 percent. Today,
unemployment is at 9.4 percent with about 400,000 new claims every week.[64]

The reality, as displayed in Chart 6 above and 6a below, is
diametrically opposite the assertions of Representative Bachmann.
The trend line of unemployment starts with a low point in October
2007 of 4.4 percent and then moves precipitously upward, with
negligible monthly variations, to 8.2 percent in February 2009,
scarcely five weeks after Obama assumed office.[64a] This amounts to a
whopping 3.8 percent increase in unemployment and all of it within
the final fiscal year of President Bush's administration - not to
mention that nearly all of that increase originated within the
chronological term of Bush 2. This leaves a remaining increment of
unemployment amounting to 1.8 percent that defines the upper limits
of unemployment accrued under Obama's watch - chronologically
construed. This was when the unemployment rate reached 10
percent in October 2009 - albeit just a month following the last fiscal
year of the Bush administration.

 The trend line that emerges is a precipitous increase into the early
chronological months of Obama's term, capped by a leveling off in
the balance of Obama's term. This underscores the reality of the
collapse of GDP In the closing months of the chronological term of
Bush 2. This is a portrait of negative economic momentum impacting
Obama's administration that is even more graphic than that of the
Johnson administration upon Nixon's.

As to Representative Bachmann's statement of "400,000 new claims
every week," this much is generally true.[65] However, statistics that
focus exclusively on unemployment claims do not give us an accurate
picture of unemployment because it fails to place them in the context
of overall job gains balanced by job loss in a given month. In addition,

her presentation also fails to place these statistics in the context of the enormous number of job losses that occurred over the preceding year. Starting in March 2008, these net monthly job losses/gains were as follows (a positive number is a net loss of jobs/increase in

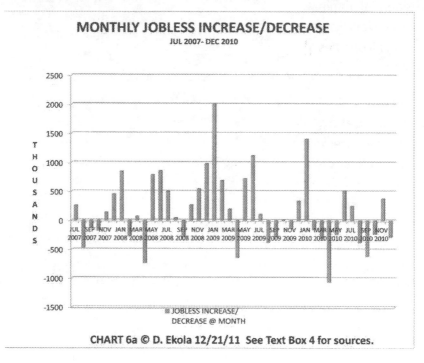

CHART 6a © D. Ekola 12/21/11 See Text Box 4 for sources.

unemployment; while a negative number is a net increase of jobs/decrease in unemployment): Mar 2008 = 74,000; Apr 2008 = -740,000; May 2008 = 789,000; Jun 2008 = 857,000; Jul 2008 = 500,000; Aug 2008 = 46,000; Sep 2008 = -280,000; Oct 2008 = 270,000; Nov 2008 = 546,000; Dec 2008 = 984,000; Jan 2009 = 2,010,000; Feb 2009 = 690,000; March 2009 = 196,000; Apr 2009 = -647,000. The total net job losses for this 14 month period attributable to the administration of Bush 2 amounts to a staggering 5,746,000. These figures are an accurate summation of monthly job gains balanced by job losses provided by the Bureau of Labor Statistics.[66]

We also need to focus on Representative Bachmann's claim that "the President's strategy for recovery was to spend a trillion dollars on a failed stimulus program, fueled by borrowed money."[67] This sound bite has been a favorite of the various contenders for the Republican presidential nomination. It is, however, nothing more than a sound bite since it lacks any support from reputable economic observers. Indeed, all one has to do is return to Charts 5, 6 and 6a to see that the Stimulus Act of February 2009 had a positive effect on the sharply negative economic trends of 2008 and the first months of 2009.

As we already have seen, Chart 5 shows this positive trend in graphic terms. It focuses on the dramatic collapse of GDP during the closing months of Bush 2's administration and its steady resurrection starting soon after the passage of the Stimulus Act. Moreover, it was essential that the administration borrow money to put this program into place because the economy was in free fall and would have collapsed into a full blown depression without it. Finally, as a footnote to this discussion of economic recovery, we ought to give credit to Treasury Secretary Henry Paulson, President Bush 2 and the Democratic Congress for their part in passing the TARP program. It played a significant role, imperfect as it was, in limiting the free fall of the economy in those turbulent months.

As to Representative Bachman's assertion that the national debt stood at 10.6 trillion dollars at the conclusion of Bush 2's term,[68] the actual gross national debt on September 30, 2009, at the end of Bush 2's last fiscal year, was 11.9 trillion dollars.[69] This misstatement by the representative often is echoed by former governor Mitt Romney - with the notable exception that Romney ratchets up the exaggeration to claim that "by the end of his first term, he will have added as much debt as all the prior presidents of this country combined." This overlooks the facts that the gross national debt already had reached $11.9 trillion at the end of Bush 2's last fiscal year on 9/30/2009 and then rose to $14.3 trillion in May 2011 - about a month prior to Romney's assertion on June 27, 2011.[70] Both Bachman and Romney not only overlook the official standards for assigning fiscal responsibility, but also, in the case of Romney, play fast and loose with the artificial distinctions between public and gross federal debt previously discussed. In addition, both ignore: the huge growth of the national debt prior to Obama as seen in Charts 1, 2, 3 and 3A; its negative impact upon Obama's administration just as the fiscal follies of the Johnson administration plagued the Nixon administration; and the limits that these enormous debts imposed upon the ability of the Obama administration to counter all of the other negative forces unleashed by the Great Recession.

We now turn to Charts 7, Average Hourly Wages 1964-2009; 7a, Analysis Missing Productivity Factor (Constant 1982 Dollars; and 7b, Analysis Missing Productivity Factor (Current Dollars), which focus on the stifling of demand in a large sector of the American economy.

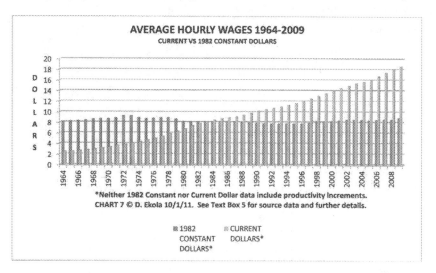

Chart 7 above illustrates how hourly wages, expressed in constant 1982 dollars, reached their peak of $9.26 in 1972-73, and then not only stagnated, but actually suffered through more than three decades of decline. At $8.57 in 2008, for example, they still were $.69 less than their peak of $9.26 in 1972-73. Meanwhile, current wages have the

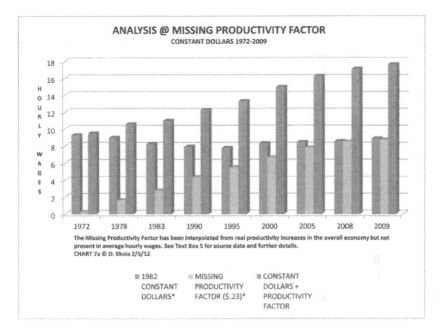

ANALYSIS @ MISSING PRODUCTIVITY FACTOR
CONSTANT DOLLARS 1972-2009

The Missing Productivity Factor has been interpolated from real productivity increases in the overall economy but not present in average hourly wages. See Text Box 5 for source data and further details.
CHART 7a © D. Ekola 2/5/12

| 1982 CONSTANT DOLLARS* | MISSING PRODUCTIVITY FACTOR ($.23)* | CONSTANT DOLLARS + PRODUCTIVITY FACTOR |

appearance of skyrocketing from $3.90 in 1972 to $18.62 in 2008. Hence, since we seldom think in terms of constant wages, the reality of declining hourly wages gets lost in the frothy ascent of current dollar wages. This naturally serves to confuse any discussion of the actual inadequacy of our current wage structure. Indeed, It has a tendency to give an aura of plausibility to the argument that hourly wages today are excessive - especially against the contemporary backdrop of high unemployment and economic suffering among those impacted most by faltering hourly wage levels. But this is not the whole story.

Charts 7a, above, and 7b, below, illustrate a dimension of the hourly wage structure that is hidden in Chart 7. This dimension is the missing productivity factor in hourly wages starting in 1972, when constant hourly wages reached their peak, and continuing up to 2009. Indeed, one reason for the decline in hourly wages is that, while the general economy experienced productivity growth during the 38 year period from 1972-2009, none of this trickled down into the sectors where

DEAN EKOLA

hourly wage earners work. This total productivity growth in the general economy for the 38 years in question amounted to .719 percent. If we were to apply this 38 year percentage increase to

---

TEXT BOX 5
Companion to Charts 7, 7a and 7b
Bureau of Labor Statistics; Labor Productivity and Costs; Productivity change in the nonfarm business sector, 1947-23009.
Federal Reserve Bank: Speech, Ferguson--Lessons from past productivity booms--January 4, 2004. Economic Report of the President: 2011 Report Spreadsheet Tables; Table B-47. Hours and earnings in private nonagricultural industries, 1964-2010.

An exact calculation of compound interest for wages that rise and fall over a 38 year period would require the patience of a saint and the skills of a mathematical guru. Since I have neither, I opted to construct a compound interest formula based on average values. This is not perfect; but it suffices for a reasonable approximation.

The average of annual constant hourly wages for the 38 year period from 1972-2009 is $8.35, or 38 year total of $317.43/38=$8.35. The 38 year average of annual productivity increases is .019, or 38 year total of .719/38=.019. When we plug these figures into the formula for compound interest we get the following: $M=\$8.35(1+.019)^{38}$ = $17.07-$8.35=$8.72/38=.229, or an annual constant productivity increment of $.23. The same process applied to current hourly wages for this 38 year period results in the following: $\$10.61(1+.019)^{38}$ = $21.69-$10.61=$11.08/38 = $.29 annual current productivity increment.

---

constant hourly wages of $8.88 for 2009, the incremental increase for the entire 38 year period would be $6.38, which would result in adjusted 2009 constant hourly wages of $15.26. In a similar manner, the incremental increase for current hourly wages of $18.62 would be $13.39 (.719 X $18.62 = $13.39), or adjusted 2009 current hourly wages

66

of $32.01. However, if we calculate these productivity gains with the formula for compound interest, we wind up with a somewhat different result.

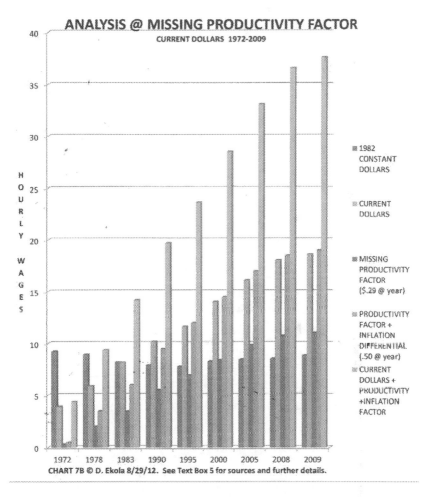

ANALYSIS @ MISSING PRODUCTIVITY FACTOR
CURRENT DOLLARS 1972-2009

CHART 7B © D. Ekola 8/29/12. See Text Box 5 for sources and further details.

An estimate of the average annual monetary increase provided by compound interest for this 38 period would be 23 cents per hour for constant wages and 29 cents per hour for current wages. The sum of these incremental increases for constant hourly wages provide us with a total missing productivity factor of $8.74 per hour and result in an adjusted constant hourly wage of $17.62. Similarly, the sum of these increases for current wages provide us with a total missing productivity factor of $11.02 and result in an adjusted current hourly wage of $29.64 (see Text Box 5 above for detailed calculations). However, as discussed in Text Box 5, we also must account for the inflation differential of $8.01, which results from the difference between the average current wage for 38 years of $10.61 and the 2009 current wage of $18.62. The combination of these two factors results in an annual Productivity/Inflation Differential increment of $.50, which results in an adjusted current dollar wage of $37.62 for the year 2009.

At this point it also should be noted that there are two additional wrinkles in this presentation of the missing productivity factor. The first is that these productivity increases are total labor productivity increases and would not flow in their entirety into hourly wages. In union shops they are the subject of collective bargaining and in non-union shops they are subject to individual bargaining. Both settings to some degree are impacted by contemporary market forces. And, of course, during the past several decades, these forces have been heavily influenced by the downward pressure of outsourcing on wages in the developed economies.

For these reasons, it is difficult to say exactly what percentage of these incremental increases would have been awarded to hourly workers in more typical times. We only can say that these annual productivity increases in the general economy describe a framework in which wage negotiations take place, and that, traditionally, such productivity increases usually have generated increased wages. But, in this case, it is striking that these increases in productivity not only failed to generate any increase in hourly wages, but actually resulted in a decline in constant wages. Moreover, the extended period of time over which this stagnation and decline occurred gives new meaning to the term 'lost generation.' The second wrinkle in this discussion of the missing productivity factor is that it reflects averages, not the actual course of annual productivity increases.

The most salient insight we derive from the three preceding charts is that the past four decades have been an era in which the promised 'trickle-down' stopped trickling. And although the preceding text focuses on the 38 years highlighting the period of greatest decline in hourly wages, the period of actual wage decline extends back another year to 1971, when constant hourly wages of $8.92 were four cents higher than those of $8.88 in 2009. Moreover, the subsequent year of 2010 also reveals hourly wages ($8.90) less than those of 1971 and all the intervening years. In short, this era of lost wages now extends to 40 years. Viewed against this background, the current Republican charges that the Obama administration initiated this period of wage stagnation is groundless. We obviously are looking at a systemic problem with very deep roots.

In addition, it also must be noted that this failure of productivity gains to 'trickle-down' illustrates an additional source of the widening gap In Income distribution. Obviously, this failure negatively impacts a very large percentage of families, who depend upon hourly wages, while it positively impacts the much smaller percentage of families who are not hourly wage earners. This clearly results in a very substantial 'trickle-up' phenomenon, bestowing the largest benefits on those at the top of the income hierarchy.

Regrettably, this is not the whole story. As bad as this story is, the 40-year span of declining wages for hourly wage earners pales in comparison with the devastation caused by skyrocketing health care costs.

The broad outlines of these increased health care costs can be seen below in Chart 8, Average Hourly Wages & Health Costs 1964-2009. This gives us a picture of the impact of health care costs on an

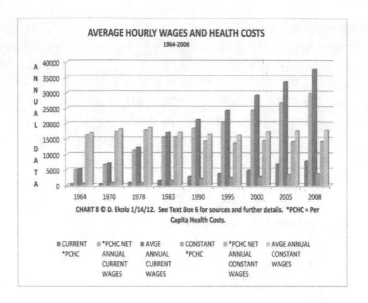

CHART 8 © D. Ekola 1/14/12. See Text Box 6 for sources and further details. *PCHC = Per Capita Health Costs.

TEXT BOX 6

Companion to Charts 8, 9 and 9a.

Economic Report of the President: 2011 Report Spreadsheet Tables; Table B-47. Hours and earnings in private nonagricultural industries, 1964-2010.

U.S. Dept of Health and Human Services (www.hhs.gov), National Health Expenditures Summary and GDP: Calendar Years 2009 to 1960.

U.S Census Bureau, Current Population Survey, Annual Social and Economic Supplements; Table H-1. Income Limits for Each Fifth and Top 5 Percent Households: 1967-2010

---

individual basis. Per Capita Health Costs, expressed in constant 1982 dollars, rose dramatically from $624 in 1964 to $3860 in 2009 - a net increase of $3,236 in constant dollars that translates into 519 percent. This contrasts with a rise of $1,601, from $16,869 to $18,470, in average annual constant wages - or a modest increase of only 9.5 percent over this 45 year period.

However, the truly destructive economic impact of these health cost increases gets blunted when we measure them as individual costs measured against the average hourly wages of an individual. There are two reasons for this. First, our economy actually functions more as household units - than as individuals - in terms of health care costs. Second, by focusing exclusively on average hourly wages we lose sight of the messy context in which health costs are shifted away from low income sectors, who cannot afford them, to those groups that barely can afford them.

The broad outlines of this more representative context are addressed below in Chart 9, Health Costs and Household Income

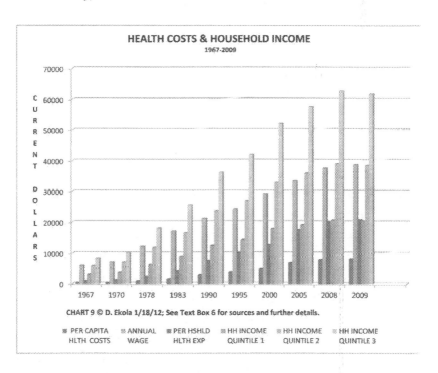

1967-2009, and in Chart 9a, Health Costs As % Household Income, Quintiles 1-3 1967- 2009. Chart 9 contrasts per capita health costs, average hourly earnings as an annual wage and household health costs with the first three quintiles of household income. As can be

seen in Chart 9a, household health costs of $833 were relatively tame in 1967, amounting to 14 percent of the average annual wage ($5928) for that year.

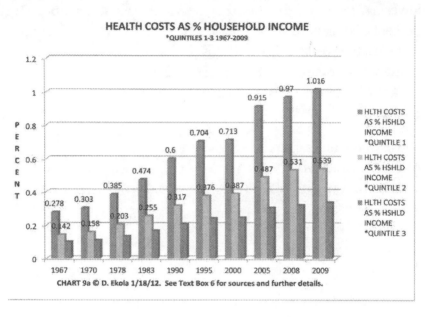

HEALTH COSTS AS % HOUSEHOLD INCOME
*QUINTILES 1-3 1967-2009

CHART 9a © D. Ekola 1/18/12. See Text Box 6 for sources and further details.

But when viewed in the context of the first three household income quintiles, a somewhat different picture emerges. While these costs amounted to a relatively modest 14.2 percent of the second quintile ($5850) and only 10 percent of the third quintile ($8303), they amounted to a considerably larger share, or 27.7 percent, of the annual household earnings ($3,000) of the first quintile. Moreover, it also should be noted that all of these figures represent an understatement of health care costs relative to household income insofar as these income figures are not the average for each quintile, but rather are the highest income for each bracket. This distortion naturally impacts all of the quintile data presented in this discussion.

Turning back to Chart 9, we can see that by 2009 household health care costs ($20,781) had soared to such heights that they became financial wrecking balls for household income quintiles 1 ($20,453) and 2 ($38,550) and a severe challenge for quintile 3 ($61,801). Chart 9a above completes the portrait of how our soaring health care costs have sucked dry the demand side of our economy. For those in the lowest quintile, their share of health care costs soared to 101.6 percent of their household income. For those in the second and third quintiles, they reached 53.9 and 33.6 percent of their respective household incomes. It is against this background that our hybrid free market/government subsidy system of health care is exposed as naked folly.

Those who argue against the role of big government point exclusively to government involvement as the Achilles heel of our health care system. And in very general terms, their argument sounds plausible. Indeed, when we compare pre-Medicare health care costs with our current health care cost structure, it's hard to dispute the contention that government's role in health care has powerfully impacted its overall costs.

A brief review of its history follows. Medicare/Medicaid became law in 1965. Spending on pre-Medicare/Medicaid health care amounted to just over 5 percent of the nation's GDP in 1960 and subsequently soared to over 16 percent in 2008. Even more suggestive is the fact that the private share of health care spending dropped from over 75 percent to less than 53 percent of GDP in 2008, while the public share of that spending climbed from less than 25 percent to over 47 percent during the same period.[70a] When these comparisons are coupled with daunting demographic changes reducing the worker/beneficiary ratio supporting Medicare/Medicaid, it is easy to draw an alarming portrait of the system's prospects. Similarly, it also is difficult to see how a reform based exclusively on increased taxes and fees can adequately confront these problems.

However, such an analysis ignores a number of significant cost drivers. First, the American health care system is not a single-payer system exclusively controlled by the government. It is a hybrid system resting primarily on free market fundamentals, increasingly subsidized by the government.   One analogy of this relationship might be that government invited the free market fox of our health care sector into the hen house of the U.S. Treasury - without giving sufficient consideration to the foxy dynamics of such a relationship.

Some of the other drivers propelling these costs up are the following: 5 percent of health care recipients account for half of health care spending;[70b] similarly, some 25 percent of Medicare expenditures have been spent on the last year of end-of-life care;[70c] but, perhaps most importantly, prior to Obamacare, government subsidies took the form of payments on a per-service basis, frequently punctuated with failed price-control measures. Payments were not tailored to patient progress; health outcomes; or most importantly, incentivized with rewards.[70d] Hence, not surprisingly, up until now the result has been escalating costs as providers gamed the fee schedule for services rendered with no reference to outcomes.

 But these cost drivers of our hybrid free market/government subsidy system have not been the only escalators of our health care costs, propelling them far beyond what most other developed economies experience. To get a more complete picture of those other cost increases, we need to return to our discussion of the relationship between household income and health care costs.

Specifically, we need to look at how unsustainable health care costs for the lowest income quintiles are redistributed for payment elsewhere. One of these is the defacto reinsurance system utilized for unpaid hospital emergency room charges: they either get added into private health insurance billings; or in the case of public hospitals, they also find their way into the property tax system. For much of the history of our hybrid health care system, most of these defacto means of funding unpaid health care charges were essentially flat rate collection systems; i.e., they were comparable to a flat rate tax system. This also has been so in the case of Medicare, which, for much of its history, imposed flat rate FICA taxes and premiums on everyone. In short, with a few exceptions these were regressive funding schemes that bore down hardest on those who could least afford them. The one exception, perversely, were the uninsured, who typically have been charged significantly more than their insured counterparts.

The upshot is that this opaque system of funding our unsustainable health care costs resulted in a snowball effect in which the inability of the lowest income groups to pay for their health care shifted these costs to the next group, which resulted in a further shift of unsustainable costs to the next group and so on. In fact, it is reasonable to conclude that the funding failures of this defacto reinsurance system actually creates a system that, whether by design or default, contributed to the inflation of overall health care costs by routinely inflating private health insurance premiums and the costs of health care services by an amount commensurate with uncollectable health care charges.

The combined thrust of all these cost drivers has resulted in a system that costs far more relative to GDP than most of the world's other developed economies.[108] It is a system that has spewed out bankruptcies for the millions who lack adequate insurance or have none at all. Similarly, It hobbles the competitiveness of our private sector and strains the fiscal resources of our public sector. It is a lose, lose paradigm for all concerned.

Worst of all, since it has been allowed to fester over a half century, it has attained a magnitude and negative momentum that chills the public's ardor for the costs of reform. In short, just as with our fiscal follies, the daunting consequences of drift and inaction lead to further inaction.

Earlier in this essay, we touched upon our renewed embrace of two obsolete economic theories: Adam Smith's theory of the invisible hand and Jean Baptiste Say's supply side theory. While these towering figures in economic history received scarcely a passing mention as we approached the 2012 elections, their concepts nonetheless provide the intellectual foundations of modern conservative economic theory.[71] Only the labels have been changed. Instead of invisible hand and supply side, these labels have been repackaged into a unified concept of the free market - focused almost exclusively upon the role of the entrepreneur. Presumably this tweaking of their identity resulted from a marketing judgment that, in America, the idea of free market forces would resonate more favorably than references to the caprice of an invisible hand or the theory of an obscure Frenchman.

This is not to say that these subjects have never been discussed on the fringes of our conventional wisdom. Certainly there was a spate of articles and columns that focused on these so-called *pointy-headed* subjects during the depths of the 2008-09 financial crisis. But given their theoretical focus, we can safely conclude they were not widely read then and have, as a practical matter, since fallen back into oblivion.[72] This provides fresh grist for George Santayana's iconic caveat that those who forget their history will be condemned to repeat it.

The first step to understanding the significance of these two concepts is to focus on their underlying assumption that free market capitalism is guided by rational players. The early proponents of capitalism shared in the same optimistic assessment of human nature that arose out of the Enlightenment and coursed through our Declaration of Independence. This optimistic assessment was based upon the-then-novel premise that rational self-interest is essentially benevolent. It also was the basis for our first attempt at a constitution: the Articles of Confederation of 1781.[73] This attempt failed miserably precisely because it failed to grant essential coercive powers to government.[74] It assumed that rational self-interest - and a commitment to the noble experiment in democratic government - would lead the citizens of the young republic to voluntarily subject themselves to the disciplines of taxation, regulation and restraint of unbridled state's rights necessary for a strong and prosperous nation.

The next six years proved conclusively that these assumptions were wrong. Lacking the necessary powers of taxation, the central government was powerless to responsibly manage the normal expenses of government - not to mention the greater burden of the infant republic's revolutionary war debt. [75] Moreover, a huge part of the war debt was owed to rank and file Revolutionary War veterans who had been paid with worthless script. Needing real money to restart their civilian lives, they had fallen victim to the rapacious terms of speculators, receiving only pennies on the dollar for their script. The speculators, in turn, successfully pressed state legislators to redeem this script at face value. The legislatures then levied taxes to fund this redemption. The shameful result was that these financially vulnerable veterans - heroes of the Revolutionary War - were not only cheated of just recompense for their service, but forced to reimburse, via taxes, the full value of their service to those speculators who had exploited them. Sadly, in too many cases they were unable to pay the taxes and were subjected to the grim prospects of forced sales of their land along with personal property - or even debtor's prison. [76]

This quickly led to armed demonstrations at courthouses and, ultimately, instances of more determined insurrection. These were epitomized by, but not limited to, Shay's Rebellion. These flames of class war were troubling not only for the wealthy interests in the North, but also for southern plantation owners. The latter were fearful that these sporadic armed uprisings were spreading a dangerous example among their slaves - who comprised a majority of the population in a number of those states. [77] Even more distressing to the *better class* of citizens was that the central government did not have a standing army to quell these disturbances or to defend against foreign interference.[78]

Equally problematic was that the reliability of the mainstay of domestic order, the militia, too often was undermined by the sympathy of its members for their compatriots. Indeed, in some instances they had defected to the side of the insurrectionists or, nearly as problematic, refused to engage against them . However, in the case of the final battles of Shay's Rebellion, the insurrectionists luck finally ran out. The force that finally put down the insurrection consisted of a federal contingent, mobilized for this specific need, and a much larger mercenary army funded by a coalition of Boston bankers.[79]

Adding more fuel to these flames of disintegration were the unbridled exercise of state's rights in the area of interstate and foreign commerce. Finally, looming over this chaos and the impotence of our *First Confederacy* was the specter of European ambition. In particular, both Britain and Spain were maneuvering to regain some of their recent territorial losses.[80] It was at this point of multiple systemic crises that the Constitutional Convention of 1787 was convened, in secret, and during which our government finally was granted the powers necessary to govern. Defending these newly granted powers in his Federalist No. 21, Alexander Hamilton blasted the want of such powers in the Articles of Confederation:

...[without these powers] the United States afford the extraordinary spectacle of a government destitute even of the shadow of constitutional power to enforce the execution of its own laws.[81]

Also driving these sea changes in the powers granted to the federal government, was an equally profound shift in how the Founding Fathers viewed human nature. The grand experiment in an essentially voluntary association that, *hopefully*, would be guided by its devotion to reason and democratic principles of government had taken them to the brink of ruin. Now they were forced to fall back on a much harsher assessment of human nature and its implications for government. James Madison acknowledged this in his Federalist No. 51:

It may be a reflection on human nature, that such devices [as checks and balances] should be necessary to control the abuses of government. But what is government itself, but the greatest of all reflections on human nature? If men were angels, no government would be necessary. In framing a government which is to be administered by men over men, the great difficulty lies in this: you must first enable the government to control the governed; and in the next place oblige it to control itself.[82]

Although scarcely noted outside today's halls of higher education, this amounted to a huge rebuke of the Enlightenment and its faith in the benign character of humanity's rational self-interest. Hence, it is remarkable just how far we have travelled away from these hard-won lessons of our Founding Fathers. But, for too many of us, no matter how well documented, this acknowledgment of the sea change in the FF's view of human nature is regarded as unpatriotic revisionist history or simply too far removed from our present era to be worthy of our attention. This is regrettable because these lessons get right to the heart of our current predicament.

To understand the connection between this example of failed rational self-interest and the Great Recession, we now turn to former Federal Reserve Chairman Alan Greenspan. During his career as Chairman of the Federal Reserve, he embraced the doctrine of rational self-interest just as our Founding Generation initially had done. As evidence of this, just three years prior to the Great Recession, he travelled to Kirkcaldy, Scotland, the birthplace of Adam Smith, to give a lecture that celebrated Smith's contributions to economic theory. He praised Smith as "a towering contributor to the development of the modern world" and his "extraordinary insight that the individual's drive for private gain will promote the public good," even though it "was no part of his intention."[83]

In his concluding remarks, he wove together Smith's theory of the 'invisible hand,' the Enlightenment concept of rational self-interest and an optimistic assessment of how the assumed self-balancing character of these forces results in a functioning economic system:

Classical economics, especially as refined and formalized by Ricardo and Alfred Marshall, emphasized competition in the marketplace among economic participants governed by rational self-interest. The value preferences of these participants would be revealed by their actions in that marketplace....Over the past two centuries, scholars have examined these issues extensively, but our knowledge of the source of inbred value preference remains importantly shaped by the debates that engaged the Enlightenment. The vast majority of economic decisions today fit those earlier presumptions of individuals acting more or less in their rational self-interest. Were it otherwise, economic variables would fluctuate more than we observe in markets at most times. Indeed, without the presumption of rational self-interest, the supply and demand curves of classical economics might not intersect, eliminating the possibility of market-determined prices. For example, one could hardly imagine that today's awesome array of international transactions would produce the relative economic stability that we experience daily if they were not led by some international version of Smith's invisible hand. [Federal Reserve Board; Speech, Greenspan - Adam Smith - February 6, 2005][84]

This was the same Greenspan, who several years previously, had thrown his support behind the 1999 legislation that jettisoned the depression-era financial regulations of Glass-Steagall, stating that such protections no longer were necessary. In his defense, though, it should be noted that he was not alone in pursuing this disastrous course. In fact, this was an instance of bipartisan folly. Both Democrats, including President Clinton, and Republicans joined in celebrating what they regarded as the beginning of a brave new age of financial innovation.

But, it also opened the floodgates to the assumption of unregulated, unmonitored and hidden levels of risk by banks. It resulted in the assumption of staggering levels of risk that not only were hidden from federal regulators, but also from the banks own officers. It was, in effect, a reincarnation of Adam Smith's invisible hand come home to roost - in its most perverse form. It would become the invisible hand of economic destruction, in the form of poorly understood, highly esoteric financial products, set loose upon the economy by a naive spirit of deregulation.[85]

One of the midwifes present at the birthing of these financial perversions had this to say nearly a decade before the onset of the 2008 financial meltdown:

In 1981-82, as a member of the finance committee of Ronal Reagan's National Commission on Housing, I became one of the authors of the plan by which housing could be financed with real estate mortgage investment conduits, permitting pension funds and mutual funds to get in and out of housing investments, and permitting Wall Street houses to slice and dice mortgage paper that carried an implicit government guarantee. The bankers created innumerable "tranches" that could be sold separately to risk-averse investors and risk-seeking speculators, hedged to reduce the dangers of changes in interest rates, or rolled over in repurchase agreements to multiply both risks and rewards. It is by no means clear that the future will regard this system of home finance as a good idea.[86]

Returning to Greenspan and shifting forward three years, we find the former Federal Reserve Chairman chastened and shocked by the economic crisis that uprooted the fundamentals of his economic worldview. In his remarks to the House Oversight Committee on 10/23/08, Greenspan stated that:

...those of us who have looked to the self-interest of lending institutions to protect shareholder's equity (myself especially) are in a state of shocked disbelief. Such counterparty surveillance is a central pillar of our financial

markets' state of balance. If it fails, as occurred this year, market stability is undermined.[87]

In response to questions, he emphasized how this market failure had impacted his fundamental view of how markets functioned. He stated that his long-standing belief in the self-interest of banking institutions as sufficient to protect equity values had been a mistake. The tsunami in the credit markets of 2008 had forced him to see the "flaw in the model that I perceived is the critical functioning structure that defines how the world works."[88]

This brings us back full circle to the ideas of rational self-interest, the invisible hand and how they are assumed to operate in tandem as a self-regulating mechanism in a capitalist economy. But, to better understand the obsolescence of this theory, we must turn to Adam Smith's specific language about the mechanics of the invisible hand:

*As every individual, therefore, **endeavors as much as he can both to employ his capital in the support of domestick (sic) industry, and so to direct that industry that its produce may be of the greatest value; every individual necessarily labours (sic) to render the annual revenue of the society as great as he can.** He generally, indeed, neither intends to promote the publick (sic) interest, nor knows how much he is promoting it. By preferring the support of domestick (sic) to that of foreign industry, he intends only his own security; and by directing that industry in such a manner as its produce may be of the greatest value, he intends only his own gain, **and he is in this, as in many other cases, led by an invisible hand to promote an end which was no part of his intention.** Nor is always the worse for the society that it was no part of it. By pursuing his own interest he frequently promotes that of the society more effectually than when he really intends to promote it.*[89] (emphasis added)

The critical element here is the economic provincialism of the capitalists of Smith's era and their reluctance to invest outside their home turf. This reluctance to invest abroad was not surprising in an age where commerce was hindered by the uncertainty of ploddingly slow communications and transportation - and a lack of confidence in the catch-as-catch-can means of contract enforcement in foreign trade. This must have been especially true in an age when capital formation was in its infancy and capital was both comparatively rare and a very precious commodity.

Today we face radically different circumstances. Chief among them has been the unprecedented surge in outsourcing production from mature economies to the cheap labor markets of the ascendant economies of the world. And therein lies the fulcrum of obsolescence for Smith's theory of the invisible hand. Today's capitalists no longer are reluctant to invest outside their homeland. Indeed, their eagerness to reap profits, flowing from the steep differential in global labor costs, is whetted further by the substantial reduction of most of their ancient apprehensions about foreign investments. More to the point, this increased sense of security has grown apace with the hunger in the third world for access to development, bringing with it an expanded range of employment possibilities for their people, and the reality that many multi-national corporations now enjoy resources and power in excess of many of the smaller foreign countries with whom they deal.

But despite the death of Smith's invisible hand in our time, we not only have failed to assemble for an appropriate wake and reassessment, we also continue to act as though its mystical provenance still provides us with the most trustworthy guidance through these deeply troubled times. The upshot is that, while we continue to mouth the same old economic bromides that are part and parcel of the invisible hand theory - not to mention deeply implicated in our near total economic collapse - our economy continues to crawl and stumble in a most unsatisfactory manner. Given such a checkered legacy, it's clearly past time we laid Smith's theory of the invisible hand to rest and acknowledged the necessary sea changes in economic policy that are implicit in its passing.

Jean Baptiste Say's supply side theory, first published in 1803, suffered obsolescence in much the same manner as Smith's invisible hand. It was overrun by the sweeping evolution of economic life during the following century. The essence of Say's theory is that supply, or the production of goods, automatically generates sufficient demand for its purchase and guarantees the continuing advance of the economy.[90] Certainly the simplicity of the economy in his day lent an aura of common-sense plausibility to it.

Indeed, to put Say's theory in historical perspective, we need to recall that 1803, the year of its publication, was the same year President Thomas Jefferson concluded the Louisiana Purchase. The following years (1804-06) bracketed the iconic Lewis and Clark expedition through uncharted territory to the Pacific coast. The year 1825 marked the completion of the Erie Canal. It created a transportation link between New York City and the Great Lakes that opened the Midwest to settlement, agricultural development and, ultimately, to carbon-fueled industrial development that surpassed the limited potential of water-driven industries of the East.

When we step back from this panorama of change following the Constitutional Convention, we are struck by several major themes. First, as regards the nation's economic development, the Constitutional Convention laid down the legal foundations of what would become the world's most expansive common market. Second, the Louisiana Purchase represented a huge step in expanding the territorial base of that common market. Third, the era's many transportation initiatives, of which the enormously successful Erie Canal was but one, started the process of knitting together this huge common market. Fourth, the creation of this transportation network, especially in the form of railroads, spurred the growth and development of extractive and heavy industries. Finally, all of these, reinforced by quantum leaps in communications and energy production/distribution, created a symbiotic dynamic that propelled the economy into previously unimagined scales of production and heights of productivity.[91]

Hence, to return to 1803, when Say published his theory, the problems of unregulated competitive markets and mass production generating enormous gluts of goods - in both the agricultural and industrial sectors - were still in the distant future. Indeed, depending on the sector, they still were nearly a century in the making. By contrast, the very limited scales of production and distribution of Say's era - still evolving out of the grip of handcrafts and guilds - certainly enhanced the concept of an unfettered competitive model. To put a finer point on it, the competitive model of that formative era was more an ideal than a tried and tested institution. Much like today, it provided a plausible abstraction against which the economic realities of the day could be measured. But, it wasn't reality.

In the end, though, the most compelling evidence against Say's supply side theory, as with Smith's invisible hand, may be found in the economic wreckage that brought on the Great Depression While World War I had generated enormous European demand for the agricultural and industrial goods of the United States, this would prove to be only a temporary bright spot. This was especially true for the U.S. agricultural sector, that, excepting the good times of WWI, otherwise was caught in a downward spiral driven by structural changes in both foreign and domestic markets.

Going back to the end of the nineteenth century, U.S. exports of cereal grains ran into stiff competition from Canada, Argentina and Australia. U.S. cereal exports plummeted from 530 million bushels in 1897-98 to 168 million in 1913-14. This was followed by a brief rebound back to 533 million bushels during the war, but soon collapsed post-war. By 1925-26 these exports had dropped back to 210 million bushels. During this nearly 30 year period, Canadian wheat production had increased ten-fold, from 52 million bushels to approximately 550 million bushels in 1928. While the increase of wheat production in Argentina and Australia was not as dramatic for the same period, it nonetheless nearly tripled in the former and more than doubled in the latter. But, when we turn to beef exports, the picture was even more bleak for U.S. exporters. Exports of beef from Argentina skyrocketed from 54 million pounds in 1900 to nearly 2 billion pounds, tallied as annual averages, for the years just prior to the Depression. By comparison, U.S. beef exports all but vanished during the same period.[92] Naturally such disruption of our traditional global markets for agricultural products was a huge blow to the profitability of America's farms. Unfortunately, these global trends in agriculture were not the whole story. Equally negative forces within our domestic farm economy also were at play.

Before we address these other negative forces, let's pause to focus upon a major source of data and interpretation for this discussion. The title of the work in question is *Recent Economic Changes in the United States*, published by the National Bureau of Economic Research in early 1929, just a matter of months before the great stock market crash of October 1929. This was a cooperative effort by the Committee on Recent Economic Changes of the President's Conference on Unemployment;[93] however, its focus actually was much broader than unemployment. Similarly, while its avowed frame of reference was the so-called prosperous post-war period of 1922-29, it actually took a more extensive view that stretched back into the late 1800s when necessary. We also should note that the NBER is a private entity; however, in the years preceding 1934 it filled a quasi-public role that had not yet been adequately filled by the federal government. In other words, it amounted to the private precursor to the Bureau of Labor Statistics and Bureau of Economic Research. Today it continues to be a highly respected private research organization.

This 1929 analysis of the U.S. economy is a seminal work in two respects. First, its discussion of the nation's agricultural economy hones in on a prime mover of the Great Depression. It reveals how the demand side of the nation's economy was eroded not just by the collapse of its global agricultural markets, but how technological change uprooted ancient pillars of the domestic agricultural economy, further undermining the livelihoods of rural America.[94] Second, it provides us with a private sector view of market forces, contrasting markedly with those of today's supply side conservatives.

Starting in the 1800s, American agriculture was impacted by technological change in several distinct phases. The initial phase consisted of the adoption of horse-drawn machinery to aid in cultivation and harvesting. It had its origins in the first half of the nineteenth century, but did not take off in earnest until the labor shortages of the Civil War provided the necessary element of urgency.[95] The second phase consisted of an ambitious program to promote and disseminate scientific farming practices by means of a national network of educational and experimental institutions ranging from land-grant colleges to county demonstration agents.[96]

Parenthetically, what is particularly interesting about the adoption of scientific farming practices is that it goes right to the heart of the controversy whether government does or does not create wealth. Certainly the record shows that, in the case of agricultural productivity, the government was a prime mover in the creation of wealth. To quote the report:

From the Civil War to the World War, we had a succession of developments of Federal and state departments of agriculture, agricultural colleges, agricultural experiment stations, extension service, and county demonstration agents or farm advisers. The pressure of war needs and 'food-will-win-the-war' campaigns resulted in a rapid development of the extension service and the putting of local educational agents in about 4,000 of the principal agricultural counties, from one end of the country to the other.[97]

All of these contributed to revolutionary advances in agricultural practices, or more precisely, in the skills of agricultural labor. When combined with the relentless mechanization of draft animal and human labor inputs, the result was the reduction in the percentage of population engaged in agriculture from some 95% at the end of the colonial period to about 2% today.[98] Moreover, this small percentage of the population not only feeds a population of some 350 million, but also plays a major role in the world market. This is an amazing spectacle of wealth creation, a large part of which resulted from government programs focused on agricultural education and research.

The third phase of this technological revolution in American agriculture consisted of the replacement of draft animals in both general transportation and on the farm. This process started in the first decades of the twentieth century as horse-drawn carriages and carts in the cities and towns were the first to be converted to the internal combustion engine. This process then expanded onto the farms, triggered initially by the labor shortages of World War I. But, with the end of the war, a deepening crisis overtook American agriculture. Overproduction and falling prices, along with rising production and distribution costs, drove farmers to produce more in a desperate bid to cover such fixed costs as mortgages. These self-defeating efforts to produce more in a glutted market led them to embrace more fully the switch from draft animals to the internal combustion engine.[99]

According to the above-mentioned report, "...the number of horses and mules on farms [declined] from 25.7 million to 19.5 million" between 1913 and 1928.[100] These declines were exceeded by the even greater transition from draft animals to motorized vehicles in America's towns and cities. Consequently, "demand for at least 15 to 18 million acres of hay and grain land....dropped away as a result of this transition from horse power to internal combustion motors."[101]

This loss of demand for forage led to even greater production of food destined for human consumption. And this, of course, led to even greater declines in agricultural price levels.

This perfect storm within American agriculture laid bare the failure of the unregulated competitive model to cope successfully with the vicissitudes in the global economy and the profound impact of technological changes. Needless-to-say, it also overturned Say's supply side theory and Adam Smith's theory of the invisible hand. What is especially ironic is that, arguably, American agriculture provided a better example of laissez-faire's competitive model than did the monopolistic tendencies of American corporations. Hence, while in theory agriculture's essentially competitive structure should have spared it from ruin; in reality it did just the opposite.

Nor was the ruin of agriculture a matter of little concern for the American economy - despite the enormous changes and seeming prosperity in the urban economy of that era. Certainly it is true that a major shift was taking place in the urban-rural make-up of the nation. The size of the farm population had declined from an estimated 95 percent, at the time of the Constitutional Convention, to 30.1 percent in 1920.[102] However, this trend could not alter the fact that the percent of the overall population dependent upon agriculture was substantially larger than suggested by this statistic and that this entire sector was struggling. It was struggling to the point that it could neither support its share of industrial production, nor, in many instances, meet its mortgage payments. The latter was made worse by the fact that mortgages of the day had short terms - typically only 8 years. In other words, they came up for renewal, review and possible termination with a frequency injecting a destabilizing degree of volatility into the overall market.

When we step back from this bleak portrait, we can see just how much the deck was stacked against the individual farmer, struggling to meet the increased costs of refinancing existing debt against a backdrop of declining land and commodity values. Forced to increase production in a market that must punish him for producing more, he was caught in a race to the bottom in a market over which he and his fellow farmers had no control. It was a situation that cried out for a guiding hand capable of controlling the destructive forces of the free market. However, in that age of relative economic innocence preceding the Great Depression, the political consensus essential to government management of the agricultural sector simply did not exist.[103] It would take the national train wreck of the Great Depression to shake the country's faith in laissez-faire.

Contrary to the dominant free market ideology of the era, the report on *Recent Economic Changes* addressed these defects of simplistic economic analysis time and again. In that spirit it made repeated calls to be mindful of the need for economic balance among the various sectors of the economy as in the following excerpt:

All parts of our economic structure from the prime processes of making and of marketing to the facilitating functions of finance, are and have been interdependent and easily affected. And therein lies the danger: That through ignorance of economic principles, or through selfish greed, or inadequate leadership, the steady balance will be disturbed, to our economic detriment. [104]

Moreover, it did not view this need for balance as a condition within a static context. Rather it introduced the-then-novel concept of dynamic equilibrium, a dynamic that must evolve and adapt its underlying equilibrium in fluid circumstances.[105] This anticipated subsequent metaphors of economic growth as a form of flight, as for example in W.W. Rostow's *Stages of Economic Growth.*[106] Nor did it hesitate to denounce the tendency within the various market sectors to aggrandize their narrow interests over those of the overall economy. Finally, what was remarkable for the laissez-faire spirit of that era - not to mention outright heresy for today's reactionaries - was the committees call for a greater role for government in maintaining this balance:

*To maintain the dynamic equilibrium of recent years is, indeed, a problem of
leadership which more and more demands deliberate public attention and
control.*[107]

When viewed in hindsight - and especially in view of the eminent
collapse of the stock market that same year - the report's description
of the economic imbalance between the agricultural sector and
general economy, along with its emphasis on the importance of
economic balance, take on an almost prophetic quality. Equally
significant, their concepts of economic balance and dynamic
equilibrium - within an economic arena of disparate competing
interests - reflected the influence of our Founding Generation, who, in
turn, were influenced by the pessimistic assessment of human nature
set forth by Thomas Hobbes. The latter famously observed that,
reduced to a state of nature, "the life of man [would be] solitary,
poor, nasty, brutish, and short."[108] As already discussed, the Founding
Generation regarded this Hobbesian view of the human condition as
a fundamental concern in designing our new Constitution as a
mediator of those competing interests.[109]

Given this legacy, the 1920s view of the economy was indisputably
more complex - and arguably more realistically grounded - than the
unitary concept of today's laissez-faire conservatives. This is
especially so since today's unitary concept is an odd blend of
complete faith in the automatic dynamic of an unregulated free
market economy - provided that no one stirs the pot of class warfare.
This caveat about class warfare conveniently transforms what the
founders regarded as a general trait of the human species - unbridled
self-interest - into one that is exclusively the province of the working
class. Typically, it is introduced in a separate context, so as not to
raise questions about the presumed perfection of the 'auto-dynamic'
of free market dogma. In a similar vein, the purported virtues of the
entrepreneur are trumpeted ad nausea so as to inoculate them

against the contagion of any unseemly spatters that might issue from the mud being cast at the less-favored classes.

This is not the whole story. New-age conservatives actually have a much grander agenda. This grander agenda rests upon the hijack of the idea of America as the exceptional nation. The details of this hijack are as follows: first and foremost, we have the time-honored proposition that America is the promised land in which democratic freedoms, both economic and political, have been enshrined in our Constitution; second, America is an evangelical beacon guiding the rest of the world to share in our moral and cultural superiority as the greatest nation on earth; and, third, according to its more enthusiastic adherents, the strength of this exceptional role arises out of its divine sanction and that, in turn, demands a reverence not unlike the worship of religious icons.[110]

In this manner, we wind up at the intersection of the sacred and profane, where contemporary partisan agendas get all dressed up in the raiment of freedom, liberty and constitutional purity. Hence, instead of a living constitution, designed to adjust as the circumstances of our lives evolve, we are confronted by the intractable demands of reactionaries, fully prepared to dismantle our government piece by piece. These demands include the elimination of the so-called 'death tax,' the income tax, the Federal Reserve Bank, a reinstatement of the gold standard, the elimination of the Departments of Education, Energy and Health and Human Services, and for some, the elimination of every department that did not have cabinet rank when the Constitution was ratified. If we opt for this more ambitious program of constitutional purity, then we can also rid ourselves of the Departments of Interior, Agriculture, Commerce, Labor, Housing and Urban Development, Transportation, Veterans Affairs and Homeland Security.[111]

Given such ambitions, it is not surprising that these reactionaries have sought to enlist divine sanction in support of their cause. Nor should we fault them for doing so. After all, should they succeed, they will have eliminated so many jobs and so much revenue, that the still struggling dynamic balance of the economy will finally collapse into the abyss. At that point, we will need divine intervention like never before - so we ought to congratulate them for being sufficiently far-sighted and well-prepared for the coming disaster. But now we must descend from these Olympian heights of *constitutional restoration* to the meaner streets of today's commerce and the rough and tumble of everyday politics.

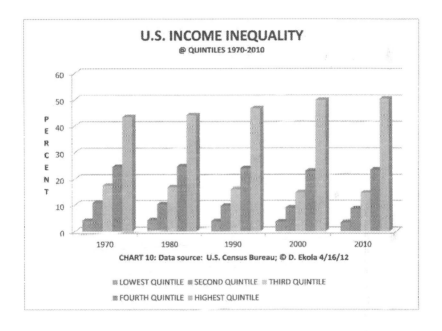

Such a descent brings us back to our earlier discussion of the stagnation, even decline, of average hourly wages and the related trends of growing inequality of income distribution over the past 40 years. Charts 10 above, and 10a and 10b below, illustrate these related trends of increasing inequality of U.S. income distribution.

Chart 10 provides us with a snapshot of income distribution with each income bracket, or quintile, calculated as a percentage against the total of national income. This has a leveling effect and dilutes the extent of changes occurring between each quintile and the highest quintile. Most discussions of income inequality are based on this kind of analysis and, as a result, lack a galvanizing sense of urgency.

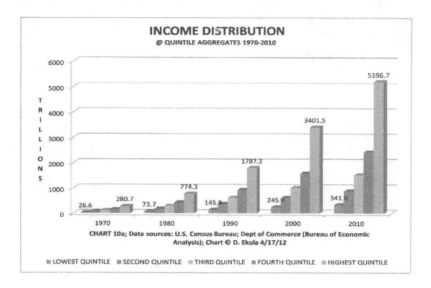

Chart 10a, on the other hand, translates these percentages into each quintiles share of total national income for the given year. This gives us a snapshot of the aggregate income of each quintile for the given year. As can be seen, the impact of this analysis is far more dramatic in showing the shift of income from the lower quintiles to the highest.

Chart 10b goes one step further and compares the aggregate income of each of the first four quintiles as a percentage of the highest income group. Once this step is completed, the incremental decreases in the aggregate income for each of the four income groups are then factored into, or added to, the highest income group. Finally, the revised income figures for the highest income group are then calculated, as a percentage, against the combined total income for the lower income groups. In short, Chart 10b actually consists of two charts in one. It portrays, on the one hand, each of the lower

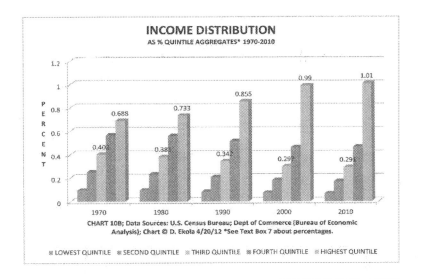

INCOME DISTRIBUTION
AS % QUINTILE AGGREGATES* 1970-2010

CHART 10B; Data Sources: U.S. Census Bureau; Dept of Commerce (Bureau of Economic Analysis); Chart © D. Ekola 4/20/12 *See Text Box 7 about percentages.

※ LOWEST QUINTILE ※ SECOND QUINTILE ※ THIRD QUINTILE ※ FOURTH QUINTILE ※ HIGHEST QUINTILE

TEXT BOX 7

Chart 10b actually consists of two charts in one. It portrays, on the one hand, the income share of each of the lower four income groups as a percentage, decreasing over time, against the share of the highest income group; and on the other, it shows the income share of the highest income group, increasing over time, as a percentage of the combined income share of the four lower income groups. This is the reason that the percentages in each quintile add up to more than 100%. These are two charts juxstaposing the evolving relationship of two distinct income groups against one another.

four income groups as a decreasing percentage against the highest income group, and on the other, the highest income group as an increasing percentage of the combined total for the four lower income groups.

Before proceeding further with our analysis of these three charts, let's first pause to consider the term 'trickle-down economics.' Simply stated, it describes a theory, destitute of contemporary validation, in which policies that benefit the wealthy purportedly trickle-down to the less well-off. In short, it often is used as a catchy substitute for saying that 'a rising tide lifts all boats.' But, the two phrases are quite different. The latter describes a broadly-based dynamic, raising all sectors of the economy simultaneously. Metaphorically speaking, it subsumes a vigorous demand sector capable of full participation in the overall economy.

By contrast, the former evokes an image of a mere trickling down of a stingy surplus from our modern iteration of the feudal manor. As a result, the former has become a pejorative term as, doubtless, intended by Will Rogers when he reportedly coined it during the Great Depression. [112] Hence, few advocates for the wealthy use this term today even though the policies they advocate are essentially 'trickle-down' in everything but name. Instead supply-side economics and Reaganomics have supplanted trickle-down in the lexicon of contemporary conservatives. But viewed as a concept, most will note a general similarity between 'trickle-down,' supply-side and Adam Smith's theory of the invisible hand.

The odd thing about this class war is not that ultra-conservatives prefer it be kept on the down-low, but that their efforts generally succeed.[113] Typically, most Americans accept class differences as necessary and proper fixtures of the economic order. They regard equality of opportunity, not equality of result, as the keystones of a well-ordered society. Unfortunately, though, there is a minimum proportionality of result that must be met to maintain sustainability of an economy. In other words, as we saw in the case of the Great Depression, there is a minimum proportionality of result that must be met to maintain adequate demand in an economy. And equally important, there is a minimum proportionality of investment that must take place in education and research to retool the human capital of an economy. Consequently, as most anyone who takes the time to focus on the preceding charts can see, these minimum levels of proportionality have not been met - and are not being met - by the grossly unequal income distribution outlined in the above charts. The lopsided nature of the result is obvious and it correlates in a common sense manner with the near collapse - and painfully slow recovery - of our economy in 2008. And to some extent, this reality has shown up in at least one recent poll.

The New York Times reported on January 11, 2012 that *Pew Social and Demographic Trends* found that perception of class conflicts had shot up from 47 percent in 2009 to about two-thirds in their most recent poll.[114] The article went on to report that these perceptions increased most among middle-class and independent voters, but also increased substantially among Republicans, rising among the latter from 38 percent in 2009 to 55 percent in 2011. These results track well with the loss of income in those groups as reflected in Chart 10b. Specifically, over the past 40 years, income groups 3 and 4 actually suffered the greatest losses in income, relative to the highest group. The overall loss for the third quintile stands at 11.1 percent, while the fourth lost 10 percent. In comparison, the lowest quintile lost 2.9 percent and the second 8 percent.

And yet - as self-evident as these facts appear to be - we lack a decisive electoral majority who understands them. Instead, we are confronted by an extremely close election contest in which the small margin of victory shifts back and forth with little reference to either the fundamental issues that confront the nation, or the interests of certain groups. Indeed, given how little the fundamentals have influenced this superficial spectacle, we might as well let the outcome be decided by a game of pin-the-tail-on-the-donkey.

A series of Gallup Polls taken during 2012 illustrates this trend. Their poll for the period April 12-16, 2012 found Romney leading Obama 48 percent to 43 percent.[115] This was followed by their poll of June 4, 2012, tracking the Obama-Romney contest by race. On the one hand, that poll found a significantly skewed percent of white voters in all income groups preferring Romney over Obama: perhaps most surprising was that white households earning less than $36,000 preferred Romney by 50 to 40; those earning $36,000 to $89,000 preferred him by 56 to 37; and those earning $90,000 or more by 54 to 40. On the other hand, there was a reversal of preference by non-white households in those respective income groups of: 80 to 12; 74 to19 and 73 to 21.[116] Obviously, there is a substantial racial undercurrent driving voter behavior in this election.

Gallup polling in the closing days of August 2012 continued to show a razor thin margin shifting back and forth between Obama and Romney, with an overall preference of 47 to 46 in favor of Obama on 8/23-8/29/2012.[117] However, what is eye-opening is that a substantial majority, of 52% to 43%, continued to maintain a preference for Romney regarding the economy.[118]   In that same poll, Romney also held a decisive advantage as being better able to handle the federal budget deficit by a margin of 54 to 39 percent.

This demonstrates a glaring incapacity of registered voters to process and retain relevant economic data. After all, Romney has set forth a program that not only continues the destructive policies of George W. Bush - he actually doubles down on them. With respect to tax cuts for the wealthiest members of society, he demands more than Bush. Specifically, Romney calls for an additional 20% cut in marginal tax rates. This would reduce the top marginal tax rate from 35% to 28%.[119] These cuts must be seen in the context of how destructive the Bush tax cuts were to the fiscal integrity of the nation's finances and to the huge role they played in fueling the financial meltdown of 2008-09. Quite simply, these tax cuts generated a capital glut that flooded the equity markets. So much money flooded into the equity markets in search of a good return on investment that it overwhelmed the traditional supply of investment opportunities. Those are precisely the conditions that generate speculative balloons.

That is the other side of the story behind the real estate boom. Wall Street was only too happy to supply investments for this capital glut.

In return for handsome commissions, they sliced and diced subprime mortgages into new-age financial instruments, marketing them as sound investments with attractive returns. Nor did this exhaust their marketing creativity. They not only profited from the sale of those derivatives, but they found additional opportunities in the sale of new-age financial 'insurance' - credit default swaps - that pretended to guarantee their customers protection against any risk of default.

Unfortunately, the reality was that there was neither real substance nor anything that resembled credible insurance underlying these so-called investments/insurance. Indeed, Wall Street might just as well have been printing money and selling it from their back door. How else can you account for the fact that, in just two years time, the mind-boggling sums of $31.7 trillion in credit default swaps and an additional $3.2 trillion in equity derivatives simply vaporized - just vanished from the books?[120] Nor do these sums include the additional loss of $16.8 trillion in household net worth during the same period.[121]

This is not wealth creation. It's wealth destruction on a scale never before experienced in the history of our republic. It is wealth destruction closely tied to: inadequate levels of taxation; inadequate levels of investment in human capital and basic research; and speculative investment of the capital glut arising out of these public sector funding failures.

But this is not the whole story of Romney's tax reform proposals resulting in future capital gluts. He also calls for the complete elimination of the estate tax, a reduction in the corporate income tax and maintaining the capital gains tax rate at its extremely low level of 15%.[122] The latter has allowed Romney to pay taxes at about a 14% rate - at least as reflected by the one complete return he has permitted us to see. It goes without saying that this percentage is less than what is paid by many Americans with much smaller incomes. With the exception of those advocates of supply-side economics, most economists view this low capital gains tax rate as too low for the fiscal health of the nation. In their view, the economy would do better if the capital gains rate were raised and the corporate income tax were lowered.

We also ought to keep in mind the origins of this low capital gains tax rate. It originated as a quid pro quo during the Reagan presidency in which this lower capital gains rate was offered as an offset to a higher corporate income tax rate. In short, at that time consideration was given to the impact of tax cuts upon revenues and the need to maintain the fiscal integrity of the nation. It was a balance that also was respected when President Bill Clinton's administration achieved a balanced budget by raising taxes during his first term. [123] That balance is lacking in Romney's approach. Indeed, the above list of his proposed tax cuts is incomplete. If you go to his web site, you will discover several additional taxes slated for reduction or complete elimination. To be fair, two of those did benefit a wider class of taxpayers than just the wealthy.[124] But taken together, they constitute an unprecedented assault on the fiscal integrity of the nation at a time when the national debt is a serious concern.

Moreover, what is especially distasteful about Romney's defense of the current low capital gains tax rate is that hedge fund operators are some of the largest beneficiaries of this low capital gains rate. They naturally are opposed to increasing it and defend it as the necessary price of the investment risks assumed by them. Such rationalizations ring hollow as doublespeak, though, when we realize that they market these new-age investments as virtually risk-free given the mathematical genius of their investment formulas.[125]   However, as will become clear in the following discussion, the levels of risk undertaken by hedge fund operators are both astronomical and an integral part of their investment strategy. This unbridled speculation played a large contributing role in the enormous wealth destruction of 2008-09.

Now let's return briefly to those Gallup Poll results reflecting the public's decisive preference for Romney's handling of economic and budget deficit concerns. As we have seen, Romney's approach to both of those problems amounts to a two-legged stool , based exclusively on tax cuts and reduced government regulation of the economy. In other words, Romney's approach to both problems is the restoration of pure supply-side economics - or what we could describe as Reaganomics on steroids. It dismisses entirely the need for increased revenue - a need that even Reagan recognized at times - and what the Democrats call 'ladders of opportunity.' The latter consist of a complementary range of programs designed to retool the nation's human capital, increase investment in basic research and rebuild the nation's physical infrastructure. When combined with a responsible program of deficit reduction, all are critical elements of a more vigorous economic recovery.

What emerges from the polls, though, is a jagged portrait of disconnected thoughts, hobbled by our lobotomized concept of wealth creation. On the one hand, Romney wins on the economy and deficits. On the other, Obama wins on taxes, health care and likability. There is no unified vision based upon a coherent understanding of: momentum and the dynamic equilibrium of the economy; how all the elements are linked together; how the economy grows, stagnates or declines with the waxing and waning of its key drivers; the sea changes accompanying the agro-industrial revolution and how they created a critical government role in the wealth creation process. Nor does this failure of comprehension show any sign of receding when it concerns something as momentous as the onset of the Great Recession. If anything it seems to grow even worse - both prospectively and retrospectively.

 Prospectively, it was as If most of the nation were either sleep-walking, or in a herd-like trance, as we rushed to exploit, on the one hand, the real estate balloon, or, on the other, the financial derivatives characterized by Warren Buffett as *financial weapons of mass destruction.* [126] Nor does the situation improve when we view it retrospectively. As we look back on the Great Recession, almost four years after it destroyed $16.8 trillion in the household net worth of Americans, nearly half of the nation cannot connect the dots between this enormous destruction of wealth and the fact that our economy still is struggling to recover fully. One cannot help but ask: why is it so difficult to understand that such an enormous loss must have a huge impact on the economy? After all, for many this amounted to nearly a lifetime of accumulated savings and, for the nation as a whole, more than an entire year of gross domestic product.

One part of the answer is that too many of us have been stripped of our economic common sense by the magical concepts of the invisible hand and a self-correcting free market. This is so because such magical paradigms promote the destructive idea that things will take care of themselves without any mental exertion on our part. As a result, we no longer feel the need to pay attention to economic details. This opens the door to ignorance and a defect of prudence - or what the Founding Fathers would have described as good judgment. And somewhere in the debris of this defect of prudence, you will find the discarded idea of economic balance.

Having said that, we must also acknowledge the impenetrable complexity of the financial products that prompted Warren Buffett to brand them with such scathing contempt. Indeed, it is Warren Buffett's experience with these financial derivatives that provides us with a key to understanding the protracted nature of our current economic struggles. In the late 1990s, Buffett's company, Berkshire Hathaway, acquired General Re Securities as part of a larger acquisition. This company was a derivatives dealer, judged "dangerous" by Buffett. Unable to sell it, Berkshire Hathaway set about unwinding the individual contracts to terminate the company.

But several years later, in 2003, Buffett acknowledged that: "It will be a great many years before we are totally out of this operation....like Hell, both [the reinsurance and derivatives businesses] are easy to enter and almost impossible to exit."[127]

There also are several other factors that contribute to our lack of comprehension about the grip exerted by these new-age financial products on our financial markets. First and foremost, the majority of these are unregulated private contracts. Hence, they are not subject to a uniform body of standards as regards leverage or reserve requirements. Second, the creative intent for the most perverse derivatives, credit default swaps, was to shift risk out of view of third parties and disguise it with a figment of insurance. This intent succeeded by virtue of two things: On the one hand, as noted above, lack of regulation enabled degrees of unmonitored leverage that escalated risk to levels capable of destroying global financial markets;[128] on the other, the inherent complexity of these instruments made them incomprehensible to all but the most mathematically gifted.[129] Third, despite being marketed as a form of insurance, there was no insurance in the traditional sense of creating adequate reserves for risks taken - not to mention the extravagant Wall Street bonuses generated by them.[130]

Fourth, there was a fundamental difference between the regulated stability of the insurance market and the unregulated volatility of this market for privately negotiated financial contracts. Losses in the former do not trigger a panic because they are part of a regulated business plan - protected by adequate reserves; whereas participants in a speculative balloon - aloft without a parachute - invariably are driven by fears of losing out to bad timing - whether the balloon be on the ascendant or descendant.[131] Fifth, the risks - and fears - for the latter were intensified by an industry that increasingly found it both necessary and advantageous to borrow enormous sums of money with very short maturities.[132]

Sixth, investors were enabled to bet on anything without having a proprietary relationship to the subject of the wager. In other words, the parties to the contract did not have to have any skin in the game. Hence, any tangible linkage between the rational self-interest of the investor and the wager was non-existent.[133] Seventh, these wagers involved outcomes that often played out over a period of years - or even decades. Eighth, they had the tantalizing feature of allowing estimated profits to be recorded and collected in the short term without actually selling the contract.[134] This naturally opened the door to a fantastic financial playground in which chickens could be counted before they were hatched. Ninth, since credit default swaps are bought and sold privately and not subject to the public scrutiny of an exchange, there is much greater price elasticity. The result: fees for CDS deals cost about 10 times more than for those on a traditional initial public offering.[135] Tenth, privately negotiated contracts have a higher priority in bankruptcy proceedings.[136]

Given this catalog of heightened risk and lack of transparency, it makes no rational sense that these credit default swaps became the darling of Wall Street. At least, it makes no rational sense if Wall Street is viewed in its traditional iteration, as a group of responsible investors, whose top priority is to act as trustees of their customers long-term financial well-being. But it does make sense if Wall Street is viewed in its contemporary, post-Glass-Steagall iteration, as a group of myopic investors most interested in their own short-term profits trading on the bank's behalf.

Hence, it comes as no surprise that, with few exceptions, Wall Street investment banks flocked to the CDS bandwagon right from the start. It started in the investment bank of J.P. Morgan in the mid-1990s with an offering of risk, valued at just under $10 billion, derived from a portfolio of Morgan loans to a field of some 300 blue chip U.S. corporations.[137] This fledgling market then soared to $6.4 trillion in

2004 and peaked at $62.2 trillion in 2007.[138] As this market evolved, the subprime mortgage market became its biggest driver.

Once it got rolling under a full head of steam, the purchase and securitization of subprime mortgages became the spice in otherwise plain vanilla investment packages. It was the spice that inflated yields for investors and commissions for brokers. And all of this speculative energy and delusion was reinforced by the roaring ascent of the real estate market. Remarkably, one of Wall Street's most venerable investment banks did have second thoughts and liquidated its holdings in these checkered contracts. Most notably, J.P. Morgan-Chase, the originator of CDS contracts, left the market before it crashed and joined Wells Fargo, who claimed to have avoided them from the outset.[139] The balance of the market would not be so level-headed and fortunate.

This brings us to the subject of leverage, loan maturities and the role they play in hedge fund operations. The most fundamental element of this subject is that hedge funds have a voracious appetite for borrowed money. This voracious appetite arises out of the basics of their investment strategy. The latter relies upon making very small profits across an enormous number of transactions. This forces them to fund an enormous number of transactions. As described by Martin Mayer in *The FED*:

They were 'selling volatility' - that is, they were betting that prices in the option markets, and in markets where assets were valued according to their 'optionality,' overcharged the buyers options by assuming greater volatility than was probable from the historical record. It was thus safe for people smarter than the market to sell options, especially when they could be paired in ways that paid off whether the market rose moderately or fell moderately. Because the gains per trade from these apparently sure things were very small, the game had to be played with enormous quantities of borrowed money.[140]

Given these huge borrowing costs, it is easy to see that the price of money becomes a significant factor in hedge fund operations.

Similarly, since the cost of a loan typically rises with the length of its term, it also is easy to see that a hedge fund operator would try to take advantage of the lower lending rates for short term loans. These pressures naturally mount against the backdrop of the very small profit margin on individual transactions and the beguiling belief that these transactions would pay off regardless of market shifts.

Of course, notwithstanding these beliefs, there is the reality that the market does shift - sometimes immoderately - and that those shifts will impact asset values. When that happens, the holder of the asset is subject to a margin call. And that makes it necessary to come up with more funds to meet the terms of the margin call. In some circumstances this will make it necessary to venture into the overnight loan market to serve as a bridge until less volatile funding is secured. These overnight loans, known as repos, also can be useful as a cheap, albeit volatile, means of increasing the leverage of a given transaction.[141]

A specific example of these hedge fund operations may be found in a *House of Cards,* by William D. Cohan. In it he describes the career of Ralph Cioffi at Bear Stearns, who, starting there in 1985, became a prime mover some 18 years later in the creation of its own hedge fund, called the High Grade Fund:

The High Grade Fund opened to outside investors in October 2003. Cioffi and [his assistant] Tannin told investors that the fund would invest in low-risk, high-grade debt securities, such as tranches of CDOs, which the ratings agencies had rated either AAA or AA. The fund would focus on using leverage to generate returns by borrowing money in the low-cost, short-term repo markets to buy higher-yielding, long-term CDOs. The difference between the interest received and the interest paid, enhanced by the use of borrowed money, would yield the fund's profits.[142]

However, as Cohan explains, this strategy shifted over the next few years:

Cioffi had supposedly figured out a way to get some long-term funding for his hedge funds by creating an 'entity' that borrowed short-term in the commercial paper market and then used the proceeds to buy his long-term mortgage securities. This scheme was called 'Klio Funding.' 'Every time you asked him, Ralph would say, 'Yeah, I just did another Klio deal. I locked up another $2 billion with Dresdner Bank for ten years, another $4 billion with Citibank for five years. Isn't it great?' We'd go, 'Wow, wish we had that.' We were jealous.[143]

But, as Cohan explained, this was just what Cioffi wanted those outside the fund to believe. Reality had a much uglier and risky side:

He kept saying to us, 'Don't worry, I have all my funding locked up on a ten-year term, non-recourse basis. I can never get a margin call. They can never pull it from me. It doesn't matter.' We were thinking to ourselves, 'Wow, that's a beautiful thing.' In fact, he had about $10 billion like that. But he had another $14 billion that was funded month-to-month.[144]

The ugly truth was that it didn't matter that he had $10 billion of secure, non-recourse funding. What mattered was that he had $14 billion in volatile 90 day funding in a market that was being battered by increasingly bad news about its exposure to subprime mortgage risk. Even worse, Cioffi had misrepresented his exposure to subprime mortgages by telling his investors that only 6 percent of his funds were subprime, whereas in reality "the funds had closer to 60 percent of their money invested in subprime mortgages."[145]

Unfortunately for Cioffi and those who were playing the same game, by 2007 there were plenty of headwinds working against them. The first signs of these headwinds started to appear in late 2005 with headlines signaling that the housing boom was peaking. An article in a mid-western daily on 11/16/2005 announced: "Home prices up 15% in third quarter," but qualified that with a sub-head: "Realtors: Sector probably peaked."[146] Two days later the same paper followed up with less ambiguous news: "Housing starts tumble; Analysts attribute October decline to rising mortgage rates."[147]

Then by late summer and fall of 2006, the tone of the housing market underwent a complete reversal from the frantic days of the boom, when buyers saw properties repeatedly snatched off the market as soon as they were listed. On 8/15/2006 the headline "Buyer's Market" concisely summed up the end of that seller's market. This was followed two weeks later with an early warning about the subprime mortgage market: "Subprime loan defaults grow."[148] Finally, the obituary for the housing boom came on 10/8/2006 with the headline: "The Housing Glut."[149]

Taken by themselves, these markers of boom's end did not lay bare the full extent of the threat it represented to the financial markets, but more explicit warnings would soon follow. Indeed, we already have seen the ARM reset chart published by Credit Suisse in January 2007.[150] This showed with awful clarity the long-term threat these ARM resets presented to the economic health of the nation. For those with sufficient attention span to absorb their meaning, the six-year span of these resets described the inevitability of a long train of future foreclosures, compounded by an equally long-train of home equity destruction. This was nothing short of an early warning of the unavoidable path of economic ruin upon which the nation had just begun.

Just months later, in March 2007, this Credit Suisse bombshell was followed by a column from Gretchen Morgenson in the New York Times: "Crisis Looms In Mortgages."[151] Her lengthy column described in great detail the seamy side of the failures in underwriting, regulating, rating and, most importantly, in ethical conduct, that triggered the crisis now coming to light in home mortgages. And, most enlightening, front and center in her column was the detailed story of the new-age financial products that were now unraveling.

Viewed more generally, though, the most perverse consequences of these new age financial products were the following: these products created a vast network of shared leverage, riddled with weak links, linking all sectors of the economy to the fate of the most vulnerable. Moreover, the sustainability of this network rested upon the flawed assumption that the real estate market, torqued up on speculative fever, would continue to rise and inflate away any immediate consequences for its underwriting sins. Equally problematic was that much of this was a shadow market.[152] As a result, no one knew exactly where the greatest risks resided. It was a daisy chain of risk obscured by countervailing mathematical equations so intricate only a PhD in mathematics and computer science could fathom them.[153]

Of course, so long as the market was rising, the bona fides of these geniuses, burnished by their immediate successes, were sufficient to overawe all doubters and add to the luster of their products. But the great flaw in these products was that their creators were relative newcomers to financial markets and lacked an understanding of the dynamics - and animal spirits - that drive markets up or down. Most importantly, their exotic algorithms lacked the historical depth to take into account the reality that not all price swings are moderate and, eventually, all booms come to an end. Consequently, once the credibility of these new-age financial gimmicks started to fray, it didn't take long for panic to overrun the vastly overextended leverage built into those algorithms. Worse yet, the impenetrable complexity of these new-age products meant that no one knew the extent of the rot, so no one could be trusted. And with the end of trust came the end of credit.

Some of the major financial institutions and mortgage lenders that fell victim to the toxic combination of CDS and subprime mortgage contracts were Countrywide Loans, Bear Stearns, Lehman Brothers, Wachovia, Washington Mutual, Merrill Lynch, AIG and Fannie and Freddie Mac. Most were absorbed by other banks. Some lived on as subordinate entities. Some went into a form of government trusteeship. Some like Lehman Brothers went into bankruptcy and completely disappeared. And as we already have seen, another measure of the severity of the meltdown that overtook these firms is that by 2008, CDS activity, as reported by International Swaps and Derivatives Association, had dropped 38 percent, from $62.2 trillion to $38.6 trillion. A year later, it had dropped further to $30.4 trillion.[154] This amounted to a mind-boggling loss of $31.8 trillion. Added to this were the losses of $7 trillion in home equity and $3.2 trillion in equity based derivatives.

That is why virtually all lending seized up in the fall of 2008 and why the economy teetered on the brink of collapse. An economy simply cannot function without credit. Banks would not lend to other banks, let alone businesses. Businesses were having difficulty funding their payrolls and other critical obligations.[155] That is why it is critical that America understand the posture of the Republican Party during this crisis. The majority of their party opposed the efforts of their President and Secretary of Treasury to restore the health of the banking sector.[156] Worse yet, they have continued to rail against those efforts as unnecessary and spendthrift, without a dime's worth of acknowledgment that the Troubled Asset Relief and Protection Act of 2008 served one of its overarching goals of reining in the financial meltdown of 2008.[157]

Obviously, measured by the polls showing a dead heat in the 2012 presidential election, it is evident that many people still share this view. For those who still hold this alternate view of the universe, it would help bring them into a closer relationship with reality if they turned to Chart 5; weighed it against the above list of financial institutions put at dire risk or obliterated; and paid sufficient attention to the relationship between these two gauges of financial and economic distress so that they understood the depth of crisis confronting the nation during the years 2007-09. Given the benefit of these insights, most reasonable observers understand that, to their credit, it was the Democrats who stepped up and shouldered the unpopular burdens of the TARP bailout of the Bush 2 administration.

Had they not done so, the credit freeze would have continued and even more financial institutions would have collapsed, dragging the rest of the economy down into the depths of a depression.[158]

Having said that, it also must be acknowledged that there is another troubling dimension to the TARP bailout. That troubling dimension is the near total failure of TARP to implement either a successful mortgage rescue program or an effective repurchase of toxic mortgage-related securities. After all, these were the objectives stressed by Secretary Paulson when he presented his rescue program to Congress. Nevertheless, these were tumultuous times and decisions were being driven by the need for haste.

Hence, it should not surprise that the passage of a few days would bring to light fresh insights. First, the sheer magnitude of these two objectives suggests that it would have been an impossible task. We already have seen the staggering losses inflicted on the related markets during the two-year period 2007-09: $31.8 trillion in credit default losses, $7 trillion in lost home equity and $3.7 trillion equity derivatives. By way of contrast, the $750,000 billion in the TARP fund looks nothing short of anemic. But that's not the whole story. The list of specific problems blocking a successful outcome was, and remains, even more daunting.

The realization of all these problems was not long in coming to the surface. TARP's initial passage was on 10/3/2008.[159] Less than two weeks later, on 10/12/2008, Treasury Secretary Henry Paulson backed away from its principal stated objectives of a mortgage rescue/toxic asset repurchase program in favor of simply injecting capital into the nation's largest banks via purchases of preferred stock.[160] Although this represented a major shift away from the policies he had emphasized in urging Congress to pass it, he subsequently would make the abandonment of those policies even more unmistakable.

On 11/13/2008, he announced a new round of capital injections into the financial sector funding student, auto and credit card loans. At the same time, he stated that: "the Treasury's bailout effort,...should not be spent helping ailing Detroit automakers or homeowners facing foreclosure because that would violate the intent of the initiative but that they deserved help in other forms." He went on to say that: "the use of bailout money to reduce foreclosures, were 'not what the American people were expecting, and it's not what many in Congress are expecting.'"[161] Nevertheless, some five weeks later, President Bush would overrule his Treasury Secretary and order a $17.4 billion auto bailout.[162]

Despite this seemingly clumsy footwork on the part of Secretary Paulson, there were substantial problems standing in the way of implementing TARP as originally proposed. In addition to the enormity of the equity destruction relative to the fiscal resources of the government, there was an equally daunting disparity between the technical skills of the government and the byzantine challenges presented by these toxic mortgage securities. The truly odious consequence of this disparity was to force the government to enlist the aid of the very people, responsible for creating this financial monster, in the task of unraveling it.[163] This placed the government in the unenviable position of embracing a tar-ball laced with conflicts of interest - both apparent and substantive.[164]

Equally odious was that both of these tasks promised to be spread out over years, not months, and not at all certain in their outcome. Such delays were a luxury the economy could ill afford as it continued on its downward spiral during the closing months of the Bush administration.[165] Indeed, to get an idea of just how painfully long this process would be, one need only revisit the experience of Warren Buffet's organization with their long-drawn-out efforts to unwind the tangle of derivatives that were a part of their General Re acquisition.[166] We already have seen how that effort dragged on for years.

Finally, they also had to reckon with the fact that the banks were opposed to marking their troubled assets down to market values and that the legal framework to compel such mark-downs was not in place.[167] Failure to achieve such mark-downs inevitably would have driven the costs of the program even higher. In the end, the path that Paulson chose saved the Treasury - and taxpayers - an enormous amount of money. The specifics of these savings are as follows: the initial authorization for TARP was $750 billion; according to the Congressional Budget Office, actual disbursements from that fund amounted to $431 billion, while "the cost to the federal government of the TARP's transactions (also referred to as the subsidy cost), including grants for mortgage programs that have not yet been made, will amount to $32 billion."[168] When measured against the magnitude of current federal budgets and the even greater magnitude of the tens of trillions of dollars lost in the financial catastrophe of 2008, this sum quite literally is like a drop in a bucket. But, as the old saying goes: you get what you pay for. Hence, it should not surprise that this bargain-basement priced TARP offered scant help to the millions facing foreclosure and the millions more that would lose their jobs as an indirect result.

Having said that, any attempt to put these very real failures of TARP in perspective must also take the following into consideration. These failures of TARP resulted from the fact that our new-age financial products not only outpaced our ability to comprehend and regulate them, but, even more importantly, they undermined the traditional credit systems that once served as the bulwarks of sound equity.[169] Those traditional credit systems drew their strength from local banking institutions well-versed in the credit worthiness of their customers. The integrity of this locally-focused system was reinforced by their rational self-interest since, in the good-old-days, these local bankers retained ownership of the mortgages issued by them. This long term ownership by loan originators gave them a vested interest in assuring the integrity of those mortgages.

This is not to say that these traditional virtues have been abandoned throughout every nook and cranny of the mortgage industry. The point is that a new breed of loan originator entered the housing market during the thirty year period beginning with securitization. As the housing market heated up, this new breed multiplied along with the fast profits built into the commission structure of the securitization/credit default swap market. Indeed, we already have seen evidence of the incredible expansion of this market. Equity derivatives increased nearly five-fold, from $2.5 trillion to $10 trillion, in the five years between 2002 and 2007; while credit default swaps soared from $919 billion to $62.2 trillion in just six years between 2001 and 2007.[170] Naturally as these profits grew, Wall Street looked for ways to increase its participation. One means of doing so was by acquiring, or establishing, firms closer to the action on the ground floor.[171] Investment banks increasingly expanded their participation in the mortgage market. This allowed them to increase the availability of mortgages by lowering standards for - and speeding up the process of - loan approval.

As previously alluded to, a principal driver of the explosive growth of these markets was the enormous amount of money needed by hedge funds. Their profits were based on amassing tiny transactional profits across an enormous range of transactions;[172] in short, their business plan was the leveraged-buy-out of the 1980s on steroids. In other words, the explosive growth of the derivatives/credit default swaps market was a reflection of the enormous leverage driving it - it rested upon a mountain of debt. Needless-to-say, this was a business plan completely antithetical to that of the traditional local banker.

Another ugly feature of these new-age financial products was that it involved not only a break-down in the valuation process, but it also impacted the integrity of the paperwork. As noted already, securitization opened the door to equity degradation by attenuating the bond between asset originator and asset owner. Indeed, in a disturbing number of cases that bond frayed so badly that mortgage securities were sent off with questionable documentation not only about their sustainability as viable loans, but also about their actual ownership.

This was the inevitable result of a process whereby a mortgage, a legal document describing the ownership of a property as a clearly delineated linkage of rights and responsibilities, between mortgagor and mortgagee, was digitized into an abstraction.[173] This abstraction fragmented the mortgagor's ownership interests into a confusing labyrinth connecting myriad bits and pieces of the original contract. The upshot of this securitization process was that it obsolesced - or arguably was incompatible with - the traditional means of legally securing it in a trail of paperwork. This reality was recognized in 1995 with the incorporation of Mortgage Electronic Registration Systems, Inc (MERS).[174]

According to the MERS website, their system was "created by the mortgage banking industry to streamline the mortgage process by using electronic commerce to eliminate paper."[175] A key component of this streamlining process was that "MERS acts as mortgagee in the county land records for the lender and servicer. Any loan - where MERS is the mortgagee - registered on the MERS® System is inoculated against future assignments because MERS remains the mortgagee no matter how many times servicing is traded."[176] However, a large number of governmental agencies take a different view of this streamlining process. As an example, upon filing a lawsuit in February 2012, Attorney General Eric T. Schneiderman of New York had this to say: "The mortgage industry created MERS to allow financial institutions to evade county recording fees, avoid the need to publicly record mortgage transfers and facilitate the rapid sale and securitization of mortgages en masse."[177]

The critical point here is the 'facilitation of the rapid sale and securitization of mortgages en masse.' As noted earlier, the enormous profits arising out of the securitization process rested on the ability to eke out very small transactional profits on massive numbers of transactions. These profits would have been jeopardized by the need to process all of these transactions - and pay the fees - associated with the traditional county-based system of record-keeping. Hence, the need for streamlining.

The problem is that the cumbersome paper-trail that leads to the county records office also served as the guarantor of the integrity of the records. Once the counties got elbowed out of the way, the paper-trail was short-circuited and diverted into what has every appearance of being an error-prone digital replacement. One of the chief flaws appears to be, that abbreviating the subsequent trail of ownership under the single identity of MERS, as mortgagee, inevitably confuses actual ownership. It also appears that confusion - or difficult-to-correct errors - would be the inevitable result of not having a paper-trail to verify subsequent changes in the event of a defect in the digital record. The third - and perhaps fatal - flaw of the system was its reliance on private sector agents overseeing the greater part of subsequent transactions - despite their conflicts of interest arising out of involvement in the securitization process.

Needless-to-say, the record of those private sector agents has not inspired much confidence in either their integrity - or their competence - when viewed through the lens of the disaster that overwhelmed the financial sector. Moreover, the general characterization of the digital process being error-prone is supported by the number of lawsuits initiated by government agencies starting in the Fall of 2010 - many of which were successful. In addition, the fact that two major banks, J.P. Morgan Chase and Washington

Mutual, stopped using MERS in their foreclosure proceedings well before 2010 also points to a growing recognition of troubling flaws in the MERS System.[178]

Returning to the Fall of 2010, nearly a quarter of the houses in the housing market were in a state of foreclosure at that time. Families were being evicted; houses were standing empty; neighborhood property values were declining. Against this painful backdrop, the airing of the scandals underlying these apparent abuses stirred a good deal of outrage. The inevitable outrage manifested itself in calls for a moratorium on foreclosures and also led to a number of lawsuits focusing on documentation of loan sustainability or actual ownership of the property, or both.[179]

All of this surfaced in the fall of 2010 - in the two months preceding the 2010 midterm elections. While all of this had its origins in the years prior to Obama's presidency, the immediate impact was to add to the present economic pain experienced by millions. Moreover, as important as they were, the questions about the legitimacy of the foreclosure process and calls for a national foreclosure moratorium nevertheless caused the housing market to slow down even more and, as The New York Times reported on 10/17/2010: "in certain parts of the country [it] has come to a near standstill."[180] As such, it's likely that this continued hemorrhaging of the real estate market further damaged the Democratic effort to maintain their control of Congress - especially since the Republican attack was alleging that TARP and the recently passed Dodd-Frank Act were responsible for the poor economy.

Another element scarcely noted in the 2012 presidential election campaign is the linkage between the collapse of the real estate market and stagnation of hourly wages. This generations-long stagnation of hourly wages for the majority of working families - and the resultant erosion of their standard of living - drove a huge appetite for home mortgages of all stripes. Rising property values created a superficial remedy, albeit a very risky one, for wages that did not keep up with the cost of living and all of the emergencies that arise in the daily round. Further enhanced by the advantages of home mortgage interest and property tax deductions, it didn't take long for homeowners to develop a piggy-bank mentality about the present, or prospective, equity in their homes. The same could be said for prospective home-buyers. All of this added fuel to the fires of speculation. The bitter result, as previously noted, was the destruction of $7 trillion of equity in the nation's housing stock and a foreclosure crisis, beginning in January 2007, that will not run its full course until January 2014.[181]

As a consequence, one of the most stubborn holdovers from the Great Recession of 2008 is the real estate market. For years now we have been hearing estimates that eventual recovery for this market will come in 2015. That is some 9 years distant from the actual onset of the real estate downturn in 2006. There are two reasons for this long-delayed recovery. First, as we have seen already, the reset schedule for adjustable rate mortgages (ARM) has extended this foreclosure crisis from its beginning in January 2007 to January 2014. This is so because each time one of these ARMs resets it forces those homeowners with underwater mortgages into the impossible situation of securing a new mortgage, with no equity, in a market with much tighter standards.[182] This naturally has unleashed an unrelenting stream of financial havoc both in the real estate markets of the nation and on the demand side of the economy.

Second, when we consider the time it took for Berkshire Hathaway to wind down the derivatives of General Re Securities, it should not surprise us that the overall economy has stumbled badly in absorbing the $31.8 trillion collapse of the credit default swap market - compounded by the $3.2 trillion collapse of the equity derivatives market. In both instances we are talking about the unwinding of assets that have been sliced, diced and scattered all over the financial landscape of not just America, but the world.[183]

It's a slow and painful process because the path is poorly marked and the assets themselves have suffered both the erosion of the overall market and the handling charges of the many middlemen involved in their journey - not to mention the obfuscation of the asset's identity by the slicing and dicing process. In short, how does anyone ever reassemble - and assign derivational values to - the Humpty-Dumpty of a mortgage that has been sliced, diced and scattered hither and yon? Indeed, how does one do this with those mortgages that were put under the derivative knife with such haste that the MERS System equivalent of the original paperwork never accompanied them through the labyrinth?

Given these considerations, it is not surprising that the recovery from the Great Recession has been painfully slow. First, there have been the enormous losses to America's capital stock: $16.8 trillion from the net worth of American households and $31.8 trillion from the CDS market.[184] These are mind-numbing losses and - apparently for most - incomprehensible. Unfortunately, if enough of us don't make the effort to understand them, we simply will blunder back onto the same path that led us into this economic devastation in the first place. So let's look at it this way: the losses from these two sectors total $48.6 trillion dollars. This amounts to three times the size of the 2011 U.S. gross domestic product of $15.1 trillion.[185] But viewed in comparison with additions to the federal debt during Obama's first term, these capital losses are even greater. The combined debt of the annual federal deficits for the years 2010-2013 is estimated to be $5.7 trillion.[186] This amounts to only 12 percent of the nation's capital stock losses of $48.6 trillion.

While this doesn't eliminate the need to work toward long term deficit solutions, it does place the current spike in deficits in a more balanced perspective. Obviously, such an enormous loss in the nation's capital stock had to be addressed with emergency spending by both the Federal Reserve and the Obama administration. That emergency spending placed a floor under the collapse of the credit markets. Like the emergency braking system of an elevator, it stopped the fall of those markets and gave the economy enough time to catch its breath and begin the recovery process. Most reputable economists concur that a failure to deploy those emergency spending measures surely would have caused the economy to collapse into the abyss of this unprecedented destruction of circulating and fixed capital.

This juxtaposition of the nation's long-brewing fiscal crisis along with urgent needs for continued emergency spending highlights the treacherous character of our current situation. The nation is caught between the rock of fiscal privation and the hard place of urgent need - both in human and economic terms. It sheds light on the delicate balancing act forced upon the government as it pursues a three-pronged strategy for recovery. These three prongs consist of: (1) the constraints placed upon the government by the size of the gross federal debt; (2) the absolute necessity to meet the urgent needs of the huge sector of our population dispossessed by the economic destruction of the Great Recession; and (3) the need to address the long-festering structural problems of the economy: health care reform, reform and updating of job training programs; energy innovation, education reform, tax reform, climate change, and infrastructure maintenance.

The fact that all of these represent critically urgent national needs in the context of strained credit resources naturally creates a climate of intense competition for funding. It is a climate that beggars the future by limiting our capacity to invest in areas of critical importance to our national agenda. As such, it limits our capacity for recovery because innovation is essential to overcoming the structural problems that hinder economic growth. Lastly, we need to keep in mind that our present mountain of debt resulted from our seldom successful efforts to control our appetite for ever-lower rates of taxation, even while confronted with two wars, a growing crisis of sustainability in the energy and health care sectors, and the gradual obsolescence of the skills of a substantial part of the nation's labor force. We could have avoided our present pains by forthrightly addressing the fiscal burdens of these challenges, but we chose not to. And from the look of it, the same chorus that led us down this prodigal path may prevail again. Such a dismal record should bar any sensible nation from considering themselves as exceptional. Those who say otherwise only can be regarded as a bunch of blowhards.

All of this serves to underscore the point, noted earlier, that the father of government deficit spending, John Maynard Keynes, did not endorse such profligate behavior when an economy was running smoothly. During those times of prosperity, Keynes maintained that government should increase taxes and moderate spending to create a reserve for the next downturn. Had the government done so, we now would enjoy a much stronger fiscal condition to meet our present crisis. Moreover, contrary to the current conservative characterization of Keynes, he was not a radical anti-capitalist.

He was a traditionalist trying to save capitalism from its inherent contradictions. Indeed, when he was formulating his ideas in the early stages of the depression, he was focused on the cyclical side of the economy and what it would take to reverse the self-perpetuating dynamics that drove an ever deepening downhill spiral in demand and employment. In the summary of his *General Theory* he states just how conservatively he viewed the limits of those remedies:

Our criticism of the accepted classical theory of economics has consisted not so much in finding logical flaws in its analysis as in pointing out that its tacit assumptions are seldom or never satisfied, with the result that it cannot solve the economic problems of the actual world. But if our central controls succeed in establishing an aggregate volume of output corresponding to full employment as nearly as practicable, the classical theory comes into its own again from this point onwards. **If we suppose the volume of output to be given, i.e. to be determined by forces outside the classical scheme of thought, then there is no objection to be raised against the classical analysis of the manner in which private self-interest will determine what in particular is produced, in what proportions the factors of production will be combined to produce it, and how the value of the final product will be distributed between them....Thus, apart from the necessity of central controls to bring about an adjustment between the propensity to consume and the inducement to invest, there is no more reason to socialise economic life than there was before.** *(emphasis added)*

To put the point concretely, I see no reason to suppose that the existing system seriously misemploys the factors of production which are in use. There are, of course, errors of foresight; but these would not be avoided by centralising decisions. When 9,000,000 men are employed out of 10,000,000 willing and able to work, there is no evidence that the labour of these 9,000,000 men is misdirected. The complaint against the present system is not that these 9,000,000 men ought to be employed on different tasks, but that tasks should be available for the remaining 1,000,000 men. It is in determining the volume, not the direction, of actual employment that the existing system has broken down.[187]

Economic policy long since has moved beyond Keynes limited concept of government involvement in the economy. Two of the most significant - and interrelated - exceptions are the following: the identification of the technostructure as a fourth factor of production by J.K. Galbraith and the idea that a competitive economy is incapable of producing certain classes of economic goods vital to its functioning. The former was recognized in its nascent form as early as the mid-1700s when Adam Smith singled out certain talents of labor sharing the same inherent qualities of fixed capital. In his Wealth of Nations, he breaks down fixed capital into four categories and describes the latter of those as follows:

Fourthly, of the acquired and useful abilities of all the inhabitants or members of the society. **The acquisition of such talents, by the maintenance of the** *acquirer during his education, study, or apprenticeship, always costs a real expense, which is a capital fixed and realized, as it were, in his person. Those talents, as they make a part of his fortune, **so do they likewise of that of the society to which he belongs.** The improved dexterity of a workman may be considered in the same light as a machine or instrument of trade which facilitates and abridges labor, and which, though it costs a certain expense, repays that expense with a profit.*[188] *(emphasis added)*

Just as today, there was a wide range of economic and cultural significance attached to these acquired and useful abilities of all the inhabitants of the mid-1700s. The continuum of such significance ranged from the craft skills transmitted through the network of craft guilds to the transformative discoveries in science and the transformative innovations arising out of new technologies in the extraction and application of various forms of carbon-based energy. The former, the craft skills, evolved steadily as they were shaped by new discoveries in scientific research and results of technological innovation. One result of this evolutionary process was the gradual replacement of the guild structure of vocational training with what eventually would become a compulsory system of public education. The latter grew in response to the growing demands of industry - and society in general - for a work force equipped with the skills essential for an increasingly refined economy.

What is most important here is that an enormous cultural and social transformation accompanied these sea-changes - and especially so in America. We started out as an essentially decentralized society in which the agrarian part encompassed nearly 95% of the population and was, to an astonishing degree, nearly self-sufficient.[189] A key feature of this agrarian society was that few Americans worked for someone else. The vast majority answered only to themselves and the awful consequences of acting improvidently. As William Graham Sumner famously exhorted his countrymen in the late 1800s, the cold hard reality was that man had "no more right to life than a rattlesnake."[190]

The Founding Fathers were very aware of the unique circumstances presented by their young republic and how these circumstances impacted its future prospects . Indeed, many of them clearly sensed that they were living in a transiently benign epoch. And while many mistakenly believed - or were guardedly optimistic - that they could maintain these benign conditions for a very long time, they also could see the forces that threatened to undermine them. After all, these forces were already at work on the European side of the Atlantic and the results were disturbing.

Several of the most prominent founding fathers - Benjamin Franklin, John Adams and Thomas Jefferson - had served as diplomats with long periods of European residence and were concerned by their first hand observations of conditions in its larger cities. Especially disturbing were the reports of raw exploitation of women and children in the new English factories and the concomitant breakdown of social structures. All of this naturally reinforced their conviction that the political virtues necessary to a democratic republic were grounded in the simple agrarian way of life.

Thomas Jefferson weighed in forcefully on this topic. He believed that the preservation of American's political liberties were dependent on the continued dominance of agriculture and the availability of land. Hence, Americans would maintain their liberties:

...as long as agriculture is our principal object, which will be the case while there remain vacant lands in any part of America. When we get piled upon one another in large cities, as in Europe, we shall become corrupt as in Europe, and go to eating one another as they do there.[191]

It is this simple agrarian context that breathed substance into his famous caveat - or what often is attributed to him - that 'that government governs best that governs least.'[192] In like manner, the primitive level of the context that spawned that caveat also forms the practical limit for its application.

But, perhaps the most succinct observation about the unique circumstances of the founding era came from Alexander Hamilton. He observed that: "In the general course of human nature, a power over a man's subsistence amounts to a power over his will."[193] Of course, while it also is true that Hamilton is better known as an advocate for manufacturing and the benefits accompanying a diversified economy, his quote about how freedom is not just a product of political institutions, but of economic ones as well, illustrates the pervasiveness at that time of this economically conditioned view of human freedom.

Moreover, what is fascinating about Hamilton's observation is that it anticipated a key insight of Marxian analysis. With just a single sentence, albeit in nascent form, it opens the door to an economic analysis framed by the factors of production. Implicit in his observation is that the agrarian economy of late 18th century America, with its widely distributed ownership of land, allowed for economic freedom based upon a wide distribution of the means of production. Conversely, it carried with it the logical implication that a shift in the means of production to an expanded manufacturing sector, accompanied by reduced access to land, would sharply reduce overall access to the means of production and result in diminished economic and political freedom.[194]

This brings us back to the revolutionary shift, commencing in the nineteenth century, away from our predominantly agrarian economy to an urban industrial economy. The social costs for this shift were staggering. Prior to this shift, America's cities were little more than what we now regard as a good-sized town. Philadelphia, the largest, had a population of 30,000.[195] As a result, no one had experience in how to manage urban populations that soared into the hundreds of thousands and soon approached a million in some cities. Equally disastrous was that this population explosion occurred decades prior to the innovations both in indoor plumbing fixtures and metropolitan sanitation infrastructure for the provision of clean water and removal of waste. This created a public health crisis of filth, squalor and overcrowding in which life expectancy actually dropped - substantially. As described by Robert William Fogel, a Nobel Laureate in Economics, America's cities during this period became "death traps:"

Between 1790 and 1850, life expectancy in the North declined by 25 percent, and the decline in New York, Philadelphia, and other large cities was twice as great. Life expectancy at birth for persons born in New York and Philadelphia during the 1830s and 1840s averaged just twenty-four years, six years less than that of Southern slaves.[196]

A key element of this human disaster was the lack of essential skills in managing urban populations. Metropolitan governments of that era lacked even the limited expertise of European cities, not to mention the infrastructure and technological skills that would eventually arise out of this crisis. In other words, this human disaster did not arise out of government invading the private sector; it arose out of its failure, or its inability, to effectively engage the disaster.[197] It arose out of the reality that these metropolitan governments were just learning how to deal with population densities previously unknown. In other words, the root cause of this disaster was a flood of immigrants that exceeded the resources of the infant republic to absorb them in a humane manner.

This flood of immigrants was driven, in part, by economic travails in the home country and romanticized expectations about the new world. But, it also was driven by concerted efforts on the part of industrialists to ease long-standing shortages in the American labor market.[198] The latter motive, of course, was directed at the price of labor and amounted to nineteenth century social engineering by American entrepreneurs. Given its drastic impact on urban life expectancy, it was this private sector social engineering that, in turn, became a significant driver of the social engineering embedded in the progressive reform agenda.

Probing more deeply into this human disaster, we find ourselves wrestling with the same problems that confronted the Founding Fathers and the authors of the previously cited 1920s study of *Recent Economic Changes*. Both provide us with a view of society dominated by competing interests that must be balanced by government. The latter, as previously discussed, cautioned about the importance of maintaining a dynamic equilibrium within the economy against the destructive forces of ignorance, selfish greed and the tendency of one economic sector to aggrandize its interests above the common good.[199] The former, authored by either Alexander Hamilton or James Madison, unequivocally places government in such an interventionist role:

Justice is the end of government. It is the end of civil society...In a society under the forms of which the stronger faction can readily unite and oppress the weaker, anarchy may us truly be said to reign as in a state of nature, where the weaker individual is not secured against the violence of the stronger; and, us in the latter state, even the stronger individuals are prompted by the uncertainty of their condition, to submit to a government which may protect the weak as well as themselves; so, in the former state, will the more powerful factions or parties be gradually induced, by a like motive, to wish for a government which will protect all parties, the weaker as well as the more powerful.[200]

What we need to keep in mind is that on February 8, 1788, when these words were written, American capitalism was but a gleam in the eye of the likes of Alexander Hamilton. The U.S. Constitution was the legal framework designed to encourage the growth of capitalism. But that was just the first step in a long journey. The actual saga of the agro-industrial revolution in America would have to wait until the 1800s to get underway in earnest. And even when it did, it would be a process inaccurately named - and greatly misunderstood - as the Industrial Revolution.

It would be misunderstood because the term industrial revolution suggests that it only transformed that part of the economy devoted to the fabrication and crafting of non-agricultural goods. This was especially misleading in the context of the overwhelmingly agrarian economy of the new American republic. Culturally, the ethos of that agrarian economy was focused upon the individual family as a production unit. Each one was deemed to be essentially self-reliant, well-versed in the skills necessary to a self-sustaining family farm, albeit supplemented by some bartering on the side. It was the era of the rugged individual in a manner completely incomprehensible to an aspiring individual today.

To be sure, the cult of the individual still thrives in America as a romanticized icon. This is due in part to countless think tanks and super PACs, celebrating individual freedom and liberty as if all three hundred million of us live in the serene precincts of Walden Pond. Thanks in part to them, many Americans like to think of themselves as rugged individuals with precious few ties to their compatriots. But the economic landscape of America long ago was transformed from a locally focused agricultural economy, congenial to such economic individualism, into a nationally framed bureaucratic industrial society. The latter would weave the fate of each individual into a web of economic interdependence, starting for most with a public education and winding its course through a lifetime of employment in a variety of organizations - both large and small.

Even now, this industrial iteration is being transformed further into a globally focused, digitally refined economy that systemically erodes, rather than increasing, overall employment within the mature economies of the world. Hence, millions of Americans, once securely employed, now find themselves in the economically untenable position of being unemployed, or underemployed, with few immediate options to resolve their crisis. So, just as occurred during the Great Depression, millions now find themselves in a personal crisis in which rugged individualism offers little in the way of effective relief. This is not a crisis born of millions of individuals turning away from work, it is a crisis born of systemic failures within the overall economy requiring a systemic response.

As the previous discussion has illustrated, there are many contributing elements to this systemic failure. However, there is one that has been discussed only in passing. That is the role of education. In 1800, nine years after the U.S. Constitution was ratified, there was no system of education in the infant republic. The length of the school career for the average American that year was a mere four months and two days. As the American economy and society gradually evolved and grew more refined, the need for increased resources directed to education also grew. School attendance naturally increased - albeit quite gradually. Overall school attendance for the average American increased to twenty-two months and ten days in 1850 - still but a fraction of the standards established in the following century. Similarly, a free education system was established in Massachusetts in 1827 and that precedent was followed by a number of Northern states in subsequent years. Massachusetts also was first in establishing a compulsory school attendance law.[201]

This initial growth spurt was capped by the creation of a Department of Education in the federal government in 1867. Its mission was for "collecting such statistics and facts as shall show the condition and progress of education in the several States and Territories, and of diffusing such information respecting the organization and management of schools and school systems, and methods of teaching, as shall aid the people of the United States in the establishment and maintenance of efficient school systems, and otherwise promote the cause of education throughout the country."[202] Of course, at that time, it was not a cabinet level department. It was led by a commissioner, not a secretary.

By the beginning of the twentieth century, the American educational effort had embraced an impressive percentage of the elementary and secondary age cohort of the country. But, while nearly 72% of those combined cohorts were enrolled in public schools in 1899-1900, this average distorted the underlying reality that grade eight was the normal cut-off point for a child's schooling at that time. Hence, only 3.3%, or 519,000, of the total enrollment for both elementary and secondary consisted of high school age students (14-17). This compared with an elementary school enrollment of 14,984,000.[203]

As the economy and society grew more refined over the course of the twentieth century, job applicants faced a market requiring ever higher levels of education/vocational training for admission. In addition, over the same period, the nation's population nearly quadrupled from 76 million in 1900 to 296 million by 2004-05. As a result of both dynamics, enrollments for both elementary and secondary age groups also soared. The former more than doubled from nearly 15 million to 34 million, while the latter skyrocketed by 2800% from 519 thousand to 14.6 million. The latter represented 30% of the total for combined elementary and secondary age groups, which suggests that the percentage for secondary school enrollment had increased to about 90%.[204]

The costs for these education programs also soared. In 1899-1900 the total national expenditures for elementary and secondary public schools were $215 million. By 2004-05, these expenditures had increased by a factor of 2,321 to $499.1 billion.[205] It is figures like these that galvanize the critics of public education and provide ammunition for their claims that public education is a waste of taxpayer's money. However, if we hone in on current expenses and also account for: population increase, changes in the cost of living and other hidden costs; we arrive at a far different conclusion.

Chart 11 below compares both total and current expenditures in current and constant 1981-82 dollars. As can be seen, an element of confusion arises out of the two different meanings for the term

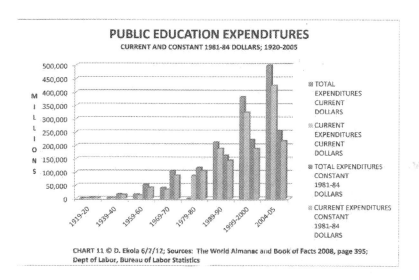

PUBLIC EDUCATION EXPENDITURES
CURRENT AND CONSTANT 1981-84 DOLLARS; 1920-2005

CHART 11 © D. Ekola 6/7/12; Sources: The World Almanac and Book of Facts 2008, page 395; Dept of Labor, Bureau of Labor Statistics

"current." Briefly, total expenses include capital costs, while current expenses do not. On the other hand, the distinction between current and constant dollars addresses the impact of inflation on expenditures over time. It also should be noted that the time frame for Chart 11 was shortened because CPI data was not available for the year 1900. For this reason the rest of our discussion will focus on the period 1920-2005.

The data presented in Chart 11 takes us through the first three steps in finding a common denominator for these educational costs spanning some 85 years of change. The first step reduces the time frame from 105 to 85 years. Starting with the years 1919-20, we have total expenditures of $1 billion, compared with total expenditures of $499.1 billion for the years 2004-05. This gives us a factor of increase of 499 to 1 [$499.1B/$1B=499] over this 85 year period. The second step reduces total expenses to current expenses. This reduces the factor of increase for this 85 year period to 471 to 1 [$424.6B/$.9B=471.1]. The third step converts current expenses from current dollars to constant 1981-84 dollars. It reduces the factor of increase to $217.7/$4.5=48.4.[206] But, while this chart provides us with a solid preliminary picture of how educational costs increased as our economy grew, it only scratches the surface in arriving at a common denominator for the evolving costs of public education.

One significant factor ignored by Chart 11 is population increase. The quickest way to shed light on it is to turn to per pupil current expense data. Per pupil current expenses will eliminate both population increase and capital costs as hidden variables. These costs in current dollars are as follows: $53.32 (1919-20); $88.09 (1939-40); $375 (1959-60); $816 (1969-70); $2,272 (1979-80); $4,980 (1989-90); $7,394 (1999-2000); and $9,995 (2004-05). This provides us with an initial factor of increase of $9,995/$53.32=187.5.[207] Applying the cost of living adjustment, based on 1982-84 constant dollars, to these per student current expenses results in the following cost revisions: $265 (1919-20); $628 (1939-40); $1,269 (1959-60); $2,100 (1969-70); $2,760 (1979-80); $3,800 (1989-90); $4,290 (1999-2000); and $5,126 (2004-05). This reduces the factor of increase from 187.5 to 19.3 ($5,126/$265 = 19.3).[208]

The next mitigating factor is special education. In the mid-1990s the Metropolitan Life Foundation sponsored two studies of education funding by the Economic Policy Institute. The first was titled *"Where's the Money Gone?"* and the second *"Where's the Money Going?"* [209] The first looked at school expenditures in nine sample districts over the period 1967-91 and the second updated this study to 1996. One of the findings of these two studies was that funding for special education increased from 3.8% to 19% of total per pupil spending over this thirty year period. Conversely, spending for regular education decreased from 80.1% to 56.8% over the same period.[210]

Expanding our focus from thirty to eighty-five years, I have adopted 1% as a reasonable estimate of special education spending for the year 1919-20. (This is based upon the fact that, in my home state of Minnesota, special education spending in 1955 was 1.8%.)[211] As a result, to maintain a reasonable basis of comparison, the revised current per student expense of $5,126 will be reduced by an adjusted special education factor (or 19%-1%) of [18% x $5,126 = $923; $5,126 - $923 = $4,203]; and similarly [1% x $265 = $2.65; $265 - 2.6 = $262.4]. This reduces the overall factor of increase from 19.3 to 16 ($4,203/$262.4=16).

When we calculate the rate of compound interest that will increase $262 (per pupil 1920 costs @ constant dollars) to $4,203 (per pupil 2005 costs in constant dollars) over 85 years, we arrive at .033 (The compound interest equation for this calculation is $262 $(1 + .033)^{85}$ = $4,138). Although this may appear on the high side when compared with productivity growth, as measured by the CPI for the same period, it is not for several reasons.[212] First, education is a labor intensive sector that does not benefit from productivity gains, technologically driven, at the same rate as are those measured by the CPI index. According to the Metropolitan Life/EPI study:

Because elementary and secondary education is inherently a low productivity industry (using a much higher proportion of labor and less technology than the average industry), inflation adjustments based on productivity and price trends in an average industry will inevitably understate inflation in education....We suggested using a modified service sector index, called the net services index (NSI), to adjust school expenditures for inflation,...Using this more accurate inflation adjustment, and examining the years 1967 to 1991, our earlier report found that about 39% of the commonly perceived doubling in per pupil spending resulted from this one mismeasurement problem alone. [213]

Applying this 39% adjustment to our revised per student current expenditure of $4,138, we get the following: .39 X $4,138 = $1,614; $4,138 - 1,614 = $2,524. This gives us a factor of increase reduced from

16 to 9.6 (2524/262 = 9.6). It also significantly reduces the rate of compound interest driving this result from .033 to .027: $262(1+.0237)^{85} = 2,522$. Nor does this exhaust all of the mitigating elements that account for the increases in public education costs.

The system also has had to deal with the growing refinement of subject matter, along with higher proficiency and salary standards for teachers, as the school system evolved from predominantly elementary to one including a greatly expanded secondary system. This dynamic was further intensified by the increasing refinement of the overall knowledge base as a result of advances in basic research and technology. We also can assume that further salary increases accompanied the shift from a female dominated elementary school staff, subject to gender driven salary discrimination, to one more inclusive of males as secondary enrollment expanded dramatically.

In addition, we also have to consider the impact of the dramatic rise in health care costs upon expenditures for benefits. Specifically, the aforementioned EPI studies found that benefits as a share of compensation rose from 8.5% in 1967 to 21.3% in 1996, for an overall increase of 12.8% over just that 29 year period.[214] Certainly a significant part of this was due to health insurance coverage. However, in the absence of better data, we must leave this as one of those yet-to-be-determined factors mitigating the cost disparity between the education costs of 1919-20 versus those for 2004-05.

 Now let's move on to the subject of the black/white disparity in educational outcomes. This is an especially difficult subject because there are several causes for this disparity - some of which appear to have nothing to do with the cultural/historical antecedents of race relations in our country and some of which do. Concerning the former, social and economic factors relating to the amount of education children receive at home and in their pre-school years are very powerful influences on the success those children will enjoy in school. Children having the benefit of a strong background in these areas typically do well regardless of race, just as children lacking the benefit of these do poorly regardless of race.

But, having said that, it still seems a bit naive to disregard the reality of who we are as a species and the long history, much of it incredibly ugly, that we share as black and white Americans. For hundreds of years this relationship was reduced to slave and master with abominable consequences for the family structure of enslaved blacks.[215] For another hundred years we continued in nearly the same relationship. We were a nation divided between an increasingly urban, industrialized society and an essentially third-world economy based on barely-concealed social and economic vestiges of slavery. These circumstances led to an enormous warehousing of human capital in a state of defacto bondage.[216]

While certainly we have made great progress in addressing this painful legacy, there still appears to be many who conclude that the country fulfilled its obligations to black Americans by fighting the Civil War.[216a] Given the apocalyptic character of that war, such an attitude is understandable. Unfortunately, it fails to take into account just how destructive the slave experience was for African-Americans. To get a better idea of what that existence was like, let's turn to Alexis de Tocqueville to get a glimpse of slavery in the ante-bellum period. After his journey through America in the 1830s, he had this to say about why race-based slavery had such a tenaciously destructive impact upon the social standing of its subjects:

The immediate evils produced by slavery were nearly the same among the ancients as among the moderns, but the consequences of these evils were different. Among the ancients, the slaves belonged to the same race as his master, and often he was superior to him in education and enlightenment. Freedom alone separated them; freedom once granted, they easily intermingled.

The ancients therefore had a very simple means of delivering themselves from slavery and its consequences; this means was emancipation, and when they employed it in a general manner, they succeeded...

What was most difficult among the ancients was to modify the law; among the moderns it is to change mores, and for us, the real difficulty begins where antiquity saw it end.

This is because among the moderns the immaterial and fugitive fact of slavery is combined in the most fatal manner with the material and permanent fact of difference in race. The remembrance of slavery dishonors the race, and race perpetuates the remembrance of slavery.

There is no African who has come freely to the shores of the New World, from which it follows that all those found there in our day are slaves or freedmen. Thus the Negro transmits to all his descendants, with their existence, the external sign of his ignominy. The law can destroy servitude; but God alone can make the trace of it disappear.[217]

In another passage, Tocqueville shifts his focus to the individual and family structure of the African-American slave:

Oppression has with one blow taken from the descendants of the Africans almost all the privileges of humanity! The Negro of the United States has lost even the memory of his country; he no longer understands the language that his fathers spoke; he has abjured their religion and forgotten their mores. In thus ceasing to belong to Africa, he has however acquired no right to the goods of Europe; but he has stopped between the two societies; he has remained isolated between the two peoples, sold by one and repudiated by the other, finding in the entire universe only the hearth of his master to offer him the incomplete image of a native country.

The Negro has no family; he cannot see in woman anything but the passing companion of his pleasures, and his sons, by being born, are his equals.[218]

Taken together, along with the history of how their Civil War emancipation was subverted during the following century, de Tocqueville's observations give us a profound insight into why the race-based slave experience of African-Americans had such a destructive impact on them - and why the perverse legacy of that system continues to impact too many of their descendants. After all, it was an experience, nearly three centuries long, that not only was designed to destroy the family structure of African-Americans along with their social standing, but also corrupted the so-called master race, giving them a myopic and corrosive sense of their own superiority, if not outright contempt for an entire race.

As a result, we have visited upon not just African-Americans, but society in general, heavy burdens of social dysfunction that have cost us far more than the substantial profits wrung from such an evil institution. Nor should it come as a great surprise that we have stumbled in trying to remedy this sad state of affairs. After all, the great genius of our species is our capacity for experimentation - our gift for the processes of trial and error - and trying new things when success eludes us.

Unfortunately, one of our great weaknesses as Americans is the belief among many of us that only private enterprise, in the pursuit of profit, is entitled to embark upon social experiments fraught with destructive consequences. Governments, on the other hand, are not entitled to experiment with programs to mitigate the dysfunctional results of such private sector social engineering. Hence, when government screws up, it becomes the poster child for government as a failed institution - regardless of how many other successes it has achieved. When private enterprise screws up, such mistakes are regarded as the price of progress and the purported remedy for it will be found only in even greater reliance on the unfettered operations of the free market.

Having said that, we need to recognize that although the painful history of African-Americans is critical to understanding our present challenges, it would be a mistake to focus exclusively upon it. After all, such an exclusive focus has the unintended consequence of reinforcing the unfortunate stereotypes and prejudices that are the legacy of that history. Even worse, it leads us to the erroneous conclusion that all is fine within the American education establishment, but for the struggles of African-Americans and other minorities.

But, before we move on, we ought not completely disregard the forgoing. It does provide a useful insight into the difficult cultural/historical forces that still intrude upon our efforts to create a genuinely productive educational experience for all of our children. And by that I mean the whole range of troubling dynamics, ranging from the 'soft bigotry of low expectations,' to the anti-social street-gang mentality of those minorities who count themselves outside the fold of American society.[219]

With those thoughts in mind, we turn to the larger picture of the following systemic shortcomings of contemporary American education: (1) we clearly do not lead the world in elementary and secondary education rankings - if we ever did;[220] (2) a principal cause of this failure is that we still draw our teachers from the bottom third of higher education students; while most leaders in international rankings draw their teachers from the top third;[221] (3) the schools that need our most talented teachers lack effective incentive programs to attract them; (4) the most economically challenged school districts needing the greatest funding, get the least;[222] (5) we need to look at teacher merit pay systems to see if there is a correlation between them and the failure to attract candidates from the top third of college students; (6) we need to look at the effectiveness of curricula and how that relates to issues of teacher evaluation and incentives; (7) we need to focus upon low-income obstacles to learning rather than those focused upon minority status;[223] (8) we need an accounting system within education that clarifies and enables program analysis, rather than obstructing it;[224] (9) this reform of education accounting is critical not only for an accurate measure of program value, but also for the creation of an equitable system of teacher evaluation; (10) we need to take a very hard look at indiscriminate mainstreaming of special education students and the impact that has on overall education outcomes.[225]

Faced with these challenges, there is a temptation to describe our current circumstances in the worst possible light. This is an easy trap to fall into when you are trying to galvanize the nation for emergency rescue measures. However, we should avoid painting with too broad a brush, whether that be vis-à-vis our shortcomings or our strengths. Indeed, the data indicates that we ought to avoid such lopsided assessments. When measured against other nations in education achievement, we are neither an abject failure, nor as accomplished as needed to compete successfully in the global market, while at the same time, equipping our citizens with the self-sustaining skills essential to a resilient economic society. Having said that, it also is worth emphasizing that our failure to provide all students with self-sustaining skills comprises a very large part of the fiscal burdens shouldered by local, state and federal government. Hence, while we may not be at 'the sky is falling' moment in education, we nevertheless have an urgent need to commence with genuine reform.

The Programme for International Student Assessment (PISA) for 2009 places the U.S. 7 points above the average score for reading, 1 point above the average for science and, more troubling, 9 points below the average for mathematics. In terms of ranking, this places the U.S. in 14th place for reading, 23rd place for science and 29th place for mathematics.[226] The good news is that these are pretty much fair to middling scores for an enormous nation - hobbled by a constitution that frustrates positive action. The bad news is that these are pretty much fair to middling scores for a nation once accustomed to being a world leader in a highly competitive global economy. And it is especially bad news in a global economy driven increasingly by advances in human capital fostered by highly competitive educational programs in other countries.

One of our challenges is that we are a nation riven by regional cultural differences relative to the value of education. The PISA 2009 report had this to say about these regional differences within the U.S:

There is, of course, significant performance variability within the United States, including between individual states. Unlike other federal nations, the United States did not measure the performance of states individually on PISA. However, it is possible to compare the performance of public schools among groups of states. Such a comparison suggests that in reading, public schools in the northeast of the United States would perform at 510 PISA score points - 17 score points above the OECD average (comparable with the performance of the Netherlands) but still well below the high-performing education systems examined in this volume - followed by the midwest with 500 score points (comparable with the performance of Poland), the west with 486 score points (comparable with the performance of Italy) and the south with 483 score points (comparable with the performance of Greece). Note, however, that because of the way in which the sample was drawn, the performance estimates for the groups of states are associated with considerable error.[227]

Another challenge results from the way we squander what should be a strength. This strength is that, for the time being , we still are one of the richest nations in the world. As such we have the opportunity to direct more resources to education than most other countries. And we do that. The PISA 2009 report ranks the United States 2nd in the world in education spending per pupil.[228] This also provides us with the potential to direct more resources to those students in greatest need of help. Unfortunately, though, unlike most of the OECD nations, we fail to take advantage of this opportunity to improve the educational outcomes for those in the greatest need. Instead, we direct a disproportionate amount of resources to those who need them the least. According to PISA 2009:

The United States is one of only three OECD countries in which, for example, socio-economically disadvantaged schools have to cope with less favourable student-teacher ratios than socio-economically advantaged schools, which implies that students from disadvantaged backgrounds may end up with considerably lower spending per student than what the above figures on average spending would suggest.[229]

An additional challenge facing our educational system arises out of our efforts to establish accurate standards of teacher evaluation. Setting aside the political controversy roiling this discussion for the moment, let's return to the aforementioned Metropolitan Life/EPI study. This study focused on the system of accounting in public education. It is an accounting system that fails to track specific program costs in a manner facilitating a meaningful analysis of their success or failure. This barrier to effective program analysis naturally undermines the effort to establish a level playing field for the evaluation of teachers. It becomes especially significant with questions that focus on whether funding for a given program has risen or fallen over time.

The second mismeasurement concerns the data used for comparison of 'resources' to 'student performance.' While our earlier report offered no conclusions about whether regular academic student performance has shown 'tangible improvements,' we noted that the resources (per pupil spending) against which the efficiency of these improvements is normally measured are devoted to a wide range of programs, academic instruction being only one. Schools also provide special education for the disabled, vocational education, lunch programs, and special instruction for at-risk youth and for economically disadvantaged students. Comparing the combined expenditures for all these programs to the outcomes of only one of them (academic achievement of regular students) provides a misleading picture.

This mismeasurement is difficult to correct because schools do not report their expenditures by program. Instead, districts, states, and the federal government report education expenditures by 'function' (administration, instruction, etc.) or by 'object' (salaries, benefits, supplies, etc.). These categories cut across varied school programs, making it difficult to discern the efficiency of spending on regular, special, or vocational education or on noninstructional programs like health or nutrition.

Because school finance is normally concerned with 'function' and 'object,' not programs, there are no conventionally accepted definitions of programmatic categories or their components.[230]

As for the analysis contained in the Metropolitan Life/EPI study, it was made possible by a laborious process of reverse engineering the budgets of the sample school districts into programmatic categories. Unfortunately, such budgetary reconstruction on a national scale is not to be expected anytime soon.

Meanwhile, there is a positive side to this subject. According to the PISA 2009 study, the United States could expect very substantial economic gains as a result of improved learning outcomes. This places the short-term costs of increased funding and appropriate reforms in the favorable context of long-term gains. It also presents us with a very positive trade-off seldom encountered in contemporary debates about investment in education:

The international achievement gap is imposing on the United States economy an invisible yet recurring economic loss that is greater than the output shortfall in what has been called the worst economic crisis since the Great Depression. Using economic modelling (sic) to relate cognitive skills - as measured by PISA and other international instruments - to economic growth shows (with some caveats) that even small improvements in the skills of a nation's labour force can have large impacts on that country's future well-being. A recent study carried out by the OECD, in collaboration with the Hoover Institute at Stanford University, suggests that a modest goal of having the United States boost its averaged PISA scores by 25 points over the next 20 years - which corresponds to the performance gains that some countries achieved between 2000 and 2009 alone - could imply a gain of USD 41 trillion for the United States economy over the lifetime of the generation born in 2010 (as evaluated at the start of reform in terms of the real present value of future improvements of GDP). Bringing the United States up to the average performance of Finland, the best-performing education system among OECD countries, could result in gains in the order of USD 103 trillion. Narrowing the achievement gap by bringing all students to a baseline level of proficiency for the OECD (a PISA of about 400) could imply GDP increases for the United States of USD 72 trillion, according to historical growth relationships (OECD, 2010b). [231]

But instead of seizing this opportunity and working toward it, we forego it. The problem is twofold. First, we have embraced a short-term focus that tends to avoid the costs of any investments, regardless of how sensible they may be in the long-term. Second, anything that requires an investment these days runs smack into our debt ceiling dilemma. So no matter how great the long-term pay-off, we are reluctant to add investments to our current debt load - even though the failure to make these investments actually will cost us more down the road.

This just adds to the sense of hopelessness that afflicts our contemporary politics. We no longer have sufficient faith in ourselves to make investments essential for the creation of our future prosperity. Instead, we adopt a grudging attitude toward the very institutions that must play a critical role in getting us out of our current predicament. Instead of investing in our future, the conventional wisdom is to wage a scorched earth campaign of budget cuts and public sector lay-offs, starving the beast of public education into submission - as if starvation ever produced plenty .

Mitt Romney's recently announced education policy provides a prime example of this scorched earth campaign. He would convert approximately one half, or about 25 billion dollars, of federal education funds into a voucher program for individual students. [232] These funds would come from federal assistance programs for schools with large populations of poor and disabled students. It would divert these sorely needed dollars away from those schools, that struggle the most, and send them to better performing schools, whether public or private, selected by those parents granted vouchers.

The effect on those struggling schools, far from propelling competitive excellence, would serve only to drive them further into failure. After all, it takes proper funding, not a spirit of desperation, to foster innovation and improved outcomes in academic achievement. And, as we already have seen in our discussion of the PISA studies, this can only serve to further exacerbate the dysfunctional trend in American public education that focuses our wealth advantage upon the wealthiest school systems - and beggars our poorest districts. [233] How anyone could expect success out of a strategy that simply doubles down on past failures just boggles the mind.

Romney's straw man in this debate is that America's education system is in a state of crisis. It is a crisis, so the argument goes, in which millions of American children are receiving a third world education largely due to Obama's inability to stand up against teacher unions. According to Romney, it is a failure so profound "it is the civil rights issue of our era...[and] the great challenge of our time."[234] But, it is not true that Obama has failed to stand up against teacher unions. In a Fact Check, posted May 25, 2012, Christine Armario of the Associated Press had this to say:

Several of the core tenets of the Obama administration's signature education initiative, the Race to the Top connection, are policies first heralded by Republicans and are in opposition to the steadfast positions of teacher unions on topics like school choice and merit pay for teachers.[235]

While it is true that the failures of the American education system are very costly in terms of lost human capital and severely diminished lives, the reality is this situation is driven, in part, by the hidden dynamics of culture. Those dynamics consist of the unspoken legacy of our race-based system of slavery as described earlier in this essay by Tocqueville. Certainly the rationalizations of that ugly system - those doctrines of inferiority maligning an entire race - have long since been laid to rest by the light of reason. But, as Tocqueville cautioned, those rational efforts, focused upon surface concerns, are just the beginning of the task.[236]

The other part of the task, the really hard work, has to deal with the irrational foundations of those doctrines of inferiority. Those irrational foundations consist of beliefs whose roots can be traced to the emotionally driven filing system of the brain, linked to the amygdala and hippocampus. These beliefs form the neuro-cultural foundations of what earlier scholars, the likes of William Graham Sumner, called mores, or folkways.[237] Although these terms have long since fallen into disuse, they are useful in that they provide us with a set of terms capturing the essence of the prejudices that drive the subterranean reality of culture. They provide us with explanations for the everyday - but really profound - things in life that raise nettlesome questions - like what drives the choice of a particular form of economic system? In Tocqueville's day that nettlesome question was about slavery and the explanation du jour was that Negroes were inferior to Caucasians. End of story. No further explanation was needed because everyone believed they knew - pretty much to the core of their being - that it was 'true.'[238]

Everyone knew that to be 'true' because that assumption had been accepted for centuries. In fact, it can be traced back to the formative years of Christianity in what formerly were known as the Dark Ages. During those centuries following the collapse of the Roman empire in the early fifth century, Christian doctrine had a brutally exclusive side to it. Those who were not Christians were not endowed with human rights. As Jaques Le Goff observed in his book, *Medieval Civilization 400-1500*:

For a long time the pagan world was a great reservoir of slaves for Christian trade, whether it was conducted by Christian merchants or by Jewish merchants in Christian territory. Conversion, which dried up this fruitful market, was not carried out without hesitation. Anglo-Saxons, Saxons, and Slavs (the last mentioned gave their name to the human cattle of medieval Christian Europe) supplied the medieval slave trade before being integrated into the Christian world and thus protected from slavery....A non-Christian was not really human; only a Christian could enjoy the rights of a man, among them protection from slavery. The Christian attitude towards slavery was a manifestation of Christian particularism, the primitive solidarity of the group and the policy of apartheid with regard to outside groups.[239]

Granted, centuries had passed in the interim, between the dark times of early medieval Christianity and those of early nineteenth century America. And for those who prefer to focus on the rational side of human experience, the passage of those centuries certainly had the appearance of mitigating the brutality of early Christian attitudes toward outsiders. Indeed, the fundamental thrust of the Enlightenment was supposed to have swept away the remnants of superstition and prejudice, leaving a clean slate upon which the western world could initiate a humane and rational destiny. In general terms, our Founding Generation stands as testimony to that revolution in thought.

The writings of John Locke (1632-1704) - an acquaintance of Isaac Newton and one of the luminaries of the Enlightenment - were a source of inspiration to our Founding Fathers as they composed both our Declaration of Independence and Constitution.[240] Both in his writing and much of his life story, Locke stands out as the personification of this liberal tradition. He still is celebrated today as an iconic figure in the establishment of political liberty.

But there is another side to the story of John Locke. It is a side that exposes the darker pathways of culture and how they work their will largely out of sight - or the control - of our more enlightened sensibilities. Similarly, his story is of particular interest because both he and our Founding Fathers fell into the same trap of flagrant inconsistency regarding slavery vis- à -vis their lofty philosophical precepts. We already have seen how the Founding Fathers stumbled in their attempt to create a utopian republic, a *confederacy* based upon a too-generous assessment of the power of the ideal over the gritty impulses of human nature. However, we have not discussed how they failed to come to terms with slavery. Indeed, they immortalized this failure by their inability to even refer to it forthrightly by name. Instead, they not only kicked the can of slavery down the road for generations, but also resorted to numerous semantic dodges that allowed them to deal with it in the Constitution without a single overt reference to it as slavery.[241]

For his part, Locke's relationship with slavery has the appearance of being just as hypocritical. In general terms, he developed a philosophy of governance resting on the fundamental importance of consent: In his *Second Treatise of Government*, he states:

MEN being, as has been said, by nature, all free, equal, and independent, no one can be put out of this estate, and subjected to the political power of another, without his own consent. The only way whereby any one divests himself of his natural liberty, and puts on the bonds of civil society, is by agreeing with other men to join and unite into a community for their comfortable, safe, and peaceable living one amongst another,...[242]

Viewed retrospectively, such a precept presents a formidable obstacle to the legality of any form of slavery, given its fundamentally coercive nature. More specifically, he also puts strict limits on slavery by declaring that the only justification for slavery is as a punishment for aggressive warfare against innocent persons:

And hence it is, that he who attempts to get another man into his absolute power, does thereby put himself into a state of war with him; it being to be understood as a declaration of a design upon his life;...for nobody can desire to have me in his absolute power unless it be to compel me by force to that which is against the right of my freedom, i.e., make me a slave.[242a]

Completing this line of thought in his chapter on slavery, Locke has this to say about those who would wage such an unjust war against innocent persons:

Indeed, having by his fault forfeited his own life, by some act that deserves death; he, to whom he has forfeited it, may (when he has him in his power) delay to take it, and make use of him to his own service,...This is the perfect condition of slavery, which is nothing else, but the state of war continued between a lawful conqueror and captive;...[242b]

Having set forth such narrow grounds to legitimize slavery, it is puzzling that slavery did not just wither away during the Enlightenment and its aftermath, but, on the contrary, actually flourished. Nor was Britain, despite Locke's great influence there, exempt from this puzzling trend.[242c] In their *History of the Modern World*, Palmer and Colton state that: "It can scarcely be denied that the phenomenal rise of British capitalism in the eighteenth century was based to a considerable extent on the enslavement of Africans."[242d]

But perhaps what is most intriguing, is that Locke himself wound up embracing slavery in a very personal way. In the years following his academic career at Oxford College, he became an investor in the Royal Africa Company, a company deeply involved in the slave trade and benefitting greatly from a government charter and subsidies.[243] His investment in that company - and others - made him a man of some means.[243a] At the same time, he also acquired an administrative view of the slave trade as secretary of the Council of Trade and Plantations.[243b] This vantage point was significant because these were the years when the Royal Africa company was laying the foundations for the subsequent explosive growth of the English slave trade during the eighteenth century.

Given his personal economic interest in the slave trade, reinforced by his administrative insights, it is difficult to imagine that he did not have a clear understanding of the risks and rewards of that trade.[244] In the same vein, his understanding of those risks must have included the horrific features of that trade as they related to the incidence of mortality and insurrection - and how they impacted profit and loss. In short, it is difficult to imagine that Locke, the philosopher, was not privy to just how egregiously the realities of that evil trade ran afoul of the theoretical proscriptions established by his own writings.[244a]

This was especially true regarding his views on the critical role of just war as the only legitimate justification for slavery. Indeed, the reality was that the profits of the slave trade were the driving force behind a centuries-long campaign of piracy and aggressive war against the peoples of Africa. In his work *The Slave Ship*, Marcus Rediker observed the following about this hypocrisy: "War was a euphemism for the organized theft of human beings."[245]

Placing slavery in the broad sweep of history, we need to see it as one institution among many in the saga of economic activity driven by animal-human power. Indeed, the fact that Locke was writing about slavery in the 17th century as a still-thriving institution speaks volumes about its visceral staying power as a form of economic energy. He was writing justifications for it - albeit tempered with a fig leaf of theoretical restraint - a thousand years after the period described by Jacques Le Goff. Moreover, it is all too plain that this fig leaf of restraint was underwritten by the ancient specter of the outsider - updated by xenophobic calumnies about racial inferiority and savagery. This not only speaks volumes about its staying power as a cultural phenomenon, but also about how such a morally odious institution continued to exercise such influence in the life of a single person - despite his carefully thought out rational condemnation of it.[246] It is precisely these apparent hypocrisies, these moral non-sequiturs, that expose the subterranean regions in which our neuro-cultural belief systems flourish.

It only has been in recent times that neuroscientists have started to probe the irrational dimensions of our brains. The results of their efforts are best summed up by the title of the book: *The Accidental Mind*, written by one of their leading lights, David J. Linden. The main thrust of his work is to topple the idea that our brain is "a beautifully engineered, optimized device, the absolute pinnacle of design." On the contrary, he regards such fawning praise as "pure nonsense:"[247]

The brain is not elegantly designed by any means: it is a cobbled-together mess, which, amazingly, and in spite of its shortcomings, manages to perform a number of very impressive functions. But while its overall function is impressive, its design is not. More important, the quirky, inefficient, and bizarre plan of the brain and its constituent parts is fundamental to our human experience. The particular texture of our feelings, perceptions, and actions is derived, in large part, from the fact that the brain is not an optimized, generic problem-solving machine, but rather a weird agglomeration of ad hoc solutions that have accumulated throughout millions of years of evolutionary history.[248]

One of the most significant legacies of those millions of years of evolution is the limbic system. It consists of the amygdala and the hippocampus, whose combined functions drive the emotionally driven filing system of the brain. This places these ancient organs at the critical juncture where incoming data from our sensory organs are assessed, both emotionally and rationally, and then filed in accordance with a system that weighs them disproportionately in favor of their survival-enhancing characteristics. In other words, fear - and its closely related emotions - play a big role in the prioritization assigned to this data in the filing process. Linden describes this process in the following terms:

The limbic system is important for emotion and certain kinds of memory. It is also the first place in our bottom-to-the-top tour where automatic and reflexive functions begin to blend with conscious awareness.

The amygdala is a brain center for emotional processing that plays a particular role in fear and aggression. It links sensory information that has already been highly processed by the cortex (that guy in the ski mask jumping out of that dark alley at me can't be up to any good) to automatic fight-or-flight responses mediated by the hypothalamus and brainstem structures (sweating, increased heart rate, dry mouth)....

The hippocampus....is a memory center. Like the amygdala, it receives highly processed sensory information from the cortex lying above it. Rather than mediating fear, however, the hippocampus appears to have a special role in laying down the memory traces for facts and events, which are stored in the hippocampus for a year or so but are then moved to other structures.[248a]

The key point is that Linden is describing the nexus of a memory-recording system that includes a system of prioritization that is weighted with emotion. We can then take this as the starting point for a concept that merges neuro-science into the study of those hard to explain dichotomies of everyday life and history - those perplexing rifts in the human experience separating: war and peace; civility and barbarity; tender nurture and eye-gouging viciousness. As previously alluded to, we will baptize this concept as the neuro-cultural foundation for the subterranean reality of everyday life. It is a concept so new that it has yet to surface in our everyday vocabulary - or for that matter, as a conventionally recognized object of research relevant to history and economics. Yet hopefully some day it will become the focus of serious attention in these latter disciplines insofar as it promises to answer some of those nettlesome questions about the darker side of human nature.[249]

As happens with new concepts, though, there is one large red flag hanging over this one. That is the red flag of Lamarckism - or the idea that acquired traits can be inherited. In this case, the idea gets even foggier because the inherited traits we are talking about are mental constructs. Such a notion faces enormous headwinds of established scientific doctrine, not to mention a leap of faith that would embarrass even the Vatican. So no. This discussion is not proposing the notion that specific ideas can be inherited as part of the evolutionary heritage of the species.

One proposal offered here is that so long as the underlying reality of a cultural construct survives, the adherents of that construct will keep it alive if it suits their needs. Hence, so long as slavery continued to exist across the millennia, the rationalizations for it continued to thrive. A big part of the reason these rationalizations survived was the context of economics. Slavery was big business and livelihoods were at stake. But an equally significant part of their survival most likely will be found in the irrational pathways now being explored in the human brain.

A race-based system of slavery conformed marvelously to the need for rationalizing such a morally repugnant system. It clothed that moral repugnance with the genetically branded stigmata of what had every appearance of being a foreign species. This foreign species was the incarnation of the threatening outsider. They were so different from the rest of us; they did not deserve the protection afforded by our provincially circumscribed limits of human society. How else explain the conspicuous inhumanity of our Constitution enumerating our slave population at the discounted rate of sixty percent of a person? Doesn't such a discount logically translate into the term subhuman?

Similarly, as demonstrated by our post Civil War experience in race relations, this context does not have to be all-inclusive or survive lockstep in identical format. Whether for good or ill, we humans can be adaptable and ingenious no matter the need. Hence, though African-Americans were freed from slavery by the terms of the 14th Amendment, the same economic interests that benefited from slavery found new means to ensnare them. Slavery simply metamorphosed into similarly exploitive labor institutions and systems of repression. These survived for another hundred years under a regime of specially crafted state and local laws. And their survival, in turn, was rationalized by the same racial theories that supported slavery.[249a]

The power of the racial antipathy - on which these rationalization were based - was noted by Tocqueville:

 In the portion of the Union where Negroes are no longer slaves, have they been brought closer to whites? Every man who has inhabited the United States will have noticed that a contrary effect has been produced.

Racial prejudice appears to me stronger in the states that have abolished slavery than in those where slavery still exists, and nowhere is it shown to be as intolerant as in states where servitude has always been unknown.[249b]

This racial antipathy continued unabated, roiled by the same nativist impulses of cultural alienation and economic competition that antagonized relations with other immigrant groups - except in this case they were deepened by the triple stigmata of race, cultural deprivation and economic disadvantage. This triple whammy served to reinforce a gratifying sense of superiority that affords some degree of psychic comfort for those in need of it.

As our continuing culture conflict suggests, many of these same dynamics are still at play. And for some the mythic antecedents of our race-based system of slavery still offer them a satisfying interpretation for our current social problems. African-Americans are no longer slaves, but for some the racial theories that rationalized that system still offer a convincing, albeit usually sub-rosa, explanation for the surviving stigmata of economic disadvantage. Others see these circumstances in a more hopeful light. They see an uneven playing field that needs to be leveled. They see the prospect of a brighter future resulting from appropriate investments in education and in choosing to support those systems that encourage self-improvement - rather than a grudging refusal to provide what Barack Obama calls 'ladders of opportunity.'

In short, what we Americans have today is the continuation of an epic struggle that began when buccaneering entrepreneurs found it profitable to get into the slave trade in a big way and convert the new world into a race-based slave empire. Their success became our bitter legacy: the most grievous burden born by African-Americans, but a nonetheless significant piece born also by the rest of us. We have been living with the consequences of that centuries-long experiment in social-engineering ever since. It was not something that could be legislated away overnight.

A Constitutional Amendment scarcely budged it - scarcely nudged it off its secure moorings of economic advantage and limbic-system apprehensions of cultural and racial degeneration. Granted, these mythic antecedents are truly ugly things to discuss. But, as we open our eyes to the power of that limbic system, it is time we revisited some of the awful moral dimensions of that part of our being and its role in sustaining that bitter heritage. We need to revisit it for the simple reason that this bitter heritage has had such staying power and, even now, hinders our efforts to get our fiscal house back in order.

This digression away from the specific subject matter of education may appear rather lengthy, but it was time well spent. This discussion of the neuro-cultural foundations of our decision-making processes has everything to do with how we evaluate and shape our public agendas - including our education agenda. It has everything to do with the prejudices driving the reality that our funding of less advantaged school districts does not match their needs. In other words, it has everything to do with the Bush administration's pointed criticism of minority education in the U.S. as the result of the "soft bigotry of low expectations."[250]

Having said that, let's return to our previous discussion about the depth of the crisis in American education. On the one hand, it is not true that the American education system is in a deepening crisis in which the achievement levels of American students grows worse year by year. On the contrary, as we have seen, the overall picture is one of a mediocre system struggling to make small improvements. [251] On the other hand, when this portrait of barely average outcomes is compared with the stellar performance of that small group of exceptional nations soaring past us, it does prompt a sense of unease - even outright alarm - for our future well-being.[252] Nevertheless, as we chart our course of reform, it is important that we not allow our sense of alarm to run wild. The worst thing we could do would be to go off half-cocked and unleash a wrecking ball instead of a well-balanced program of reforms that builds on the successes of specific programs.

For example, instead of providing marginal gains to a select group of students awarded federal funds at the expense of their fellow students, we need responsible funding increases that will provide the opportunity for improved outcomes for all the students in a given school.[253] This is especially true since voucher programs do not have a consistent record of success in raising the achievement levels of those students transferred to them from struggling schools.[254] To the greatest extent possible, we need programs that will lift all boats, not just a chosen few.

Similarly, we should not rush headlong into teacher evaluation programs without the essential analytical tools providing an accurate assessment of resource allocation and how that correlates with the effectiveness of curricula and individual teacher skills.[255] Instead we should approach this project with the restraint, patience and a dedication to fairness that we owe to a teacher corps that was recruited and trained under one set of standards and is now being plunged pell mell into a radically changed environment. Perhaps most importantly, we should not hastily erect an evaluation system that can be corrupted into one that sacrifices skilled senior teachers on the altar of a school district's fiscal convenience.

We also would be well-advised to focus upon those countries presenting the greatest competition in this race for academic excellence. Let's start by classifying the top performers on the PISA mathematics scale into two groups: stellar performers with scores of 520 and above and those above average with scores of 500 and above. The stellar group consists of 12 nations (and/or 'city-states'), only one of which could be considered a super-state: Japan with a population of 126.8 million and which ranks number 9 with a PISA mathematics score of 529 (average PISA math = 496; U.S. = 487, which ranks it at number 31). Only two others have a population that exceeds 10 percent of the 2010 U.S. population of 308.7 million: Korea, which ranks number 4, with a population of 48.6 million and a PISA math score of 546 and Canada, which ranks number 10, with a population of 33.7 million and a PISA math score of 527.[256]

The entire list of the stellar performers is as follows - in rank order/followed by PISA math score/population: (1) Shanghai-China/600/16.3 million; (2) Singapore/562/4.7 million; (3) Hong Kong / 555/7 million; (4) Korea/546/48.6 million; (5) Chinese Taipei/543/2.6 million; (6) Finland/541/5.2 million; (7) Liechtenstein/536/.03 million; (8) Switzerland/534/7.6 million; (9) Japan/529/126.8 million; (10) Canada/527/33.7 million; (11) Netherlands/526/16.8 million; (12) Macao-China/525/.5 million.

The above-average group consists of the following countries: (13) New Zealand/519/4.3 million; (14) Belgium/515/10.4 million; (15) Australia/514/21.5 million; (16) Germany/513/82.3 million; (17) Estonia/512/1.3 million; (18) Iceland/507/.3 million; (19) Denmark/503/5.5 million; (20) Slovenia/501/2 million; (21) Norway/498/4.7 million; (22-tied) France/497/64.8 million; (22-tied) Slovak Republic/497/5.5 million.[257]

The average country is (23) Austria/496/8.2 million.

The below average list consists of the following countries: (24) Poland/495/38.5 million; (25) Sweden/494/9 million; (26) Czech Republic/493/10.2 million; (27) United Kingdom/492/62.3 million; (28) Hungary/490/10 million; (29) Luxembourg/489/.5 million; (30-tied) Ireland/487/4.6 million; *(30-tied) U.S./487/310.2 million;* (30-tied)Portugal/487/10.3 million.[258]

These are sobering comparisons for anyone who likes to think of the U.S. as an exceptional nation. There is nothing exceptional about a nation that performs at this level. But equally important, we did not arrive at this level overnight. Indeed, this is not a crisis that suddenly developed during the administration of Barack Obama. Quite to the contrary, the trend in recent years has been one of modest improvement. In fact, the National Assessment of Education Progress found that:

In 2007, mathematics scores for both Black and White public school students in grades 4 and 8 nationwide,. ...were higher than in any previous assessment, going back to 1990. This was also true for Black and White fourth-graders on the NAEP 2007 Reading Assessment.[259]

The PISA 2009 assessment provides us with generally similar findings:

The United States has seen significant performance gains in science since 2006, which were mainly driven by improvements at the bottom of the performance distribution (visible in higher performance at the 10th and 25th percentiles) while performance remained unchanged at the top end of the performance distribution. Student performance in reading and mathematics has remained broadly unchanged since 2000 and 2003, respectively, when PISA began to measure these trends.[260]

One country that gives us insights into getting the American educational establishment out of the ditch is Finland. It provides a stunning example on how to reform a third-rate educational system into one of the world's most competitive. Thirty some years ago Finland had a largely agrarian economy with a school system to match.[261] Compulsory school attendance - at just six years - was a relic of the late 1800s and provided Finland with commensurately poor living standards.

In recent years Finland has either led, or been among the top performers, in the PISA assessment of student achievement. In the 2004 assessment it was number 1 among the OECD countries.[262] In the 2009 assessment, which included an expanded group of nations (OECD Partners), it ranked among the top three depending on the subject being assessed.[263] This expanded group included a number of

Asian countries, or city-states, that have become heavyweights in the global education competition.

Finland now boasts an economy that ranks it as one of "the most prosperous, modern and adaptable countries on the globe."[264] They have achieved this by raising the revenues necessary to fund a system that promotes high expectations for both students and staff and succeeds in motivating them accordingly. Teachers are well-paid relative to other job categories and respected for the vital functions they perform. They also are supported by complementary staff. Psychologists and teachers who concentrate on special needs students are available to work closely with classroom teachers on a case-by-case basis as needed.[265]

This, of course, stands in marked contrast to the U.S. system in which support staff such as guidance counselors are vulnerable to budget cuts, while a staff psychologist could easily become a tea party cause célèbre in the negative. More importantly, these resources are available regardless of the economic resources of a given neighborhood or region. This also stands in marked contrast to the U.S. system, in which the resources and quality of teachers in a given district are tightly linked to the wealth quotient of the district.[266]

A more detailed study of the correlation of education with economic success focuses upon the state of Minnesota. This study, "Business Cycles and Long-Term Growth: Lessons From Minnesota," was conducted by Terry J Fitzgerald and published in *The Region* in June 2003. In this study, Fitzgerald tracked the course of Minnesota's per capita income growth against national and regional rates over a period of 70 years. He found that between 1929 and 2001, Minnesota's per capita income grew from a point "14 percent below the national average" to "8 per cent above U.S. per capita income."[267] More specifically, he found that:

Since 1929, real U.S. per capita income has grown at a rate of 2.23 percent, while Minnesota per capita income rose 2.56 percent annually. Although this difference is small on an annual basis, the cumulative effect over 70 years is substantial. While U.S. income rose almost 500 percent over the entire period, Minnesota income grew more than 600 percent....Put in today's dollars, if Minnesota average income were still 86 percent of the U.S. average, state income would be almost $7.000 per person lower.[268]

In terms of its ranking among the states, Minnesota "averaged around 25th from 1929 to 1959, with some small, short-lived variations."[269]

This situation changed after the 1950s. Minnesota's per capita income ranking began climbing during the 1960s, rising to 17th by the late 1970s, and reaching the top 10 during the latter half of the 1990s. In 2001, Minnesota stood eighth. Between 1959 and 2001, Minnesota's annual per capita income growth rate of 2.76 percent outpaced 38 of the 50 states, and only five states grew at rates above 2.90 percent.[270]

He then correlated these findings against the rising levels of education among Minnesotans relative to national levels:

The relative increase in labor productivity, labor earnings and employment per capita all suggest that there may have also been a rise in the relative human capital, or skills, of Minnesota residents.....Education levels have increased dramatically throughout the country over the past 50 years. If education is to play a role in the explanation for Minnesota's incomes rising faster than the nation's as a whole, it must be that education levels have risen more rapidly in Minnesota's population. There is some evidence that this is the case.

In 2000, Minnesota ranked seventh among the states in the percent of residents 25 years and over with at least a bachelor's degree (31.2 percent compared to 25.6 percent in the nation), and third in the percent of residents with a high school degree (90.8 percent vs. 84.1 percent for the nation).

Earlier in the century, however, the education level of Minnesota's population was not especially impressive relative to the country as a whole. For example, in 1950, the percent of Minnesotans aged 25 and over with four or more years *of college was 5.6 percent, the same as the national figure. The fraction of the population with four or more years of high school was also much closer to the national average in 1950 (34.7 percent in Minnesota vs. 33.4 percent for the United States). Finally, the median duration of schooling in 1950 for Minnesotans was nine years, lower than the national figure of 9.3 years.*[271]

We still are missing one key ingredient in Minnesota's steady climb toward educational excellence as contrasted with the national average. This ingredient came to be known as the Minnesota Miracle, the miraculous designation of which was warranted for the following reasons: First, Governor Wendell Anderson embraced the substantial political risk of running on a platform of raising state taxes for the benefit of education and won quite handily - with 54 percent of the vote. Second, he managed to pass this tax reform/increase against the odds of having to work with a Republican dominated legislature.[272]

In the end, this bi-partisan effort resulted in a compromise that secured most of Anderson's school funding objectives. According to a MINNPOST article, of 10/27/2010 by Iric Nathanson:

As finally adopted, the plan raised the state share of education funding to 65 percent of the total cost and established a new formula for allocating supplemental state aid based on the number of low-income students in the individual school districts.

This school finance overhaul was funded with a revenue package totaling $580 million. It included a 22 percent increase in state income taxes, a 5 cent per pack increase in the cigarette tax, a 25 percent increase in the liquor and beer tax, and a boost in the state sales tax from 3 percent to 4 percent.[273]

Finally, what made this all the more miraculous was that Anderson did not go down in defeat in 1974, but that he actually won re-election with an even more stunning 63 percent of the vote.[274] Measured against our current anti-tax, anti-spend, ideologically gridlocked conventional wisdom, such a turn of events not only has the appearance of a miracle, but as something from another planet.

The results of this reform in education funding were dramatic. In 1969, Minnesota ranked 17th in the nation in per capita income, just an 8 point improvement from its long-standing ranking of 25th place from 1929 into the 1950s. But since that time, it increased 10 more places from 17th to 7th place between 1969 and 2003.[275]

Certainly substantial credit for these improvements in Minnesota's per capita income was due to the underlying reforms in how the Minnesota Miracle generated revenues for education. Specifically, a critical point was reducing the predominant role of the property tax in favor of state-wide funding sources. This was critical because the property tax is notorious for being an extremely uneven source of revenue. This is so because school districts vary greatly in the comparative wealth of their respective property owners, whether individual or corporate. They also vary greatly in their relative share of tax exempt properties, whether religious, charitable or governmental. These variations deeply impact their capacity to fund educational programs, which in turn impacts the ability of their school districts to successfully educate the next generation of productive citizens.

The intellectual backbone of this tax reform program came from The Citizens League, an influential Minnesota think-tank. It published a report September 1, 1970 entitled "New Formulas for Revenue Sharing in Minnesota." This report championed the idea that property taxes were a poor source of revenue for education funds. It stated:

Locally imposed taxes, particularly in urban areas with many independent units of government, such as the Twin Cities area, tend to benefit the few communities which happen to have the tax resources located within their borders at the expense of others.[276]

This idea anticipated by a generation the previously cited view of the PISA group about the importance of distributing a nation's resources according to the needs of individual school districts and students, rather than according to the accidental distribution of the nation's wealth.[277]

Before leaving this subject, we should note two additional points of great significance. The first is the cautionary point of just how debilitating the consequences are for the individual student and society in general when adequate resources are not distributed throughout the education system of a nation. According to the PISA 2009 report:

Level 2 on the PISA reading scale can be considered a baseline level of proficiency at which students begin to demonstrate the reading competencies that will enable them to participate effectively and productively in life.[278]

Conversely, of course, those students who fail to achieve a level 2 baseline proficiency in reading, as did 18 percent of fifteen-year-olds in the U.S., will face difficulties in participating effectively and productively in life.[279] This naturally translates into substantial social costs for those who either have difficulty in finding work, then become beneficiaries of safety net programs and/or become offenders and wards of the criminal justice system. It is in this sense that we ought to briefly reprise the economic rewards of improvements in educational achievement.

As previously cited, the PISA 2009 report on the U.S. found that a modest performance gain of 25 points over 20 years could generate "a gain of USD 41 trillion for the United States economy over the lifetime of the generation born in 2010."[280] This gain would result, on the one hand, from decreased economic drag arising out of lowered social costs, and on the other, from the increased productivity of enhanced human capital. In other words, the investments made to produce these performance gains deliver a one-two punch of improved economic efficiency: the first reduces dead weight on the negative productivity side of the equation, while the second boosts the rate on the positive productivity side.

This PISA 2009 analysis adds weight to John K. Galbraith's hypothesis that the technostructure amounts to a new factor of production.[281] Galbraith's concept of the technostructure receives further validation from Fitzgerald's findings, previously cited, about long-term growth in Minnesota. But just as conservative voices have managed to roll back many of the gains made by the Minnesota Miracle, they also have prevailed across the nation. They have prevailed with an argument short on facts, but long on ideology, powered by sentimentality and a distorted rendition of some of the most significant chapters in our history. To the great injury of our nation and our future well-being, we are being sold a bill of bogus goods. And this brings us to the second point of great significance.

Hidden away in the PISA 2009 report is another insight with profound implications for our current political debate. In fact, we might call it a twenty-first century addendum to the common sense views of Alexander Hamilton. So let us first refresh our focus on Hamilton's views, as interpreted by Broadus Mitchell, a biographer of Hamilton:

Hamilton never took refuge in a rule dictated by theory....Legislators and administrators, not to speak of individual enterprisers, must be prepared for constant adjustment to changing circumstances. A country's economy could not rely on the proposition of automatic operation. Hamilton's contemporary Antifederalists (Madison and Jefferson, for example) who rested their faith in laissez faire, the policy of let-alone, or the policy of, in fact, no policy, were wearing blinders. Hamilton plumped for the continuing exercise of judgment. This was the arduous, courageous system of conduct in a statesman.[282]

Given Hamilton's rejection of laissez faire, we could reasonably expect him to reject the non-policies of Mitt Romney as an insult to the intelligence of well-informed voters. Similarly, we also could reasonably expect him to be disgusted with Romney's deeply flawed version of the period leading up to the Great Recession of 2008 and his failure to acknowledge the depth of the crisis that naturally followed. After all, an accurate assessment of that seminal event was essential to arriving at a sensible policy to counteract the lengthy downturn that ensued. However Romney's assessments of this period and his criticism of President Obama's economic remedies are so shallow and bereft of accurate detail that they lack any credibility - especially for those who actually paid attention to the crisis as it unfolded.

This brings us back to the PISA 2009 report and its definition of the twenty-first century intellectual tools essential for what Hamilton regarded as the "continuing exercise of judgment." The first item describes the reading competencies required by level 6, which is the highest level and achieved by only 0.8% of students across the OECD:

Tasks at this level typically require the reader to make multiple inferences, comparisons and contrasts that are both detailed and precise. They require demonstration of a full and detailed understanding of one or more texts and may involve integrating information from more than one text. Tasks may require the reader to deal with unfamiliar ideas, in the presence of prominent competing information, and to generate abstract categories for interpretations. Reflect and evaluate tasks may require the reader to hypothesize about or critically evaluate a complex text on an unfamiliar topic, taking into account multiple criteria or perspectives, and applying sophisticated understandings from beyond the text. A salient condition for access and retrieve tasks at this level is precision of analysis and fine attention to detail that is inconspicuous in the texts.[283]

At the other extreme, we find level 1b, the lowest level, which is attained by 98.9% of students across the OECD:

Tasks at this level require the reader to locate a single piece of explicitly stated information in a prominent position in a short, syntactically simple text with a familiar context and text type, such as a narrative or a simple list. The text typically provides support to the reader, such as repetition of information, pictures or familiar symbols. There is minimal competing information. In tasks requiring interpretation the reader may need to make simple connections between adjacent pieces of information.[284]

Somewhere between these two levels lies the nemesis of American democracy, the level of reading competence and intellectual predisposition that embraces automatic formulae instead of a commitment to facts and rigorous analysis.[285] It is a predisposition that finds it origins in the 'catchy', high impact messaging that arose out of the 'roaring twenties.' The marketing of that new automotive age was abbreviated to the fast-paced needs of roadside messaging. It commenced with an intuitive preference for short and sweet, but over the course of a century has morphed into a cacophony of all manner of sentient disturbances and intrusions. These range from the seductive and comedic, to the numbingly repetitive, through the blatantly in-your-face, to the downright offensive.

But, all the while the initial impetus for cutting quickly to the quick was being reinforced by the axe of cost effectiveness, the medium itself, along with the size of its audience, was evolving and expanding from roadside sign to radio to TV to the internet. In the end, we have been left with a cost structure for marketing political discourse that crams the message into a fraction of a minute. It is a ruthlessly abbreviated process - tilted decisively against the intellect - that stifles meaningful discussion of complicated issues. Given these low-brow market forces, it should not surprise that important lessons of history, along with level 6 skills of precision of analysis and fine attention to detail, are routinely sacrificed to the need to provide the listener with a simple narrative, reinforced by constant repetition, as in level 1B. The real tragedy here is that, while we were the victors in WWII, the ghost of Joseph Goebbels, master of Nazi propaganda, has been resurrected in the guise of new-age marketing.[286]

But now let us shift our focus from the abstract terrain of reading skills back to what or, more importantly, to what is not in the nation's head. Without question, the two most significant concepts missing from American conventional wisdom are economic momentum and Galbraith's concept of technostructure. Both of these are so basic that it is impossible to conduct a meaningful conversation about things economic without them. Oddly enough, the concept of economic momentum probably is the most elusive - precisely because the more general phenomenon of momentum is so ubiquitous. It is so much a part of our everyday life that it has seeped into our thought processes and language as if it were second nature - which is exactly what it is. Whether you consider the relative braking difficulties of a light vehicle versus a mile-long train, or the relative thrust required to lift a single-engine aircraft versus a 747, the world around us is filled with examples of Newton's laws of motion. Unfortunately for our perception of it, though, that reduces it to the level of habit; which more often than not operates in a subconscious, taken-for-granted manner.

Hence, the very ubiquity of momentum as part of the fabric of life hides the significance of it. And the ironic result is that a culture supposedly endowed with an appreciation for Newton's laws of motion is incapable of comprehending their significance - especially as they relate to the near collapse of the behemoth of our fifteen trillion dollar economy. After all, in a fully rational world, one would expect that familiarity with Newton's laws relating to the mass of an object - its inertia and momentum - would translate into an intelligent understanding of how the momentum of a fifteen trillion dollar economy, whether ascendant or descendant, would continue over a period of years, even a decade, rather than a few months. However, as we have seen when we turn to polls about President Obama's handling of the economy, we do not live in a fully rational world. We live in a partially rational world in which those who comprehend economic momentum are outnumbered by those who don't.[287]

Notwithstanding this intellectual handicap, let's take a closer look at Newton's laws of motion:

Newton's Laws of Motion (1687)
Isaac Newton (1642-1727)

First Law: An object at rest will remain at rest and an object in motion will remain in motion at that velocity until an external force acts on the object. Second Law: The sum of the forces (F) that act on an object is equal to the mass (m) of the object multiplied by the acceleration, or F = ma. Third Law: To every action, there is an equal and opposite reaction.[288]

Roughly translating this into economic terms, we get the following equation for the economic growth of a $14 trillion economy: F = $14T X % of increase. In an economy with a moderate rate of growth, say 3 percent, the above equation would look like this: $420B = $14T X .03. In other words, it takes a positive $420B economic force to move a $14T economy at a moderate 3% rate of increase. Now to translate this equation into the force requirement for moving an economy out of recession, we will plug in the following rates of GDP contraction for Q4 2008 as perceived on the following dates: -3.8% (1/30/2009), -5.4% (2/11/2010), -6.8% (2/23/2011), and -8.9% (10/27/2011).[289] The resultant equations for these negative forces, calculated on an annual basis, are as follows: -.038 X $14T = $532B (1/30/2009); -.054 X $14T = $756B (2/11/2010); -.068 X $14T = $952B (2/23/2011); and -.089 X $14T = $1.246T (10/27/2011). The next step is to convert these to quarterly values: 532B/4=133B; 756B/4=189B; 952B/4=238B; and 1,246T/4=311.5B. Having illustrated just how much these Q4 2008 GDP values varied over time, we now will focus on the four deepest quarters of the Great Recession, as seen in January 2009 and October 2011.

The four deepest quarters of the recession were April 2008-March 2009. The average percentage change in GDP for those four quarters as perceived in 2009 was -.0197%; in 2011 that percentage change was -.045%.[289a] In short, this perceived drop in GDP more than doubled over that period. The respective amount of stimulus needed to offset these losses and bring the economy back to moderate growth works out as follows: .0197 X 14T = 276B + 420B = 696B (2009); .045 X 14T = 630B + 420B = 1.05T.

This exercise discloses two important points. First, the amount of stimulus signed into law on 2/17/2009 ($862 billion) was inadequate to the task at hand.[289b] Second, the actual depth of the economic decline during the fourth quarter of 2008, a disastrous drop of 8.9 percent, did not fully materialize until 10/27/2011 - a full year after the 2010 election.[290] Indeed, the preliminary assessment of a 3.8 percent decline did not come to light until 1/30/2009 - a week after Obama took office.

As a general rule, such delays in arriving at an accurate estimate of changes in the GDP are not unusual. Under normal circumstances early estimates of GDP may be adjusted up or down over a several year period.[291] Consequently, judged by any fair assessment, it must be acknowledged that, during the tempestuous period when the Obama administration took office, it was shadow-boxing with a dramatically shifting once-in-a-century reality. They knew the situation was difficult; they just didn't know how bad it was and precisely how much stimulus it would take to counteract the downturn.

It is against this background that we return to the estimate by Obama's economic team - and the unfounded allegation they made a disingenuous promise to the nation: that unemployment would not exceed 8 percent if the stimulus package were enacted.[292] The reason for taking another look at this episode is because it provides an excellent example of the 'Big Lie' in the 2012 presidential election campaign. It is a 'Big Lie' that accuses the Obama administration of making a 'Big Lie' on the basis of very distorted facts. It makes a fine example because it is a serious distortion of the factual record that has been repeated ad nausea throughout the campaign - with scant correction from the media. First, unemployment already had reached 8.2% by the end of February 2009, less than two weeks after the American Recovery and Reinvestment Act (ARRA) was signed into law.[293]

Second, it is important to take note of the actual date of this estimate. It was announced on January 9, 2009, some two weeks prior to President Obama actually taking office, in a report written by Christina Romer, slated to be the Chairperson of the Council of Economic Advisers, and Jared Bernstein, an assistant to Vice-President-elect Joe Biden.[294] More specifically, it was drafted in the period that preceded the preliminary -3.8 percent GDP estimate of 1/30/2009. Moreover, we have seen how this early estimate of -3.8 percent GDP gradually evolved over the next two-and-one-half years into a truly severe depression-like drop of -8.9 percent GDP.[295] In other words, the administration and the entire country were only gradually realizing the full extent of the unfolding crisis. Having said that, they nevertheless realized that their estimates were being made in the midst of a severe downturn and that the full extent of that downturn was yet to be determined. Hence, far from promising the country that passage of the yet-to-be-determined stimulus measures would guarantee specific results, they clearly stated the tentative character of their estimates:

It should be understood that all of the estimates presented in this memo are subject to significant margins of error. There is the obvious uncertainty that comes from modeling a hypothetical package rather than the final legislation passed by the Congress. But, there is more fundamental uncertainty that comes with any estimate of the effects of a program. Our estimates of economic relationships and rules of thumb are derived from historical experience and so will not apply exactly in any given episode. Furthermore, the

*uncertainty is surely higher than normal now because the current recession is
unusual in its fundamental causes and its severity.*[296]

 Similarly, it is against this same background of a shifting reality that
we must assess the success of the enacted stimulus measures. First,
when measured by any reasonable standard, it is clear that the
stimulus legislation of 2009 succeeded in halting the economic
collapse that was unfolding at that time. By the end of June 2009,
although GDP growth had not been restored in absolute terms, the
decrease in GDP for the quarter just ending (2009-Q2) had fallen to
less than 1 percent (-0.7%). This was a huge improvement from the
loss of -8.9% in 2008-Q4 and -6.7% in 2009-Q1; then, as a further
indication of economic improvement, by the end of the third quarter
2009 (2009-Q3),[297] GDP was back in positive territory at 1.7 percent.[298]

GDP has remained in positive territory since July 2009, although you
would be hard-pressed to realize it, given the constant barrage of
anti-stimulus invective. There even have been quarters of respectable
GDP growth starting with the fourth quarter 2009. That quarter
produced GDP growth of 3.8 percent. The record for the first half of
2010 continued with similarly decent rates of GDP increase: 2010-Q1:
3.9% and 2010-Q2: 3.8%. The second half of 2010 was not as solid, but
it was respectable for a period following a major financial crisis.
Those growth rates are as follows: 2010-Q3: 2.5% and 2010-Q4: 2.3%.
Subsequent growth rates have not done as well, but they remained in
positive territory. Those figures are as follows: 2011-Q1: .4%; 2011-Q2:
1.3%; 2011-Q3: 1.8% and 2011-Q4: 2.8% (partial data for 2011-Q4).[299]

This return to positive territory for GDP - and its comparatively strong
showing during 2009-Q4 and the first two quarters of 2010 - can
hardly be considered as a failure of the stimulus program. This is
especially true given that the majority of economic experts, whether
private or public, say that a financial crisis as deep as that of 2008-09
necessarily results in a very protracted period of recovery. We

already have discussed the depth of that crisis. Total losses amounted to $51.8 trillion, including losses of $16.8 trillion in household net worth, $3.2 trillion in equity derivatives and $31.2 in credit default swaps.[300] Only a child could fail to comprehend the devastating impact of such losses on the demand side of the economy. Only someone with stunted reading skills could fail to comprehend the devastating impact of such losses on the economy's potential for recovery.[301]

But this is not the whole story. We must not forget the Credit Suisse chart outlining the reset schedule for adjustable rate mortgages. That schedule spanned six years beginning in January 2007 and ending in January 2014. As we already have seen, that ARM reset schedule describes an intractable course of economic misery as those mortgages came due - and will continue to come due - in a real estate market of drastically reduced values.[302] It is a market that doomed millions of additional homeowners to foreclosure and loss of their homes. It is an intractable problem that has continued to undermine both the recovery of the real estate market and the demand side of the economy. And it still has not run its course. We have yet another year to go.

These are structural problems that no president could banish with just a few clever strokes of political maneuvering - especially when confronted by an equally intractable opposition party.   Other contributing factors to this slowing of the recovery included the continuing financial crisis and recession in the European Union and the slow-down in the Chinese economy. In June 2009, the World Bank issued a "surprisingly bleak forecast for the world economy."[303] It predicted that the "global economy will shrink 2.9 percent in 2009" and that the "expected recovery is projected to be much less vigorous than normal."[304] In addition, the winding down of the stimulus program removed sorely needed support despite the continued need for it. Hence, it is not surprising that most responsible economists projected that recovery for an economy as deeply troubled as ours would take the greater part of a decade. Those who say otherwise are drinking the kool-aid of supply-side economics. Indeed, the fact that there is an international component in this list of obstacles to economic recovery just adds one more element of similarity between the Great Recession and the Great Depression.

Meanwhile, as long as we're focused on the silly side of American conventional wisdom, let's turn our attention to the auto bailout. We'll begin with a brief review of the events that preceded it. First of all, this started out as a bipartisan effort - at least when viewed through the lens of administrative action. It built upon initiatives of the Bush administration during their final months in office. Nor does one have to look far for the reason why both the incoming Obama administration and the outgoing Bush administration found a good chunk of common ground between them on this issue. Mike Jackson, president of AutoNation, the largest U.S. car dealer group, set the grim tone of the Detroit auto show in January 2009 when he observed that: "I have seen a better mood at funerals."[305]

Whether you take the long view or short view, the reason for this black mood was not hard to find. In the long view, the Big Three U.S. automakers had been losing market share to foreign imports for decades; while in the short view, this dismal process finally had reached an end game of dire consequences. Since the 1960s, GM's market share had fallen from over 50% to 22% in 2008 - and it still had not reached bottom. Focusing upon GM, an article in Time magazine on 11/14/2008 summed up the bleak choices facing the country: "The automaker may not deserve a bailout, but losing it could wreck the economy."[306] The Bush administration affirmed this view when it reluctantly overrode the Senate's rejection of federal aid to GM and

Chrysler. The administration cited the danger of: "A precipitous collapse of this industry [that] would have a severe impact on our economy."[307]   One week later, the administration approved a $17.4 billion bailout that would keep the two auto companies in business into the next year.[308]

The enormity of the downside consequences lay in the unique nature of the auto industry. Although the core industry of the Big Three only employed about 240,000 at that time, the vast network of suppliers and subcontractors greatly expanded the overall number of industry employees to nearly 1 million. Nor does this take into account the crippling impact that the collapse of the supplier network would have had on production of foreign makes within the U.S. Such a collapse would, in the view of industry analysts, have resulted in a shutdown of the entire U.S. auto industry - regardless of the nationality of ownership of individual plants. All of this, along with the multiplier effect of their wages, would have further expanded the number of affected workers by an estimated 1.5 million employees.[309]

When viewed against this backdrop, the statements by Mitt Romney that he would not have intervened on behalf of the auto industry are incredible.[310] The loss of some 2.5 million additional jobs - on top of the millions of job lost prior to and following Obama's inauguration - would have cancelled out any benefit from the ARRA of February 17, 2009. Job losses of that magnitude would have propelled the country right back into a steep downturn.[311] After all, as the Obama administration turned its focus from passage of the ARRA act to the reorganization of GM and Chrysler, the nation's GDP still was racking up a deep -6.7% 2009-Q1 loss, following on the heels of an even deeper -8.9% 2008 Q4 loss.[312] It hardly takes a genius to see that adding 2.5 million more job losses to this tableau of a deeply damaged economy would erase the hard won gains won by the monetary measures of the Federal Reserve Bank - along with the legislative remedies of TARP and ARRA. These efforts soon would result in the

much improved GDP of -.7% in 2009-Q3.[313] But without the auto
bailout such prospective gains clearly were at risk.

Another measure of the severity of this crisis was that it brought
about a spirit of cooperation within the industry. Rather than
exploiting the crisis for the benefit of their individual companies, the
industry joined ranks in voicing support for government aid to their
stricken rivals. Following the refusal of Senate Republicans to join the
House and pass an auto bailout of their own, Ford was quick to voice
support for that aid.[314] Within days, the top three Japanese auto
makers in the U.S. followed suit. As one analysis pointed out, the very
success of the Japanese in the U.S. auto market made them equally as
vulnerable to the unfolding crisis within that market: "By growing
more American, they have become such a part of the U.S. industrial
landscape that the collapse of any of Detroit's Big Three would be a
blow to the Japanese manufacturers."[315]

Especially important, though, is the point only briefly alluded to
earlier. Specifically, the shared network of parts suppliers ties the
entire U.S. auto industry together in a web of interdependence. And
that includes both foreign and domestic auto brands. Hence, the
success of the Japanese auto manufacturers within the U.S. is tied
not only to the general health of the American market, but to the
sustainability of the part suppliers who support the automotive
industry. As noted by another analysis early on in the crisis: "When
suppliers big and small start failing, the flow of parts to every
automaker in the country will be disrupted, because suppliers
typically sell their products to both American and foreign brands with
plants in the United States."[316]

The Achilles heel of this web of interdependence was the credit
freeze that arose out of the financial meltdown. In more normal
times the ups and downs of the auto industry could be absorbed by

the availability of credit from a variety of sources to keep the show on the road. Whether from commercial banks or credit extensions from the supplier network itself, funds could be found to maintain payrolls and daily operating expenses during a downturn. But this time, there was no credit.[317]

This was the reason the auto bailout was so critical. GM and Chrysler were dangerously short of cash and about to close their doors. Indeed, by early March 2009, GM's auditors raised the specter of "substantial doubt" whether GM could "overcome its staggering losses and generate enough cash to stay in business, or remain a 'going concern'..."[318] Moreover, as the enormous industry-wide drop in sales showed, this contagion was spreading. For the first time in 70 years, Toyota was anticipating an operating loss in 2009.[319] March 2009 sales losses were nothing short of horrendous - across the board. Sales for GM were down -45%, Ford -45%, Chrysler -39%, Toyota -39%.[320]

The lack of credit put the government in the driver's seat. Just days before the announcement of these dismal sales figures, the Obama administration requested the resignation of Rick Wagoner, GM's CEO - although few doubted that it was an outright demand.[321] Obama also made it clear that: "the White House would oversee, and heavily influence, decisions about what plants to shutter, what brands of cars to abandon, and how much workers and managers will get paid."[322]

Nor was this the full extent of White House control over the fate of GM. The government also: guaranteed the warranties of Chrysler and GM; reminded GM of its resolve to force them into bankruptcy under the terms of its bailout agreement; and continued to play a forceful role in gaining the agreement of GM creditors to the government's preferred settlement terms in advance of a bankruptcy.[323] In short, the actions of the Obama administration were, at once, decisive, bold and unprecedented. But, as David E.

Sanger stated in his New York Times analysis of 3/31/2009: "Obama is not relying on a statute. His powers derive from the fact that the White House and the Treasury control the last piles of cash available to keep General Motors a going concern."[324] Moreover, the reality, as clearly indicated by Sanger's article, was that there was no private cash available to fund a successful bankruptcy operation outside of government.

Notwithstanding the controversy besetting the auto bailout going back to December 2008, this was a legitimate role for government. The administration had done nothing more than exercise sound judgment in carrying out a vital industry reorganization in the midst of a national crisis. Moreover, GM and Chrysler opened that door to government intervention when they sought government assistance. They asked for the funds and they signed the agreements that gave the government the leverage it needed to oversee the reorganization.

Having said that, Mitt Romney was not the only one who viewed the auto bailout as a dangerous intrusion of the federal government into the affairs of private industry.[325] There were numerous critics who saw the government's unprecedented role as the specter of a new age of socialism or as picking favorites in a free market economy - or as throwing good money after bad. All of this fed the fires of a growing backlash that delivered a sharp rebuke to the Democrats in the 2010 congressional elections. The terrible irony in all of this was that the more Obama succeeded in meeting the challenges presented by the Great Recession, the more Obama's coalition eroded under the weight of all the unprecedented emergency measures he was forced to take. And this was capped by the greatest irony of all: his successes mitigated more dire consequences that would have proved the need for the actions taken.

These risks and political headwinds made the auto bailout a genuine exercise in political courage. Taking the bull by the horns, the administration confronted the reality that a crown jewel of American capitalism was about to collapse and did everything in its power to see that did not happen. It assumed the risks and unprecedented political burden of conducting a bankruptcy operation out of the White House. It waded into this high-risk venture despite: nearly universal Republican opposition, the counsel of high-level members of its own administration who also opposed it and, perhaps most importantly, despite the gut instincts of much of the country against government intervention in the basic operations of individual companies.

Before moving on, though, there are two additional points about the auto bailout that need discussion. Both concern issues of national security, macroeconomic myopia and the efficacy of supply-side economic theory. First, and most importantly, the national security element of the auto bailout seldom, if ever, gets mentioned. But national security becomes a part of this discussion because the auto industry, including its parts suppliers, played a huge role in America's victory in WWII. It provided, as apparently many have forgotten, one of the pillars of America's role as the Arsenal of Democracy. We not only armed ourselves; we provided the arms for our most important allies - Great Britain and the Soviet Union. Our failure to remember the amazing role of this industrial sector in a moment of national peril is a classic example of America as prisoner of the present tense.

Turning to Mitt Romney, the fact that he failed to make this connection undermines his seriousness as a candidate for national office - especially in view of his aggressive international agenda. Moreover, such an oversight is not only myopic in the extreme, but also raises the question of the efficacy of supply-side economics. The specific question being: how can we expect the free market to automatically maintain a vital defense industry when a pretender to the throne can't even see the need to protect its foundation. The critical role of Hamiltonian due diligence is obvious here - as is the vital role of government involvement in the economy.

The second point involves Republican opposition to the auto bailout vis-à-vis the foreign-owned, non-union, automobile manufacturers found in many of their districts. As a group, Republicans represent Southern states having a significant number of foreign-owned automobile manufacturers. Viewed in that light, it could be argued that they have a parochial interest in not assisting domestically-owned, union-shop, auto manufacturers. Admittedly, though, this interpretation does get a bit thin given the other possible motives for their opposition - especially since not all foreign-owned automobile manufacturers are located in the South.

What does really stand out, though, is that Republicans, as a group, did oppose the auto bailout, while foreign-owned auto manufacturers, as a group, supported the bailout. The latter understood the dire consequences resulting from the imminent collapse of GM and Chrysler, while the former did not.[326] This not only speaks volumes about the lack of economic common sense in the new-age Republican party, it also suggests an alternate explanation for their opposition. Namely, they were so committed to the goal of making Barack Obama a one-term president, that, as a group, it did not suit their political interests to play a bi-partisan role in saving the American auto industry. Both Representative Michele Bachmann and Senate Minority Leader Mitch McConnell proclaimed this goal of making Obama a one-term president from soon after his inauguration.

As this essay winds toward a conclusion, so too does the 2012 presidential election campaign. A recurring theme of this campaign has been the fundamental choice facing the electorate. Both sides characterize this moment as prelude to a critical turning point in American history. Both claim that the choices presented will have epic consequences for the future well-being of the nation. Such an assessment is fully supported by the tumultuous events of the past decade and the depth of our ensuing economic crisis. However, despite all the chatter about our predicament, it is but a gloss over a superficial discussion focused largely on style and campaign strategy. When it comes to matters of substance like: the questionable validity of supply-side economics; the long-term wisdom of adopting an investment strategy to solve our current fiscal problems; or constitutional barriers to an effective governing majority - you encounter nothing but silence from our chattering class.

The result is a massive shroud of ignorance clouding the nation's understanding of the past several decades and how the economy works. Meanwhile, new-age Republicans skate around historical contributions to our present economic crisis and the carbon-copy similarity of their economic proposals to the ones that got us into our current mess. As for Obama, he is penned in by his 2008 campaign promise to not raise taxes on the middle-class. Clearly, that promise grows more untenable as the national debt mounts ever higher. Hence, notwithstanding the slow, but steady recovery his policies have produced, the tide appears to be turning against Obama.[327]

The country is tired of slow, but steady progress and wants quick, dramatic change. It matters little that quick, dramatic change is utterly unrealistic for an economy burdened with: the negative momentum of long-standing structural problems; its financial hangover from the Great Recession; and its massive size. What matters is the underlying reality that Americans love tax cuts. Consequently, a very large part of the country appears willing to overlook the budget-busting character of Romney's $4.8 trillion tax cut.[328] And as for the similarity between Romney's program and that of Bush the Younger, well, that's ancient history and long forgotten.

This shroud of ignorance clouding the nation's understanding is not all that mysterious. It is a view of the economy that has been sold to us over the past several generations.[329] As discussed in the introduction, it was originally called laissez-faire. More recently, it has been called supply-side economics or free-market economics. All of these have two generally similar goals: reduced government involvement in the economy and lower taxes. But as you might expect, there is not universal agreement among the adherents of these policies about their fine points. Hence, some supply-siders argue that lower taxes generate so much economic growth that these reduced rates actually generate more revenue than the higher rates.[330] While this has a marvelous ring to it, in reality it doesn't work. Specifically, the Reagan tax cuts did the opposite. As we have seen in the charts accompanying our earlier discussion of the national debt, they generated chronic deficits that quickly accumulated into a huge increase of our gross national debt. Similarly, the George W. Bush tax cuts also failed to compensate for lost revenue. And they propelled us even further down the path toward our current national debt nightmare.

What is especially instructive for our current national debate are the views of those who played major roles in these tax-cutting episodes. Generally speaking , they fall into two camps: the zealots and the realists (my terms). One of the most significant of the zealots was Arthur B. Laffer, "widely regarded as the intellectual father of supply-side economics."[331] He was an ardent proponent of the extreme view that "tax revenues will 'rise dramatically' when tax rates are cut."[332] On the other hand, you have the realists who acknowledge the reality that tax cuts will not replace lost revenue dollar for dollar, but who do argue that tax cuts will generate enough economic expansion to replace a part of the lost revenue. Unfortunately, though, even such limited gains cannot be expected to appear immediately. According to Bruce Bartlett, who was "present at the creation of 'supply-side economics' back in the 1970s,...Even the most rabid supply-sider knew we would lose $1 of revenue for $1 of tax cut in the short term, because it took time for incentives to work and for people to change their behavior."[333]

But with the passage of time, the moderating influence of the realists has faded. The ascendancy of the new-age Republicans has amplified the influence of the zealots who believe tax cuts will generate more revenue than the higher rates - regardless of the contrary experiences of Reagan and Bush the Younger. Hence, according to Bartlett:

...today [April 2007] it is common to hear tax cutters claim, implausibly, that all tax cuts raise revenue. Last year, President Bush said, 'You cut taxes and the tax revenues increase.' Senator John McCain told National Review magazine last month that 'tax cuts, starting with Kennedy, as we all know, increase revenues.' Last week, Steve Forbes endorsed Rudolph Giuliani for the White House, saying, 'He's seen the results of supply-side economics first hand - higher revenues from lower taxes.'[334]

The fact is that supply side economic theory has been very influential over the past two generations. It not only has played a big role defining the limits of our public debate relative to tax and spend, but also has heavily influenced the fiscal policies of two administrations. While it did play a positive role in the economic recovery during the Reagan years, it also had a negative economic legacy. It contributed to a massive increase in our national debt, while simultaneously failing to make the necessary investments in alternate fuels research that would have mitigated the destructive impact of peak oil during the administration of Bush the Younger.

One need only look to the example of Brazil to see just how beneficial such investments were to that nation. Starting in the 1970s, Brazil invested heavily in research aimed at finding a clean burning, cost effective source of ethanol. Under a dictatorship at that time, Brazil not only subsidized the production of sugar-cane based ethanol, but also mandated that all service stations have an ethanol pump. [335] The result of these timely efforts was that by the end of 2006, Brazil was slated to be free of imported oil.[336] By contrast, in the summer of 2008, the U.S. was wracked by energy sector price distortions brought on by peak oil.[337] These price increases heavily impacted the commuting public and exacerbated the downturn in the housing market.[338] While these energy price increases were not the only driver of the collapse of the housing market, they did make a bad situation even worse. The high cost of fuel not only added to already high commuter costs tied to McMansions in the exurbs, but also contributed to the woes of the auto industry.

This contrast between our approach to energy research and that of Brazil exposes one of the fundamental failings of supply-side economic theory. Brazil was proactive in identifying and attacking **a** systemic weakness in their economy. We were not. Brazil achieved its goal by using government resources and regulatory powers. One of the results of this process is that Brazil now is a leading exporter of ethanol, provided by its private sector.[339] As for us, we chose to follow Reagan's advice about these matters. He had this to say In his 1987 State of the Union Address:

It's widely said that America is losing her competitive edge. Well, that won't happen if we act now....It is now time to determine that we should enter the next century having achieved a level of excellence unsurpassed in history. We will achieve this first, by guaranteeing that government does everything possible to promote America's ability to compete. Second, we must act as individuals in a quest for excellence that will not be measured by new proposals or billions in new funding. Rather, it involves an expenditure of American spirit and just plain American grit.[340]

In short, we chose not to spend billions on big government programs. We chose to let the free market solve this problem. It should not come as a surprise that we still are years away from energy independence.

Naturally, with a poor track record like this, supply-side theory does not have a lot to crow about. It has a poor track record both as regards the fiscal condition of our government and as regards the kind of government-assisted research that can reduce our trade deficit and boost our private sector. Perhaps that is why Bruce Bartlett, who served such influential supply-siders as Jack Kemp, has had a change of heart. He now believes:

...it is long past time that the phrase be put to rest. It did its job, creating a new consensus among economists on how to look at the national economy. But today it has become a frequently misleading and meaningless buzzword that gets in the way of good economic policy.[341]

Taking a broader view, just as Keynesian theory was abused and distorted far beyond its original limits by careless successors, so too has supply-side theory. (Although, in the case of the latter, it must be noted that Laffer himself was a zealot.) Having said that, both examples do provide an insight into a tendency to stray from disciplined fiscal policy into the swamp of self-indulgence. In that sense, President Obama's call for the nation to "eat it's peas" was right on the mark.

The economic policies of New-age Republicans may suffer from crippling defects, but their grasp of the marketing power of labels is second to none. That no doubt explains why these days you seldom hear a Republican singing the praises of supply-side economic theory.

Instead they talk incessantly about the free market. But this change of labels is little more than a shell game. In reality, their free market policies are nearly identical to the most extreme versions of supply-side economics. However, since the overwhelming majority of the public cares nothing for such theories, this marketing shell game works just fine. And so, with the slippery grace of a chameleon, they simply go forth with the enthusiasm of a salesman peddling the hottest new thing in town. And it works. The proof of that is in the poll results.

The fundamentals of Mitt Romney's free market policies are not much different than those of George W. Bush. They both rely on tax reductions and reduced government involvement in the economy - especially as regards regulation.[342] They both rely on the underlying assumption that tax cuts, over time, will eventually produce a balanced budget. Romney's proposed $4.8 trillion cut in a smorgasbord of taxes is a case in point. It is such a massive tax cut, encompassing nine categories of taxes, that it is impossible to make up for the lost revenues by reducing exemptions - without saddling the middle class with a substantial increase in taxes and user fees.[343]

More importantly, it is such a massive tax cut, that it amounts to nearly seventy percent of the Non-Defense Discretionary Outlays of the 2010 Federal Budget. Specifically, it amounts to sixty-nine percent of the entire 2010 non-defense sector of the government minus the entitlement programs of Social Security, Medicare and Medicaid.[344] Clearly such a massive revenue reduction cannot be reconciled with spending cuts alone - or even with a majority of spending cuts. Despite such crippling flaws in the linchpin of his economic program, Romney has consistently bested Obama in opinion polls that measure approval of their economic programs.[345]

The deeply troubling thing about these tax-cutting proposals is that both Romney and his running mate, Paul Ryan, adamantly insist that these proposals are something the country can handle without extraordinary sacrifice or disruption. And when confronted with the contrary findings of a responsible centrist organization like the Tax Policy Center, they simply denounce the findings as flawed and stone-wall the whole argument.[346] Of course, they have little choice. These Romney tax cuts are the linchpin of his economic program. Without them the Romney-Ryan team has no economic program worth talking about. Moreover, when put in a historical context, this resort to stonewalling is not all that different from the marketing approach of the Reagan administration. No one then publicly acknowledged that their tax cuts would result in immediate dollar-for-dollar revenue losses in lock-step with the rate cuts. [347] However, unlike today, the Reagan economic program benefited from the fact the national debt was not nearly as big then as now.

Now we are confronted with an entirely different reality. The dollar-for-dollar revenue losses of the Romney rate cuts will be added to our already ponderous national debt. Moreover, they will prompt more cuts in government spending that will trigger more rounds of layoffs of public employees . Those layoffs will not prompt a boost in the economy. They will have the opposite effect of further reducing demand, holding down the rate of economic growth and job creation. It is for this very reason that President George H. W. Bush, Reagan's successor, who was no fan of supply-side economics, called it 'voodoo economics.'[348] In fact, faced with continuing deficits resulting from the Reagan tax cuts, he eventually agreed to raise taxes.[349]

Arguably, those tax increases, when combined with those of the Clinton administration, served to finally bring the federal budget into balance during Clinton's second term. The important thing to remember here is that these changes did not occur overnight. It took nearly a decade for a process that started in the administration of George H.W. Bush, then nourished by Clinton, to eventually produce a balanced federal budget. And contrary to supply-side theory, it also produced one of the longest peacetime economic recoveries on record - with an enviable record of job growth.[350] It is no wonder that new-age Republicans have an aversion to history.

In fact, this aversion to history is one of the hallmarks of supply-side economic theory. A classic example of this aversion recently appeared in *Newsweek* magazine of August 27, 2012. That issue included a cover-article, titled "Why Obama Must Go," by Niall Ferguson, who is the Laurence A. Tisch Professor of History at Harvard University.[351] Given his credentials as a high-profile professor of history, one would assume he has a regard for history elevated well beyond the rest of us. But that assumption is not supported by the shaky scholarship of his Newsweek article.

In discussing what he characterizes as Obama's economic failures, he rests his case upon estimations of GDP growth and reductions in unemployment made in Obama's FY2010 Budget Message to Congress of February 26, 2009.[352] These estimates were made approximately one month after Obama's inauguration. More importantly, as we already have seen, they were made two and one-half years before the full extent of the damage to the American economy came to light. That full realization came to light in a Bureau of Economic Analysis report of August 5, 2011, revising the 2008-Q4 loss in GDP to -8.9 percent.[353] The reality, as previously noted, was that it takes time to produce an accurate assessment of economic growth or contraction in an economy as vast as ours. One would expect that a historian focused upon the economy would realize that and take it into account as a pertinent piece of information impacting the judgment of a given administration. That critical sense of nuance is completely lacking in Ferguson's essay.[354]

In another example, he takes Obama to task for the fact that "the total number of private-sector jobs is still 4.3 million below the January 2008 peak."[355] This is a very convenient reckoning point, since it glosses over the fact that 4,329,000 jobs were lost in the thirteen-month period 1/1/2008 through 1/31/2009 - the period that immediately preceded Obama's assumption of the presidency.[356] Ferguson also takes repeated swipes at the Stimulus Act (ARRA), while ignoring one of its most significant companion efforts: the so-called auto bailout. As we already have discussed, the latter was a politically courageous act that saved the strategically significant crown jewel of American capitalism: General Motors and, by extension, the rest of America's auto industry.

The combined impact of these two programs was that job losses for the thirteen-month period, including Feb 2009 through Feb 2010, were substantially less than the preceding thirteen-month period under Bush's tenure. Specifically, they amounted to 2,146,000 - or 2,183,000 fewer - lost jobs.[357] This was a good start given the depth of the economic calamity that was unfolding in those early months of the Obama administration. Even the president of the U.S. Chamber of Commerce (C-of-C), Thomas Donohue, recognized that the economy was in such desperate condition that the government had to intervene. Taking a position diametrically opposed to typical C-of-C policies, he stated on 2/12/2009:

The bottom line is that at the end of the day, we're going to support the [stimulus] legislation. Why? Because with the market's functioning so poorly, the government is the only game in town capable of jump-starting the economy.[358]

Equally important, when we compare the job-creation records of Obama and Bush the Younger, we find that Obama has the better record. According to an article from The New York Times, dated 9/15/2012:

The job numbers in recent months have been disappointing,...But buried in the numbers was one accomplishment that serves only to emphasize how poorly the U.S. economy has performed since 2000. The pace of creation of jobs in the private sector during the current administration is now greater than the pace in either of President George W. Bush's terms in office.[359]

While there are numerous other points to take exception to in Ferguson's screed, some of the most significant are his open embrace of supply-side economic theory and, not surprisingly, the Romney-Ryan ticket. Although he is not a huge fan of Romney, he nearly idolizes Ryan:

Over the past few years Ryan's 'Path to Prosperity' has evolved, but the essential points are clear: replace Medicare with a voucher program for those now under 55 (not current or imminent recipients), turn Medicaid and food stamps into block grants for the states, and - crucially - simplify the tax code and lower tax rates to try to inject some supply-side life back into the U.S. private sector. Ryan is not practicing austerity. He is preaching growth.[360]

His enthusiasm for Ryan becomes almost embarrassing elsewhere in his piece. Excerpts of his devotion to Ryan include: "Ryan blew me away....There is literally no one in Washington who understands the challenges of fiscal reform better...[and]...He is one of only a handful of politicians in Washington who is truly *sincere* about addressing this country's fiscal crisis."[361] All of this would mean a great deal coming from a prestigious Harvard professor of history, if only he followed some of the elementary rules of scholarship in his text. But he doesn't. Two charts in his piece titled "Epic Budget Fail' and "What Recovery?" do not include any documentation.[362] The result is that anyone bent on confirming the accuracy of his data finds themselves up a creek without a paddle. This is not the work of a world-class scholar. It is not even the work of a rookie scholar. It is a slap-dash polemic lacking in credibility.

Even more egregiously, he places all the blame on Obama for the failure of the attempted 'grand bargain' between Obama and John A. Boehner, Speaker of the House: "Obama effectively sidelined its [Simpson-Bowles] recommendations of approximately $3 trillion in cuts and $1 trillion in added revenues over the coming decade. As a result there was no 'grand bargain' with the House Republicans..."[363] And he does so despite the fact that Obama and Boehner were negotiating a similar 'grand bargain' with an equivalent balance of tax cuts and increased revenues. This attempt failed on 7/9/2011, when Boehner advised reporters:

Despite good faith efforts to find common ground, the White House will not pursue a bigger debt reduction agreement without tax hikes. I believe the best approach may be to focus on producing a smaller measure, based on the cuts identified in the Biden-led negotiations.[364]

Since a central pillar of the Simpson-Bowles plan called for a mix of tax cuts and increases in revenues, it is clear that the failure of the Obama-Boehner negotiations resulted from Boehner's unwillingness - or perhaps more accurately his inability to fulfill the requirement for increased revenues.[365]

Although all of these ought to represent major embarrassments for a Harvard scholar, there is one more that strikes right at the heart of education itself. In pressing his case against Obama's vastly misunderstood 'you didn't build that' remark, he attacks Obama for citing: "(bizarrely) the creation of the middle-class...[as one of]...the greatest achievements of big government."[366] But, there is nothing bizarre about Obama's assertion that one of big government's greatest achievement was the creation of the middle class. The

Nobel laureate economist, Robert William Fogel, provides us with a convincing account of how government achieved this result:

One should not leap....to the conclusion that the egalitarian state played a minor role in the equalization of pre-tax incomes. Quite the contrary, the state did much to equalize incomes through the subsidization of education. By making primary and secondary education compulsory and free, the state endowed poor and middle-class children with large amounts of highly valuable human capital. The endowment of the relatively poor was further extended by the establishment of the free state and city universities and by the GI Bill (1944), which enabled more than 8 million veterans of World War II to obtain vocational and college educations.[367]

In short, as already has been discussed in detail, public education, funded by government, played a huge role in the creation of human capital. And that, in turn, became a primary driver of both the wealth creation process and the creation of the middle-class. Moreover, in general terms this is a uniquely American story because America, true to its puritan heritage, was a pioneer in public education. Indeed, the only bizarre thing here is Ferguson's denial of a fundamental dynamic in America's story. Moreover, this is not something peculiar to Ferguson. It also reflects the fundamental flaw in supply-side economic theory. It is a theory that assumes that the free-market economy will automatically provide all the education resources - and human capital - required by our post-agro-industrial economy. It is this theory that is unsupported by American history. It is this theory that is bizarre to its core.

By way of conclusion, we need to focus on one more bedrock theme scarcely noted up until now. That theme is the evolutionary character of economic reality. With the passage of time, our economic reality changes as a result of technological and/or sociological innovations in the way we do things and the products we produce. Over time these can have such a profound impact on the way our economy works that parallel changes occur in our social organization. The rise and fall of legally-sanctioned, race-based slavery as an adjunct to the animal/human powered sector of our economy is one example of such an innovation. The obsolescence of the draft animal powered sector of our economy is another example. As we have seen, the consequences of the former are still with us today, while the latter contributed greatly to the economic collapse of the Great Depression.

More generally, the agro-industrial revolution set in motion radical changes in the socio-economic organization of the Western world. It transformed the agrarian economy of our infant republic from one with widely dispersed ownership of the means of production into one with highly concentrated ownership of those means. It transformed our predominantly rural economy from an economically democratic, individual-centric society into an increasingly urban, bureaucratic economy in which a relatively small number of wealthy individuals controlled the livelihoods of many. In short, power and wealth increasingly were concentrated in the hands of an upper class.

At the same time, these profound structural changes were accompanied by rising demand for enormous amounts of capital, both human and traditional. Needless-to-say, these changes have had such a profound impact on the way we live and earn our living, that we cannot make responsible choices about critical investments in our future without understanding their significance. Moreover, a further consequence of these changes was that formerly individual decisions about investments of fixed capital were transformed into a hybrid decision-making process: both individual and social.

At this point, we need to return to our good friend Adam Smith for his take on gross revenue, net revenue and fixed capital:

The gross revenue of all the inhabitants of a great country comprehends the whole annual produce of their land and labour; **the net revenue, what remains free to them after deducting the expense of maintaining - first, their fixed,** *and, secondly, their circulating capital; or what, without encroaching upon their capital, they can place in their stock reserved for immediate consumption, or spend upon their subsistence, conveniences, and amusements.* *Their real wealth, too, is in proportion, not to their gross, but to their net revenue.*

The whole expense of maintaining the fixed capital must evidently be excluded from the net revenue of the society. *Neither the materials necessary for supporting their useful machines and instruments of trade, their profitable buildings, etc., nor the produce of the labour necessary for fashioning those materials into the proper form, can ever make any part of it...*

The intention of the fixed capital is to increase the productive powers of labour, *or to enable the same number of labourers to perform a much greater quantity of work.* *In a farm where all the necessary buildings, fences, drains, communications, etc., are in the most perfect good order, the same number of labourers and labouring cattle will raise a much greater produce than in one of equal extent and equally good ground, but not furnished with equal conveniences.* *In manufactures the same number of hands, assisted with the best machinery, will work up a much greater quantity of goods than with more imperfect instruments of trade.* *The expense which is properly laid out upon a fixed capital of any kind, is always repaid with great profit, and increases the annual produce by a much greater value than that of the support which such improvements require.* *This support, however, still requires a certain portion of that produce.* *It is upon this account that all such improvements in mechanics, as enable the same number of workmen to perform an equal quantity of work, with cheaper and simpler machinery than had been usual before, are always regarded as advantageous to every society.* [368] *(Emphasis added.)*

As can be seen, Smith makes it abundantly clear that the part of gross revenues pertaining to the maintenance/upgrade costs of fixed capital cannot be diverted into net revenue, circulating capital or consumption. It must be invested in the maintenance/upgrades of fixed capital. It must be invested in those things that enhance "the productive powers of labour, or to enable the same number of labourers to perform a much greater quantity of work."[368a] In other words, when we translate Smith's views on fixed capital into the context of our modern era, it is clear that his views represent a resounding endorsement of the critical need to maintain a robust public education system capable of supplying the human capital needed by our modern civilization.

Yet despite the synergetic thrust of both Smith's views on fixed capital and the previously mentioned systemic changes to our new-age economy, there is no consensus within the country about them. One-half of public discussion about our current economic difficulties proceeds in complete ignorance of both these structural changes and the Smithian insights into the overlapping qualities of fixed and human capital. New-age Republicans do not acknowledge these structural changes or our need to invest in human capital because their economic theory assumes that free market forces will automatically provide these investments. Hence, we are left with a one-sided discussion of these critical issues that leads into the cul-de-sac of gridlock.

As a result, there is scant mention of how the foundations of our economy have shifted. There is some mention of how the economic rug has been pulled out from under the individual, but little effort to put this into its historical context of transformational change. All of this tends to frame the discussion more in traditional terms of individual initiative, rather than as critically needed investments in human capital. The result is a vision focused on the past and an economic structure that no longer exists. It is a historical vision blind to processes like momentum or basic concepts like concentrated ownership of the means of production.

Perhaps most profoundly, it is blind to the reality of adaptability and evolution as two of the most basic qualities of life. This blindness has descended into such an abyss of ignorance that we have arrived at the end game of a cultural schism - more than two generations in the making - which pits two versions of reality against each other. One version is an essentially fact-based vision of reality, whereas the other is a vision of an alternate reality - untethered to facts.

Indeed, we have arrived at a point where new-age Republicans routinely deny the science of climate change, affirm the discredited tenets of supply-side economics (albeit camouflaged as free-market economics), deny the role of supply-side economic theory in exploding the national debt, deny the positive roles of TARP and ARRA (stimulus act) in limiting the damage of the Great Recession (despite objective evidence to the contrary), deny the findings of responsible centrist organizations (as in Romney's defense of his indefensible $4.8 trillion in tax cuts, compounded by an additional $2 trillion in increased defense spending) and reject moderate Republicans as traitors to their extreme agenda.

The demographic foundations of this cultural schism can be traced in polls focusing on religious beliefs. A *USA Today* poll of 10/10/2005, titled "The whole world, from whose hands?" illustrates a wide-spread hostility toward the idea of evolution. In a segment focused on Bible Vs. Evolution, the poll asked whether the following statement agreed with their views: 'God created human beings in their present form exactly as described in the Bible.' Fifty-three percent (53%) of all respondents agreed with that statement. More women (60%) agreed with it than men (45%). With regard to income level, the lowest income groups agreed the most (70% of those earning less than $20K) compared with only 37% of those earning $75K and up. Concerning religious affiliation, Protestants agreed with it the most (66%), with Catholics (38%), Non-Christians (15%) and None (16%) agreeing with it considerably less.[369]

Similar results were reported by a CBS News poll of 10/23/2005. It found that 51% believe that "God created humans in present form." Other options ranked as follows: Thirty percent (30%) believed that "Humans evolved, God guided the process" and 15% believed that "Humans evolved, God did not guide the process."[370]

These polls provide us with a portrait of our nation in which about one-half of us reject something as fundamental as the Darwinian theory of life evolving on this planet from simpler to more complex forms. It is a theory supported by a growing body of evidence - both in geological and genetic research. As such, the implications of this rejection are enormous. It is a rejection of the scientific method arguably as profound as the Catholic Church's rejection - in centuries past - of the Copernican system and its persecution of Galileo for his defiant support of it. It is a rejection that asserts the incredible corollary that a divine power intervened in natural/human history to bestow on humanity a special act of creation.

Some argue that this Christian propensity to embrace an alternate reality has been there from the beginning. A venerable, albeit all-but-forgotten, proponent of this view was George Santayana. He was a Spanish-American philosopher and humanist who took on this subject in his *Interpretations of Poetry and Religion*. First published in 1900, he had this to say about the Christian rejection of science and objective reality:

And yet that counter-Copernican revolution accomplished by Christianity....which put man in the centre of the universe and made the stars circle about him, must have some kind of justification. And indeed its justification (if we may be so brief on so great a subject) is that what is false in the science of facts may be true in the science of values. While the existence of things must be understood by referring them to their causes, which are mechanical, their functions can only be explained by what is interesting in their results, in other words, by their relation to human nature and to human happiness.[371]

As suggested by the above, far from being inalterably opposed to Christianity as a religion, Santayana goes on to carefully describe how even its factually challenged myth provides a compelling moral lesson for humanity:

Christian fictions were at least significant; they beguiled the intellect, no doubt, and were mistaken for accounts of external fact; but they enlightened the imagination; they made man understand, as never before or since, the pathos and nobility of his life, the necessity of discipline, the possibility of sanctity, the transcendence and the humanity of the divine. For the divine was reached by the idealization of the human. The supernatural was an allegory of the natural, and rendered the values of transitory things under the image of eternal existences. Thus the finality of our activity in this world, together with the eternity of its ideal meanings, was admirably rendered by the Christian dogma of a final judgment.[372]

As a practical matter, though, Santayana cannot escape the reality that a huge gulf separates the objective world of science and the fantastic world of imagination and subjective values. There is an intriguing - albeit perplexing - link between Santayana's 'science of values' and what conventional wisdom describes as today's 'values voters.' Indeed, one cannot help but conclude that Santayana was trying to build a bridge-too-far by concocting such an oxymoron. In the end, he attempts to paper over this gulf with the following:

Human life is always essentially the same, and therefore a religion which, like Christianity, seizes the essence of that life, ought to be an eternal religion. But it may forfeit that privilege by entangling itself with a particular account of matters of fact, matters irrelevant to its ideal significance, and further by intrenching (sic) itself, by virtue of that entanglement, in an inadequate regimen or a too narrow imaginative development, thus putting its ideal authority in jeopardy by opposing it to other intuitions and practices no less religious than its own.[373]

 With just these few paragraphs from a century long gone, Santayana anticipated our contemporary cultural schism and political gridlock. It is a cultural schism in which one side rejects the theory of Darwinian evolution and, by extension, collides head-on with the fact that our way of life rests on the nuts-and-bolts reality of a changing economy. At bottom, it is a theological rejection of the reality that we live in a world continually driven and shaped by economic evolution.

Hence, the fact that half our population believes in a divine intervention in human history - not once or twice, but thrice or more -

speaks volumes about our failure to come to terms with the dysfunctional side of our economy. Indeed, such a failure is linked closely to the predisposition to think in terms of the magical paradigms characteristic of Christianity. These include not only the virgin birth and physical resurrection of Jesus Christ, but also extend to the divine birth of the entire human species - not to mention His Divine Dispensations on behalf of the United States of America.

These magical propositions of Christian faith bear a fundamental similarity to the automatic phenomena of economic doctrines like Adam Smith's 'invisible hand' and Say's 'supply-side' theory. No matter whether secular or religious in the specifics of their content, all of them are driven by similar thought processes. They all rely on doctrines that are gems of concision and require scant intellectual energy. They all rely on a circular form of logic - supported by the authoritative character of the doctrine. The doctrine produces a given result because the doctrine says so. And so as political operatives like to say: the imperative is to stay on message. Keep repeating the message because repetition serves to enhance the currency - and therefore - the credibility of the message. The incantation of the name - whether that be free market economics, or liberty, or physical resurrection assumes that salvation, whether spiritual or economic, is assured so long as the fine points of doctrine are observed. And perhaps most appealing, adherents are spared the exertions of due diligence or a careful study of context.

So pity the poor politician. It is their task to thread the needle of a plausible narrative through this mine-field of an impossible-to-reconcile cultural schism. One-half of the country is wedded to the self-destructive delusion of economic salvation bestowed by a free-market economy and further larded with the magical predilections of a mystery religion. The other half, if that, needs to be engaged in a conversation guided by a rational discussion of dynamic equilibrium and economic evolution. Meanwhile, this quest for an electoral majority takes place in the shadow of a constitutional framework that was designed to frustrate positive action. As Madison/Hamilton observed in their Federalist No. 51:

Whilst all authority in it [the federal republic of the United States] will be derived from and dependent on the society, the society itself will be broken into so many parts, interests and classes of citizens, that the rights of individuals, or of the minority, will be in little danger from interested combinations of the majority.[374]

This insight, coupled with their elaborate system of checks and balances, informed their vision of statecraft designed to frustrate the will of a democratic majority. It was a vision wedded to the political realities of a democratically structured agrarian society, recently threatened by the economic grievances of badly treated Revolutionary War veterans. It also was the vision of a fledgling nation-state, poor in capital, and focused on creating those precious capital resources. At the same time, it was a vision constructed in the shadows of a vanishing feudal regime, whether viewed domestically in terms of our own slave economy, or in terms of the ancient landowning barons of Europe. In short, it was a vision deeply rooted in the parochial concerns of our founding generation. It was a vision tempered by keenly felt apprehensions about the synergetic dangers arising out of a democratically-structured economy and the intrigues of more powerful European states. Most evocative of their apprehensions was the fact that their deliberations were conducted in secret.

Prospectively, it was a vision scarcely able to anticipate the sporadic ebb and flow of trends toward a new-age feudalism over the course of the past century and a quarter. Certainly the Gilded Age of the late 1800s was an instance of plutocratic enrichment and empowerment posing the threat of a new feudal age. We now see similar trends unfolding in the dynamics of globalism and the emergence of a new global plutocracy. The emergence of this new global plutocracy is the natural result of a centuries-long evolution of the multi-national corporation. The predecessors of multi-national corporations started out as the vulnerable agents of emergent nation-states, both striving to gain a foothold in the risky pursuit of global commerce. As such, they provide us with a glimpse into those earlier instances of hybrid public-private endeavors, based upon mutual need:

Merchants trading with such countries needed a good deal of capital, they often had to obtain special privileges and protection from native rulers, and they had to arm their ships against Barbary or Malay pirates or against hostile Europeans. Merchants and their respective governments came together to found official companies for the trans-ocean trade....Each of these companies was a state-supported organization with special rights. Each was a monopoly in that only merchants who belonged to the company could legally engage in trade in the region for which the company had a charter.[375]

But that time of pirates and privateers now has receded to a level of acceptable risk. No longer vulnerable and dependent on the nation-states that once protected them, these multi-national corporations have long since evolved into self-confident masters of the new global commerce. They have learned to play the variations in prices and costs of global commerce and earned enormous profits in the process. Meanwhile, they no longer feel the same degree of patriotic loyalty born of their former vulnerability. They no longer feel the need to pay the piper of government, instead striving for tax avoidance whenever possible.[376]

The result is a fatal disconnect in the traditional chain of fixed capital investment by the public sector: tax avoidance. Another result is that a substantial part of what once went into the treasuries of nation-states is now being diverted into the pockets of these newly emergent global plutocrats. They owe no allegiance to any state - and their concerns are so present tense - they care little for long-term consequences of the ongoing destruction of dynamic equilibrium. The future for society as a whole may be increasingly fraught with impending disaster, but that is not their concern. We have their assurance the free-market will take care of that.

AFTERWORD

Time flies. The election of 2012 is history. Obama and the Democrats confounded the polls and won a surprisingly solid victory. But not enough to decisively tip the balance of power in Washington. As a result, we're still in the grip of political gridlock, driven by a culture war so intense it threatens to derail the economy once again and split the nation in two. With few exceptions, the onus for these dire circumstances appears to be the responsibility of the Republicans.

One major exception is the political cul-de-sac in which Obama and the Democrats find themselves. This political cul-de-sac is Obama's promise of no new tax increases on the middle class - formulated during the more optimistic pre-meltdown economic context of campaign 2008. While it is true that this promise resulted from an economic context quite unlike that which issued from the economic crisis of 2008-09, it also is true that the realities of our new global economy limit our ability to seek new revenues exclusively within the highest income groups.

At the same time, our economy desperately needs not only increased investment in human capital, research, and infrastructure, but also, bridge funding for our health care commitments while the cost reduction measures in Obamacare take effect. In short, the nation has a critical need for increased revenue to address these long-neglected problems in our health care system, our educational system, and our infrastructure. For many the sheer magnitude of these problems is enough to justify doing nothing. But the bad news is that while they already impact our ability to compete in the global economy, continued neglect will only accelerate this economic deterioration. On the bright side, the good news is that we still have the resources to overcome this grim scenario.

Oddly enough, one very attractive solution comes right out of the Republican play book. Specifically, if we were to implement a very modest national sales tax, or alternatively, a value-added tax as a supplement to our existing tax structure, we could raise sufficient revenue to fund essential investments and offer a credible path forward in our efforts to tame the deficit. Granted, these new revenues would not cure the deficit overnight. But in conjunction with some modest additional spending cuts, they would accelerate the downward trajectory of our deficit, while forestalling job losses arising out of a heavy-handed austerity program. This would create a virtuous cycle in which our gradual economic recovery drives continued reductions in recessionary spending, while the downward trajectory in our deficit would be further augmented by the positive feedback from our investments in both physical and intellectual capital.

Given this gradual approach, the rate of this national sales tax need not be that high. It could start at one percent. A one percent national sales tax might be expected to produce about $108 billion per year - or about $1.08 trillion per decade. This is based upon a 2012 estimated GDP of $15.4 trillion and a consumer economy amounting to 70 percent of that, or $10.8 trillion. Similarly, two percent and three percent rates would produce, respectively, about 216B and $324B annually - or about $2.16T and $3.24T per decade. These increases could be phased in on an annual basis, or modified in conjunction with the progress of tax reform, should the latter occur. One advantage of these taxes is that they could be implemented without exemptions or deductions, thus assuring the broadest possible base and maximum revenues. The critical point, of course, is that these taxes are not intended to be revenue neutral. Their purpose is to increase revenues critically needed to address deficiencies in our public infrastructure - both physical and intellectual.

Viewed retrospectively, the critical need for such revenue increases may be seen in view of the substantial shrinkage of federal revenues relative to GDP in recent years. According to the Congressional Budget Office:

Over the past 40 years, federal revenues have ranged from nearly 21 percent of gross domestic product (GDP) in fiscal year 2000 to less than 15 percent in fiscal years 2009 and 2010, averaging 18 percent of GDP over that span.[377]

In a similar vein, according to Bruce Bartlett, a moderate Republican:

The postwar annual average [for federal taxes] is about 18.5 percent of G.D.P. Revenues averaged 18.2 percent of G.D.P. during Ronald Reagan's administration; the lowest percentage during that administration was 17.3 percent of G.D.P. in 1984.

In short, by the broadest measure of the tax rate, the current level is unusually low and has been for some time....The Congressional Budget Office estimated that federal taxes would consume just 14.8 percent of G.D.P. this year [2011]. The last year in which revenues were lower was 1950, according to the Office of Management and Budget.[378]

Notwithstanding the need, the implementation of a national sales, or value-added, tax would amount to a huge reversal for Obama and the Democrats. Not only would it amount to going back on a fundamental campaign promise, it also would go against the conventional wisdom that such taxes are regressive - which in the narrow sense is true. However, when viewed in the broader context of maintaining programs for the poor and less-favored, they have the advantage of not only increasing overall revenues, but also preserving those programs and accelerating the rate of economic recovery.

It also addresses the troubling reality of how the burdens of our federal tax system have shifted predominantly onto the middle and upper income groups. But also, on the positive side for Democrats, it would show that they have the courage to face reality and act in a statesman-like manner for the good of the country. As for the Republicans, if they could get over their obsession with the conventional wisdom of the nineteenth century, they might see that such a tax does take a page or two out of their play book and amounts to a political victory of sorts. Indeed, if they were to cooperate with this venture and immigration reform, it just might pump new life into their fading prospects.

ENDNOTES

1 - This shift in attitude toward the Iraq war was noted in a New York Times/CBS News Poll of 4/4/2008: "When the presidential campaign began last year, the war in Iraq and terrorism easily topped Americans' list of concerns. Almost 30 percent of people in a December poll said that one of those issues was the country's most pressing problem. About half as many named the economy or jobs.
But the issues have switched places in just a few months' time. In the latest poll, only 17 percent named terrorism or the war as their top concern, while 37 percent named the economy or the job market." ["81% in Poll Say Nation Is Headed on Wrong Track," @ David Leonhardt and Marjorie Connelly, nytimes.com, 4/4/2008]

2 - This assessment is based upon the haste with which Bush2 rushed into a second war with Iraq, before first securing his victory in Afghanistan. It betrayed an ignorance about not only the culture and history of those two countries, but also about our own. This ignorance was rooted in the mistaken belief that the moral superiority of our crusade for freedom and democracy, facilitated by an initial burst of military prowess, was all we needed to prevail in those two wars. It was, in effect, a belief in laissez-faire that had grown so powerful that it seeped into - and corrupted - the administration's thinking about statecraft and nation-building. As the center-right-leaning columnist David Brooks observed: "...members of the Bush administration did not respect government enough to understand that a strong one had to be established in postwar Iraq. They had too much faith in spontaneous social order, a libertarian myth that has been sadly refuted by events." ["From loose conservatism to tight conservatism," @ David Brooks, *Pioneer Press*, St. Paul, MN, 5/16/2006, page 9B.]

Serving as a precursor to the views of Mr. Brooks was a RAND Corporation report of 2005, commissioned by the U.S. Army. (Mr. Brooks did not say whether he was familiar with this report when he wrote his column, however, the report provides considerable support for his views.) According to a newspaper summary of the report: "One serious problem the study described was a failure by the Bush administration to anticipate the scale of the burden it had assumed to keep order and rebuild Iraq's infrastructure and institutions. Another problem described was a general lack of coordination. 'There was never an attempt to develop a single national plan that integrated humanitarian assistance, reconstruction, governance, infrastructure development and postwar security,' the study said." ["RAND report on Iraq kept hush-hush," @ Michael R. Gordon (*The New York Times*), *Pioneer Press*, 2/11/2008, page 3A]

The administration's laissez-faire view of the world resulted in them excessively downsizing invasion force requests by military commanders because, by the sheer force of their blind faith in 'spontaneous social order,' there was no need to guarantee the peace with transitional garrisons. Presumably, it was enough that we had bestowed freedom and democracy upon these two countries at gunpoint. The fact that they lacked the cultural and institutional precursors guaranteeing the successful transplant of this bold adventure was not seen as a problem. After all, these were not the sort of considerations to bog down the agenda of *real men* - if they occurred to them at all. As a result, what originally were sold as military interventions carried out with lightning speed - culminating in a smooth transition to democratic republics - bogged down into a decade-long quagmire with enormous costs for all three nations, not to mention the costs to the allies who joined the struggle.

3 - *The FED*, Martin Mayer, PLUME (The Penguin Group), 375 Hudson St, New York, NY 2001, pages x-xi; see also: *An Empire of Wealth*, John Steele Gordon, Harper - Perennial, 10 East 53rd Street, New York, NY 10022, 2004, pages 366-67.

4 - *The FED*, pages 42, 178-79. In these pages, copyrighted in 2001, Mayer anticipated the financial crisis of 2008 in his discussion of the enormous changes within the mortgage market: "...by which housing could be financed with real estate mortgage conduits, permitting pension funds and mutual funds to get in and out of housing investments, and permitting Wall Street houses to slice and dice mortgage paper that carried an implicit government guarantee....It is by no means clear that the future will regard this system of home finance as a good idea." On the following page, he remarks that: "The health of the economy in the 1990s,...[has] masked the great truth that conceptually - looking ahead as central banks are supposed to look ahead - we no longer understand what we are doing."

5 - The specifics of this $51.7 trillion loss are as follows: the value of credit default swaps dropped from $62.173T in 2007 to $30.428T in 2009, for a loss of $31.745T and the value of equity derivatives dropped from $9.9T in 2007 to $6.7T in 2009, for a loss of $3.2T [ISDA Market Survey @ International Swaps and Derivatives Association, Inc]; the value of U.S. household and nonprofit organization's net worth dropped from $65.3T in 2007-Q3 to $48.5T in 2009-Q1, for a loss of $16.8T ["Americans net worth ekes up again," @ Daniel Wagner, *Pioneer Press*, St. Paul, MN, 12/11/09, page 1C].

6 - The current tendency is to characterize any government involvement in the economy as socialist, whereas, my dictionary defines socialism as follows: "...a theory or system of social organization that advocates the vesting and the ownership and control of the means of production and distribution, of capital, land, etc., in the community as a whole." [Webster's New Universal Unabridged Dictionary, Barnes and Noble Books (by arrangement with Random House Value Publishing, Inc. ©1996), page 1811] (Admittedly, my view of this has evolved somewhat since it was first written.)

7 - "Historical Highest Marginal Income Tax Rates," Tax PolicyCenter.org/Tax Facts/overview/ toprate.cfm.

8 - In addition, Charts 10, "U.S. Income Inequality @ Quintiles 1970-2010," and 10a, "Income Distribution @ Quintile Aggregates 1970-2010," which can be found below, will provide further details on this concentration of income.

9 - *The Wealth of Nations*, Adam Smith, Penguin Books, New York, NY 1982, page 359.

10 - Starting with the administration of Bush2, we can label one of the major themes of these polls as the 'Bush paradox.' It centers on the odd turn that sizable percentages, even pluralities, of Americans were dissatisfied with specific important points of the Bush agenda to the point of considering the country on the wrong track - but that he nonetheless won reelection in 2004. Just weeks after the 2004 election, a New York Times/CBS News Poll found that: "Americans Still Concerned About Bush Agenda, Poll Shows," @ Adam Nagourney and Janet Elder, nytimes.com, 11/22/2004. This poll found major differences between majorities of poll respondents and Bush's agenda regarding tax policy, abortion rights and same sex marriage, along with ambivalence toward his Social Security reform proposals and Iraq policy. In

addition, a majority believed the country was on the wrong track. The latter represented a substantial increase from the 35 percent in 2002 who felt the same way. ["81% in Poll Say Nation Is Headed on Wrong Track," @ David Leonhardt and Marjorie Connelly, nytimes.com, 4/4/2008]

Just two months later, those who believed the country to be on the wrong track had increased to 56%. ["Public Voicing Doubts on Iraq and the Economy, Poll Finds," Adam Nagourney and Janet Elder, nytimes.com, 1/20/2005. Another two months later, just four months after his reelection, a New York Times/CBS News Poll found that: "63 percent of respondents say the president has different priorities on domestic issues than most Americans." More specifically, support for Bush's social security reform proposal, adding private accounts, had eroded significantly - with only 51% supporting it generally. But that support tanked to 69% disapproval when "respondents were told that the private accounts would result in a reduction in guaranteed benefits." ["New Poll Finds Bush Priorities Are Out of Step With Americans," @ Adam Nagourney and Janet Elder, nytimes.com, 3/3/2005]

Another year later, after a disastrous response to Hurricane Katrina and the unending fiscal and human agony of Iraq, the 'wrong track' numbers had increased to 70 percent, while Bush's overall job approval rating had fallen to 31 percent. ["Bush hits new public opinion low," @ Ron Fournier (Associated Press), *Pioneer Press*, 4/8/2006, page 9A; "Poll shows worry over gas, Iraq," @ Adam Nagourney and Megan Thee (*The New York Times*), *Pioneer Press*, 5/10/2006, page 5A]

By 2008, as the recession that began in 2007-Q4 worsened, the percentages believing the country to be on the wrong track increased to as much as 81%, while Bush's overall job approval rating had fallen a few more points to 28 percent. ["81% in Poll Say Nation Is Headed on Wrong Track," @ David Leonhardt and Marjorie Connelly, nytimes.com, 4/4/2008] But perhaps the most significant observation in this poll was that this grim public perception of the country's prospects materialized in those early stages of recession, when the official determination that it is a recession had not yet been made: "The dissatisfaction [reflected in this 81% disapproval rating] is especially striking because public opinion usually hits its low point only in the months and years after an economic downturn, not at the beginning of one. Today, however, Americans report being deeply worried about the country even though many say their own personal finances are still in fairly good shape."

This introduces the idea of momentum in the form of a sociological, or cultural, phenomenon. The idea that public opinion has a gestation period over which a worrisome economic event is assimilated by the public until it eventually materializes in the form of a new configuration of public opinion. It also suggests that this gestation period can involve a significant period of time, lasting several years. This is especially interesting in that it sheds light on the very brief honeymoon period of positive public ratings enjoyed by the Obama administration. After all, it was less than a year after its inauguration, when that same sense of dissatisfaction and the country being on the wrong track quickly shifted to Obama. In just over six months, his approval rating dropped from 69% to 50%. ["A fast drop in Obama's approval rating," (McClatchy-Tribune Information Services) *Pioneer Press*, 8/30/2009, page 8B]

11 - "Poll: Americans say no one has a good jobs plan," @ Lucy Madison, cbsnews.com, 10/25/2011; see also endnote 1.

12 - *The New Industrial State*, John Kenneth Galbraith, Houghton Mifflin Company, 2 Park Street, Boston, MA 02107 (Paperback edition: Signet Books: New American Library, New York, NY) 1967, page 72.

13 - The first thing one needs to know when discussing the budget of the U.S. federal government Is that: "All years referenced for economic data are calendar years unless otherwise noted. All years for budget data are fiscal years unless otherwise noted." [www.gpoaccess.gov/usbudget/fy10/pdf/fy10-newera.pdf]

The second thing one needs to keep in mind is that it takes an enormous amount of work to prepare the budget for a nearly $4 trillion operation, which is the approximate size of the budget of the U.S. government. The result is a very substantial lag between the onset of work on the budget for a given year and its completion. Hence, fiscal years in the U.S. federal government always lag the calendar year anniversaries of their term in office by 8 months. This is spelled out in a Congressional Research Service Report for Congress, titled: "Submission of the President's Budget in Transition Years," @ Robert Keith, updated 9/15/2008 [Order Code RS20752].

It is not especially succinct and to the point about this lag, probably because it has been a feature of U.S. budgets for a very long time and therefore not assumed to require much explanation. Nevertheless, a close reading reveals that this lag is a built in feature of the budget process that dates back to the Budget and Accounting Act of 1921. This means that a recently elected president spends his/her first 8 months in office working with a legacy budget provided by the retiring administration. The incoming administration naturally has the latitude to revise this budget, assuming the cooperation of the Congress. But the reality is that the outgoing administration is both officially acknowledged as the owner of that fiscal year and, also as a practical matter, does have a profound influence upon the character of that segment of the incoming administration.

14 - A Citizen's Guide to the Federal Budget, Budget of the United States Government Fiscal Year 1998, page 15; Citizen's Guide to the 2010 Financial Report of the United States Government, page vi.

15 - "President's FY2009 Budget Submission" (CRS-5), CRS Report for Congress, Consolidated Appropriations Act for FY2009 (P.L. 110-329): An Overview, Updated 11/3/2008 @ Robert Keith (Order Code RL34711).

16 - See endnote 14: A Citizen's Guide...FY1998, page 15.

17 - "Productivity change in the nonfarm business sector, 1947-2009," U.S. Bureau of Labor Statistics, 8/11/2010; data.bls.gov/cgi-bin/print.pl/lpc/prodybar.htm, page 1. See also: "U.S. Productivity Growth, 1873-2003; Federal Reserve Bank, Speech, Ferguson - Lessons from past productivity booms, 1/4/2004, page 16.

18 - "U.S. Markets Open With a Steep Fall," @ Vikas Bajaj and Keith Bradsher, nytimes.com 1/22/2008. This article reported: "Stocks opened sharply lower in volatile trading on Wall Street Tuesday morning after markets fell around the world over the last two days and the Federal Reserve announced an emergency rate cut." The statement from the Federal Reserve explained their rate cut in the following terms (quoted in the above article): "The committee took this action in view of a weakening of the economic outlook and increasing downside risks to growth. While strains in the short-term funding markets have eased somewhat, broader financial market conditions

have continued to deteriorate and credit has tightened further for some businesses and households."

See also: "Answering an SOS," @ Jeannine Aversa and Andrew Taylor (AP), *Pioneer Press*, 1/18/2008, page 1C; "Rate cut spurs new rush to refinance," @ Leslie Wines (AP), *Pioneer Press*, 1/28/2008, page 5B; and "Foreclosure rescue plan expands," @ Martin Crutsinger (AP), *Pioneer Press*, 2/13/2008, page 1C.

19 - "Table B-4. Percent changes in real gross domestic product, 1960-2009," *Economic Report of the President, 2010*; "Table B-4. Percent changes in real gross domestic product, 1962-2010," *Economic Report of the President, 2011*; "Table B-4. Percent changes in real gross domestic product, 1963-2011," *Economic Report of the President, 2012.*

20 - "Frequently Asked Questions: Why has the initial estimate of real GDP for the fourth quarter of 2008 been revised down so much?" (8/5/2011; bea.gov/faq//index.cfm?faq_id=1003; "FAQ: How did the recent GDP revisions change the picture of the 2007-2009 recession and the recovery? (8/5/2011); bea.gov/faq/index.cfm?faq_id=1004.

21 - See endnote 19.

22 See endnote 20: id=1003, page 1.

23 - "*The Job Impact of the American Recovery and Reinvestment Plan,*" 1/8/2009, @ Christina Romer, Chair Designate Council of Economic Advisers and Jared Bernstein, Office of the Vice President-Elect.

24 - "The White House promised us that all the spending would keep unemployment under 8 percent." Re: Michele Bachmann's response to the State of the Union Address; PolitiFact.com; *St Petersburg Times*, 1/26/2011. In their very thorough assessment of Bachmann's charge, the Times initially judged it to be "Barely True." Six months later they revised it to "Mostly False."

25 -"*Mortgage Liquidity du Jour: Underestimated No More,*" Credit Suisse Equity Research, @ Ivy L. Zelman, Dennis McGill, CFA, Justin Speer and Alan Ratner, 3/12/2007.

26 - See endnote 25.

27 - See endnote 25.

28 - "*Mortgage Liquidity du Jour,...*" page 47.

29 - *The Great Crash 1929*, John K. Galbraith, Mariner Books/Houghton Mifflin Company, New York, 1955, pages 46-51.

30 - *The Great Crash 1929*, page 48.

31 - *The Great Crash 1929*, page 47.

32 - nytimes.com/Times Topics/Glass-Steagall Act (1933).

33 - nytimes.com/Archives/"Congress Passes Wide-Ranging Bill Easing Bank Laws," @ Stephen Labaton, 11/5/1999.

34 - "More subprime hazards lurk in special pipelines," @ David Reilly and Carrick Mollenkamp (*Wall Street Journal*), *Pioneer Press*, 9/2/2007, page 5D. See also: "*The FED*, page 178; "The Monster That Ate Wall Street," @ Mathew Philips, *Newsweek*, a0/6/2008; and businessdictionary.com/conduit, conduit-finance.

35 - "More subprime hazards..."

36 - "More subprime hazards..."

37 - See endnote 5: "ISDA Market Survey."

38 - See endnote 37.

39 - "*The U.S. Housing Market: Current Conditions and Policy Considerations,*" federalreserve.gov/publications/other-reports/files/housing-white-paper-20120104.pdf, page 1.

40 - See endnote 37.

41 - See endnote 33.

42 - See endnote 33.

43 - See endnote 33.

44 - See endnote 33.

45 -*The FED*, page 7.

46 - *The FED*, page 7.

47 - *The FED*, page 266.

48 - *"Hedge Funds, Leverage, and the Lessons of Long-Term Capital Management,"* Report of the President's Working Group on Financial Markets (Robert E. Rubin, Alan Greenspan, Arthur Levitt, Brooksley Born), April 1999, pages viii-ix.

49 - *"Hedge Funds,..."* page ix.

50 - See endnote 49.

51 - see endnote 33.

52 - *The FED*, page 176. See also: "Nixon's Fight Against Economic Problem No. 1," 2/21/1969, time.com/time/archive; "The Rising Risk Of Recession," 12/19/1969, time.com/time/archive; "The Economy: Crisis of Confidence," 6/1/1970, time.com/time/archive. Regarding Congressional opposition to, and business support for, Johnson's surtax, see: "Moribund Surtax," 9/22/1967, time.com/time/archive. Regarding eventual passage of the surtax, see: "Taxes, What's in the Package," 7/26/1968, time.com/time/archive.

53 - "The Economy, Crisis of Confidence," 6/1/1970, time.com/time/archive.

54 - *"The end of the Bretton Woods System (1972-81),"* International Monetary Fund (imf.org/external/about/histend.htm); also see: *The FED*, pages 74, 182-83.

55 - A significant exception to the international scope of this exchange rate system was that it did not apply to Britain's sterling zone. See: "The Classical Gold Standard: Some Lessons for Today," @ Michael David Bordo, The Federal Reserve Bank of St. Louis, May 1981, page 7.

56 - "The Classical Gold Standard..," page 7.

57 - See endnote 56.

58 - *The FED*, pages 182.

59 - "Business, Rising Cry for Reform," 12/6/1968, time.com/time/archive.

60 - "*The Economic Consequences of the Peace*," John Maynard Keynes, BN Publishing, Lexington, KY, 2010. Keynes account of the punitive measures adopted by the European victors in WWI, written in the 1920s, reads like a preamble to WWII. The differences in the economic program adopted by the victorious Western Allies at the conclusion of WWII, compared to that of their European predecessors at the conclusion of WWI, were just as stunning as the results. The latter became the source of bitterness and renewed war, while the former became the cradle of peace and reconciliation.

61 - See endnote 52.

62 - See endnote 59.

63 - *The FED*, pages x-xi, 178-79.

63a - This figure was not seasonally adjusted. The adjusted figure for January 2009 was significantly lower; however, the overall adjusted figures for the period March 2008-April 2009 actually were higher than those not seasonally adjusted. See endnote 66.

64 - "Response to the State of the Union," 1/25/2011, Michele Bachmann, bachmann.house.gov, page 1.

64a - "*Economic Report of the President 2011*;" table B-42, Civilian Unemployment Rate, 1964-2010.

65 - See endnote 64.

66 - Bureau of Labor Statistics Data: http://data.bls.gov;pdq/SurveyOutputServlet; Series Id: LNU03000000; Labor force status: Unemployed. These figures were not seasonally adjusted. Seasonally adjusted figures for the same period were somewhat higher: 5,941,000 vs. the 5,746,000 stated in the text. Seasonally adjusted figures were obtained from "Tables B-36. Civilian employment and unemployment by sex and age, 1962-2009 and 1964-2010." These can be found in the *Economic Reports of the President 2010 and 2011*.

67 - See endnote 64.

68 - See endnote 64.

69 - "*Economic Report of the President: 2011* Report Spreadsheet Tables, Table B-78. Federal receipts, outlays, surplus or deficit, and debt, fiscal years, 1944-2012.

70 - By the end of Fiscal Year 2011, the gross federal debt had reached $14.8 trillion. "*Economic Report of the President: 2012* Report Spreadsheet Tables, Table B-78. Federal receipts, outlays, surplus or deficit, and debt, fiscal years, 1945-2013.

70a - *The New York Times 2011 Almanac*, Ed. @ John W. Wright, 375 Hudson St., NY, NY 10014, 2010, page 381.

70b - "5% of patients account for half of health care spending," @ Kelly Kennedy, usatoday30, usatoday.com, 1/12/2012.

70c - "Long-Term Trends in Medicare Payments in the Last Year of Life," *Health Services Research*, @ Gerald F. Riley and James D. Lubitz, April 2010.

70d - "Saving Medicare from Itself," @ Avik Roy, *National Affairs*, Issue No. 8, Summer 2011, page 4.

70e - *The New York Times 2011 Almanac,* page 382.

71 - The first several days of the 2012 Republican National Convention offer an excellent case in point. Nearly every speaker paid their obeisance to supply side doctrine and came close to deification of the entrepreneur as fundamentally the most important factor in any economy.

72 - Serving as the exception that proves the rule, Alan Greenspan wrote an essay commemorating Adam Smith and his theory of the invisible hand, which he delivered at the Adam Smith Memorial Lecture, Kirkcaldy, Scotland, on February 6, 2005. "Remarks by Chairman Alan Greenspan: Adam Smith" [federalreserve.gov/boarddocs/speeches/2005/20050206].

73 - See endnote 72. Although Greenspan does not specifically tie the benevolence of rational self-interest to the crafting of our Articles of

Confederation, he does link it to Adam Smith and the period coinciding with the labors of our Founding Fathers. This is significant because it philosophically links the failure of our *First Confederacy* to Greenspan's role as an advocate for this sanguine view of human nature and, most importantly, the role it played in the economic disaster of 2008-09 with its similar overemphasis upon the rationality of economic man.

74 - *The Federalist*, No. 21, Hamilton, The Modern Library, Random House, New York, NY, page 126.

75 - *A More Perfect Union*, Peters, William, Crown, 1987, pages 6-7.

76 - *10 Days That Unexpectedly Changed America*, pages 31-36.

77 - *10 Days That Unexpectedly..*, pages 36-38, 43. *See also*, endnote 74, pages 126-27.

78 - *The Federalist*, No. 25, Hamilton, pages 156-58; *The Thomas Jefferson Reader, Konecky & Konecky, 72 Ayers Point Rd., Old Saybrook, CT 06475*, page 131.

79 - *10 Days That Unexpectedly..*, page 40-42

80 - *The Federalist*, No. 25, Hamilton, pages 153-56.

81 - See endnote 74.

82 - *The Federalist*, No. 51, Madison, page 337.

83 - See endnote 72.

84 - See endnote 72.

85 - See endnotes 32 and 33.

86 - *The FED*, page 178; For a retrospective view, also see: "Testimony of Dr. Alan Greenspan," Committee of Government Oversight and Reform, 10/23/2008: "The breakdown has been most apparent in the securitization of home mortgages. The evidence strongly suggests that without the excess demand from securitizers, subprime mortgage originations (undeniably the

original source of crisis) would have been far smaller and defaults accordingly far fewer."

87 - "Testimony of Dr. Alan Greenspan;" see also: "Greenspan Concedes Error on Regulation," nytimes.com, 10/23/2008.

88 - See endnote 87, "Greenspan Concedes Error..."

89 - *An Inquiry Into The Nature And Causes Of The Wealth of Nations, Vol. 1,* Adam Smith, Liberty Fund, Indianapolis, Indiana, 1981, page 456.

90 - The following works all contributed to the views expressed here: *The Worldly Philosophers*, Robert L. Heilbroner, Touchstone (Simon & Schuster), Rockefeller Center, 1230 Avenue of the Americas, New York, NY 10020, 1953; *The Century*, Peter Jennings and Todd **Brewster,** Doubleday, 1540 Broadway, New York, NY 10036 1998; *The United States Since 1865*, Foster Rhea Dulles, The University of Michigan Press, Ann Arbor, 1959.

91 - Federal Reserve Bank: Speech, Ferguson--"*Lessons from past productivity booms*," Remarks by Vice Chairman Roger W. Ferguson, Jr., 1/4/2004. The strategic thought processes that inform Ferguson's remarks, along with the details of the economic evolution it describes, contributed greatly to this view of America as the leading common market of the modern era.

92 - *Recent Economic Changes in the United States,* @ Committee on Recent Economic Changes of the President's Conference on Unemployment, National Bureau of Economic Research, 1929, pages 550-53.

93 - See endnote 92.

94 - See endnote 92, page 549.

95 - See endnote 92, page 556.

96 - See endnote 92, page 555.

97 - See endnote 92, page 555.

98 - *The New York Times 2009 Almanac*, John W. Wright (General Editor), Penguin Books, 375 Hudson St, New York, NY 10014, 2008, pages 316-17.

99 - See endnote 92, pages 550, 553, 556.

100 - See endnote 92, page 553.

101 - See endnote 92, page 553; for a complementary discussion of the dramatic increase in auto production and its impact on agriculture, see: *An Empire of Wealth*, pages 296-301.

102 - See endnote 98, page 316; see also endnote 94.

103 - *The United States Since...*, pages 344-45.

104 - See endnote 92, page xx.

105 - See endnote 104.

106 - *Stages of Economic Growth*, W.W. Rostow, Cambridge University Press, 32 East 57 Street, New York, NY 10022, 1960, pages 4-9. In these pages, Rostow discusses the transition from a traditional society to take-off. He describe this transition by focusing on the fundamental differences between these two stages of economic development:

"A traditional society is one whose structure is developed within limited production functions, based on pre-Newtonian science and technology, and on pre-Newtonian attitudes toward the physical world. Newton is here used as a symbol for that watershed in history when men came widely to believe that the external world was subject to a few knowable laws, and was systematically capable of productive manipulation."

His follow-up comment gets right to the heart of the importance of human capital in creating economic growth and wealth. "But the central fact about the traditional society was that a ceiling existed on the level of attainable output per head. The ceiling resulted from the fact that the potentialities which flow from modern science and technology were either not available or not regularly and systematically applied."

In addition, we should not fail to note his use of the dynamic term, "take-off," suggestive of acceleration and flight, nor his penetrating insight into how "compound interest" gets integrated into the very "habits and institutional structure" of the economy once it does take-off. Taken together, these not only bear a resemblance to the concept of dynamic equilibrium as espoused in the 1920s, but also to the concept of momentum as detailed elsewhere in this essay.

Finally, his linkage of the role of compound interest with the habits and institutional structure of the economy raises a warning flag about the impermanence of the cultural footings of these "potentialities flowing from modern science and technology." In short, the fact that they spring from the malleable stuff of culture points to the vulnerability of not only these economic virtues, but, more importantly, the technologically advanced life style dependent upon them. This, of course, brings us full circle back to our failure to comprehend the underlying significance of our transition from an individually-centric agrarian economy to a socially-centric technocratic economy. After all, it is our failure to comprehend the significance of this transition that has contributed to the corruption of the economic virtues essential to the sustainability of our refined economy.

107 - See endnote 104.

108 - *Leviathan*, Thomas Hobbes, The Liberal Arts Press, Inc., New York, NY 1958 (Orig. 1651), page 107.

109 - See endnote 82.

110 - These ideas were elaborated extensively by President Ronald Reagan. See especially his descriptions of America as the City on a Hill.

111 - These assertions may sound unreal for those who did not follow closely the 2012 Republican presidential primaries. But, for those who did there is nothing surprising here. Ron Paul, Michele Bachmann and Rick Perry did not hesitate to roll out an extreme Tea Party agenda for the radical restructuring of the U.S. government.

112 - There is some doubt as to whom originated this term. Some attribute it to Williams Jennings Bryan.

113 - "In Class Warfare, Guess Which Class Is Winning," Ben Stein, *New York Times*, BU3, 11/26/2006.

114 - "Survey Finds Rising Perception of Class Tension," Sabrina Tavernise, 1/11/2012, nytimes.com/2012/01/12/us/more-conflict-seen-between-rich-and-poor-survey-finds.

115 - "Gallup Politics," Election 2012 Trial Heat: Obama vs. Romney; gallup.com/poll/150743/Obama-Romney.aspx. This web site has a tracking poll that extends from 4/12-16/2012-8/29-9/4/2012.

116 - "Romney Edges Obama in Battle for Middle-Income Voters," Jeffrey M. Jones, 6/4/2012; gallup.com/poll/155030/romney-edges-obama--battle-middle-income-voters.asp...

117 - See endnote 115.

118 - "Obama Still Wins on Likability; Romney, on the Economy," Frank Newport, 8/24/2012; gallup.com/poll/156857/obama-wins-likability-romney-economy.aspx?...

119 - "Tax, Fairer, Flatter, and Simpler: Mitt's Plan," mittromney.com/issues/tax.

120 - See endnote 5.

121 - See endnote 5.

122 - mittromney.com/issues/tax-mitt's plan.

123 - See endnote 7. These days Republicans like Newt Gingrich take credit for working with President Clinton to balance the budget. However, they do not acknowledge the fact that the Democrats laid the fiscal foundation for this balanced budget by raising taxes during Clinton's first term, before the Republicans regained control of both the House of Representatives and the Senate. Similarly, neither party acknowledges the fact that tax increases during the administration of George H.W. Bush also contributed to Clinton's balanced budget.

124 - See endnote 122. The two that would benefit taxpayers in general are the Alternative Minimum Tax and the across-the-board 20 percent cut in marginal rates. However, both of these also carry with the them the inevitable reverse Robin Hood effect. The loss of revenue is so great that it

forces the resort to an increase in fees in all manner of services that ultimately depended upon federal government subsidies to make them affordable. Hence, as we have seen with previous reductions in federal income taxes, college tuition has shot up along with major rate increases for local and state property taxes. The reason for this is that federal support for various state programs - or revenue-sharing - gets cut as federal revenues decline. And, of course, since the wealthy control a vastly disproportionate share of the wealth in this country, their rate reductions amount to a very large part of the revenue loss. The take-away lessons from this are: first, middle-income taxpayers always lose in the long run when it comes to tax cuts and, second, discussion of these realities of our tax structure will always trigger accusations of class warfare.

125 - *The FED*, page 222; See also, "The Monster That Ate Wall Street," Matthew Philips, *Newsweek*, 10/6/2008, pages 46-47; "A Look At Wall Street's Shadow Market," 10/5/2008, cbsnews.com/stories/2008/10/05/60minutes.

126 - "Financial time bombs that threaten mass destruction," TIMESONLINE, From *The Times*, 12/8/2004; business.timesonline.co/uk/tol/business/columnists/article400350.

127 - See endnote 125.

128 - *The FED*, pages 222, 266-67; See also endnote 5: "ISDA Market Survey" and endnote 125.

129 - *The FED*, pages 266-67.

130 - See endnotes 125 and 126. See also: *House of Cards*, William D. Cohan, Anchor Books (Random House, Inc.), New York, NY 2009, pages 332, 336.

131 - See endnote 125: "A Look At Wall Street's Shadow Market."

132 - *House of Cards*, pages 335, 408-09; "More subprime hazards lurk...;" See also: "Hedge Funds, Unhinged," @ Louise Story, *The New York Times*, 1/18/2009, page BU6. The latter provides a sense of the generally short-term funding typical of the industry. It states that the hedge fund, Citadel, did not worry about surviving the Great Recession because it had "arranged for credit lines at dozens of banks with durations as long as a year,..."

133 - "Lenders with no skin in the game don't care if you can't pay," @ Caroline Baum, *Pioneer Press*, 10/12/2008, page3D; also see: "Lenders didn't expect walk-aways," Rachel Beck (AP), *Pioneer Press*, 2/17/2008, page 3D.

134 - See endnote 126.

135 - See endnote 126: "Financial time bombs that threaten..."

136 - "Credit default swap," en.wikipedia.org/wiki/Credit default _swap, page 1.

137 - See endnote 125: "The Monster That Ate..."

138 - See endnote 5: "ISDA Market Survey."

139 - "Dimon: 'The buck stops with me," @ Marcy Gordon (AP), *Pioneer Press*, 6/14/2012, page 6A.

140 - *The FED*, page 267.

141 - For a detailed description of repos, see: QFinance: "Understanding and Using the Repos Market;" qfinance.com/asset-management-checklists/understanding-and-using-the-repos-market. See also endnote 132: *House of Cards*, page 335.

142 - See endnote 141: *House of Cards*, page 335.

143 - See endnote 141: *House of Cards*, pages 408-09.

144 - See endnote 141: *House of Cards*, page 408.

145 - See endnote 141: *House of Cards*, page 383.

146 - "Home prices up 15% in third quarter," @ Kathleen M. Howley (Bloomberg News), *Pioneer Press*, 11/16/2005, page 6C; or for a view that better captured the uncertainty of this leading edge moment, see "Slippery Devil, That Real Estate 'Bubble," @ Motoko Rich and David Leonhardt, *The New York Times*, 11/23/2005, page WK3.

147 - "Housing starts tumble; Analysts attribute October decline to rising mortgage rates," @ Martin Crutsinger (AP), *Pioneer Press*, 11/18/2005, page 1C.

148 - "Buyer's Market," @ Gita Sitaramiah, *Pioneer Press*, 8/15/2006, page 1C; "Subprime loan defaults grow," @ Lingling Wei (Dow Jones Newswires), *Pioneer Press*, 8/30/2006, page 3C.

149 - "The Housing Glut," @ Gita Sitaramiah, *Pioneer Press*, 10/8/2006, page 1D.

150 - See endnote 28; also see: "Reasons To Worry," @ Niall Ferguson, *The New York Times Magazine*, 6/11/2006, page 50. In this article, Ferguson focuses upon the perverse dynamics resulting from the reset of ARMs. In doing so he anticipated the work of Credit Suisse analysts.

151 - "Crisis Looms In Mortgages," @ Gretchen Morgenson, *The New York Times*, 3/11/2007, page 1.

152 - See endnotes 125 and 126.

153 - These risks were compounded by the margin requirements typically found in derivative and credit default swap contracts. See, for example, endnote 34: "More subprime hazards..."

154 - See endnote 5: "ISDA Market Survey."

155 - See endnote 141: *House of Cards*, page 529.

156 - "House Passes Bailout Bill in 263-171 vote," dealbook.nytimes.com/2008/10/03/house-passes-bailout-bill-in-263-171-vote. According to this article, the specifics of the vote were as follows: "The vote was 263-171: Most Democrats were in favor (172 yeas to 63 nays), while a slighter majority of Republicans voted against (91 yeas to 108 nays), *The New York Time's* David Herszenhorn reported."

157 - "Credit Crisis - Bailout Plan (TARP)," topics.nytimes.com/ top/reference/timestopics/subjects/c/ credit_crisis/bailout_plan. This overview of the Troubled Asset Relief Program credited it with playing "a crucial role in pulling the global economy back from the brink." Regarding its $700 billion authorization, it reported that "The Treasury never tapped the full $700 billion. By the time its authority to spend the money expired on Oct. 2, 2010, it had committed $470 billion and disbursed $387 billion, mostly to hundreds

of banks and later to A.I.G., the car industry - Chrysler, General Motors, the G.M. financing company and suppliers - and to what has been, so far, a failed effort to help homeowners avoid foreclosures. Regarding its ultimate costs, it quoted a Congressional Budget Office assessment from November 2010, estimating "the final cost at roughly $25 billion,..."

158 - See endnote 157. See also: "Nightmare on Main Street," @ Martha Brannigan (McClatchy Newspapers), *Pioneer Press*, 9/25/2008, page 1C.

159 - "What did TARP Accomplish?" @ Simon Johnson, *The New York Times*, Economix, economix.blogs.nytimes.com/2009/11/19.

160 - "As economic crisis unfolds, the Bush administration is CHANGING GEARS," @ Edmund L Andrews and Mark Landler (*New York Times*), *Pioneer Press*, 10/12/2008, page 4A. See also: "Missing the Target With $700 Billion," @ Alan S. Binder, *The New York Times*, 12/21/2008, page Bu 4.

161 - "Treasury takes new tack with faltering bailout," @ Peter Whoriskey, David Cho and Binyamin Appelbaum (*The Washington Post*), *Pioneer Press*, 11/13/2008, page 1A.

162 - "Bush Approves $17.4 Billion Auto Bailout," @ David M. Herszenhorn and David E. Sanger, *The New York Times*, 12/20/2008; nytimes.com.

163 - "Got $700 Billion? Sweat the Details," @ Alan S. Blinder, *The New York Times*, 10/12/2008, page BU 1; see also: "Administration Is Seeking $700 Billion For Wall ST.; Bailout Could Set Record," @ David M. Herszenhorn, *The New York Times*, 9/21/2008, pages 1, 19.

164 - See endnote 163: "Got $700 Billion?"

165 - "$33B to 21 banks in bailout," @ Martin Crutsinger (AP), *Pioneer Press*, 11/18/2008, page 15A. This article reported: "Paulson said the severity of the financial crisis made him realize it would take too long to get the troublesome program into operation." See also: endnote 160: "As economic crisis unfolds,.."

166 - See endnote 126: "Financial time bombs that threaten..."

167 - See endnote 163: "Administration Is Seeking $700 Billion..." See also: "No 'fire sale' in bailout," @ Marcy Gordon (Associated Press), *Pioneer Press*, 9/24/2008, page 3C; "Accounting rule change demonic or divine?" @ Kevin G. Hall (McClatchy Newspapers), *Pioneer Press*, 4/2/2009, page 1C; "FASB adopts new guidelines," @ Marcy Gordon (Associated Press), *Pioneer Press*, 4/3/2009, page 3C.

168 - "Report on the Troubled Asset Relief Program - March 2012," Congressional Budget Office; cbo.gov/publications.

169 - See endnote 3: *The FED*, pages 178-79.

170 - See endnote 5: "ISDA Market Survey @ International Swaps..."

171 - See endnote 151 - "Crisis Looms In Mortgages."

172 - *The FED*, pages 267-68.

173 - *The FED*, pages 42, 178, 267-68.

174 - According to Wikipedia it was incorporated in 1995, at which time MERS "awarded a contract to Electronic Data Systems (EDS) to develop and service the technology systems," but was not officially launched until April1997.

175 - www.mersinc.org/about-us/about-us.

176 - See endnote 174.

177 - "New York Sues 3 Big Banks Over Mortgage Database," @ Reuters, 2/3/2012; www.nytimes.com/2012/02/04/business/new-york-suing-3-banks.

178 - "Chase Acts to Broaden Foreclosure Reviews," @ Eric Dash, *The New York Times*, 10/13/2010; www.nytimes.com/2010/10/14/business / 14morgan.

179 - "Mortgage questions multiply for banks," @ Alan Zibel and Alex Velga (Associated Press), *Pioneer Press*, 10/13/2010, page 7A; "Lawsuit exposes 'robo-signers," @ Michelle Conlin (Associated Press), *Pioneer Press*, 10/13/2010, page 9A; "Lenders far from ending debacle," @ Alan Zibel (AP), *Pioneer Press*, 10/20/2010, page 7A; "BofA pressured to buy back Countrywide securities," @ Alistair Barr (Market Watch), *Pioneer Press*, 10/20/2010, page

9A; "BofA won't buy back bad assets," @ Eileen AJ Connelly (Associated Press), *Pioneer Press*, 11/6/2010, page 15A; "Mass. foreclosure case could ripple through banks, mortgage markets," @ Denise Lavoie and Michelle Conlin (Associated Press), *Pioneer Press*, 1/8/2011, page 1A; "Pace of foreclosures slows as banks face many probes," @ David Streitfeld (*New York Times*), *Pioneer Press*, 1/9/2011, page 3A.

180 - "White House Urges Calm on Foreclosures," @ David Segal, *The New York Times*, 10/17/2010; www.nytimes.com/2010/10/18/business/18foreclosure.

181 - See endnote 25: "Mortgage Liquidity du Jour," page 47; and endnote 39 - "The U.S. Housing Market: Current Conditions and Policy Considerations."

182 - See endnotes 151: "Crisis Looms In Mortgages;" and endnote 25: "Mortgage Liquidity du Jour." Taken together, these two sources provide an insight into the perverse dynamic that accompanied the bursting of the mortgage balloon. A downward spiral ensued where prices peaked, then faltered as those dependent on a rising market were unable to refinance and went into foreclosure. These failures prompted a tightening of credit that only served to raise the refinance bar and increase the number of foreclosures.

183 - See endnote 126: "Financial time bombs that threaten..."

184 - See endnote 5.

185 - See endnote 19.

186 - See endnotes 69 and 70.

187 - "*The General Theory of Employment, Interest, and Money;*" John Maynard Keynes, A Harvest Book, Harcourt, Inc., San Diego, New York, London, 1964; pages 378-379 (bold face added).

188 - See endnote 9: *The Wealth of Nations*, page 377; see also pages 382-83 for Smith's definition of fixed capital and the restrictions against diverting it into any purpose other than fixed capital.

189 - *The New York Times 2011 Almanac*, ed. John W. Wright, Penguin Books, 375 Hudson St., New York, NY 10014, 2009, page 316.

190 - *American Minds*, Stow Persons, Henry Holt and Company, New York, 1958, page 245.

191 - *American Minds*, pages 138-39.

192 - Despite a good deal of searching, I have not found a clear indication that Jefferson was the source.

193 - *"The Federalist;"* No 79 (Hamilton), page 512.

194 - Both John Adams and Thomas Jefferson had similar views about the political and economic importance of widely distributed land. See endnote 190: *American Minds*, pages 138-40.

195 - 1776, David McCullough, Simon & Schuster Paperbacks, 1230 Avenue of the Americas, New York, NY 10020, 2005, page 148.

196 - *The Fourth Great Awakening*, Robert William Fogel, The University of Chicago Press, Chicago, IL 60637, 2000, pages 58-59.

197 - *"The United States Since 1865,"* Foster Rhea Dulles, The University of Michigan Press, Ann Arbor, Michigan, 1959, pages 93-94.

198 - See endnote 197, pages 94-95.

199 - See endnote 92: *Recent Economic Changes in the United States, page xx*.

200 -See Endnote 74: *The Federalist*, No. 51, February 8, 1788, page 340.

201 - *Guardians of Tradition*, Ruth Miller Elson, University of Nebraska Press, Lincoln, Nebraska, 1964, pages 5-6.

202 - *THIRTY-NINTH CONGRESS. SESS II. CHAP. 158. March 2, 1867.*

203 - *The World Almanac and Book of Facts 2008*, A Reader's Digest Company, New York, NY, page 395.

204 - See endnote 203.

205 - See endnote 203.

206 - See endnote 203; also see: Consumer Price Index (1913-2010), U.S. Department of Labor, Bureau of Labor Statistics (1982-84=100); Annual Averages: 1920=20.0; 1983=99.6; 2005=195.3. Applying these CPI adjustments to current expenses results in the following: 1920: (5 x $.9 = $4.5); 2005: ($424.6/195.3 = $217.7).

207 - See endnote 203.

208 - See endnote 206: "Consumer Price Index (1913-2010)."

209 - "Where's the Money Going?" @ Richard Rothstein, Economic Policy Institute, 1660 L Street N.W., Washington, D.C. 20036, 1997.

210 - See endnote 209, page 9.

211 - "Minnesota School Finance History 1849-2005," page 3.

212 - Average productivity growth for the 95 year period 1900-2005 is 2.26 percent. See endnote 17 for references to: Bureau of Labor Statistics and Federal Reserve Bank, Speech, Ferguson - "Lessons from past productivity booms - January 2004."

213 - See endnote 209: "Where's the Money...," page 2.

214 - See endnote 209: "Where's the Money..., page 10.

215 - *The Slave Ship*, Marcus Rediker, Viking (The Penguin Group), 375 Hudson St, New York, NY 10014, 2007, pages 338-39, 348-50. Rediker's entire work serves as a study on the slave ship as a brutal exercise in *vocational training* for slaves.

216 - A concise history of African-Americans in the U.S. may be found in the *U.S. Riot Commission Report; Report of the National Advisory Commission on Civil Disorders*, Bantam Books, The New York Times Company, 1968, pages 206-50; see also *"Slavery By Another Name,"* a 90-minute documentary that challenges the belief that slavery ended with the Civil War; www.pbs.org/tpt/slavery-by-another-name.

216a - To get a sense of how little progress our country made in race relations between the Civil War and WWII, see *Notes of a Native Son*, James Baldwin, Bantam Books, Inc., 271 Madison Ave, New York 16, NY 1964 (Original Baldwin copyright 1949).

217 - *Democracy in America*, Alexis de Tocqueville, Harvey C. Mansfield and Delba Winthrop, The University of Chicago Press, Chicago, IL 60637, 2000, Page 327.

218 - See endnote 217, page 304.

219 - *OECD 2010, PISA 2009 Results*, Executive Summary, page 13.

220 - *OECD 2010, PISA 2009 Results*, Executive Summary, page 8.

221 - "A call for the courage to challenge a status quo that serves adults - too often at kids expense," @ Joel Klein, Michael Lomax and Janet Marguia, Pioneer Press, 4/11/2010, page 9B.

222 - *OECD 2010, PISA 2009 Results*, Executive Summary, page 9; see also: *OECD 2011, Lessons From Pisa For The United States*, page 28. The perversely unique ranking of the U.S. as reflected by the latter warrants recognition: "It is not just the volume of resources that matters but also how countries invest these, and how well they succeed in **directing the money where it can make the most difference.** The United States is one of only three OECD countries in which, for example, socio-economically disadvantaged schools have to cope with less favourable student-teacher ratios than socio-economically advantaged schools, which implies that students from disadvantaged backgrounds may end up with considerably lower spending per student than what the above figures on average spending would suggest. With respect to spending on instruction, the United States spends a far lower proportion than the average OECD country on the salaries of high-school teachers." (emphasis in original)

223 - "Education Gap Grows Between Rich and Poor, Studies Say," *The New York Times*, @ Sabrina Tavernise, 2/9/2012; nytimes.com/2012/02/10/education.

224 - See endnote 209, pages 2-3.

225 - *OECD 2010, PISA 2009 Results*, Executive Summary, page 16

226 - *OECD 2010, PISA 2009 Results*, Executive Summary, page 8

227 - *OECD 2011, Lessons From Pisa For The United States*, page 26.

228 - *OECD 2011, Lessons From Pisa For The United States*, page 28.

229 - See endnote 227.

230 - See endnote 209, pages 2-3. See also: "State spends more than most per student, puts more into classroom," @ Christopher Magan, *Pioneer Press*, 7/1/2012, page 1B.

231 - *OECD 2011, Lessons From Pisa For The United States*, page 38.

232 - "Romney attacks Obama, says teachers unions block reform," @ Steven Thomma (McClatchy Newspapers), *Pioneer Press*, 5/24/2012, page 3A. See also: "Vouchers Unspoken, Romney Hails School Choice," @ Trip Gabriel, *The New York Times*, 6/11/2012; nytimes.com/ 2012/06/12/us/politics.

233 - See endnote 228.

234 - See endnote 231; see also: "Romney Calls Education 'Civil Rights Issue of Our Era' and Urges Shift," @ Trip Gabriel, *The New York Times*, 5/23/2012; nytimes.com/2012/05/24/us/politics.

235 - "FACT CHECK: Romney off on Obama's love for unions," @ Christine Armario (AP Education Writer News Fuze), 5/25/2012; www.twincities.com/ ci_20708668/fact-check-romney-off-obamas-love-unions? See also: Endnote 233: "Romney Calls Education..."

236 - See endnote 217.

237 - See endnote 190, pages 223-24.

238 - See endnote 217.

239 - *Medieval Civilization 400-1500*, Jaques Le Goff, Barnes and Noble Books 2000 (English Translation by Blackwell Publishers), pages 151-52.

240 - *A History of the Modern World*, R.R. Palmer and Joel Colton, Alfred A. Knopf, New York, NY 1961, pages 286-87.

241 - *The Constitution of the United States of America*, see Article 1, Section 2: "Representatives and direct Taxes shall be apportioned among the several States which may be included within this Union, according to their respective Numbers, *which shall be determined by adding to the whole Number of free Persons, including those bound to Service for a Term of Years, and excluding Indians not taxed, three fifths of all other Persons.*" (emphasis added)

See also: Article 1, Section 9: " *The Migration or Importation of such Persons* as any of the States now existing shall think proper to admit, *shall not be prohibited by the Congress prior to the Year one thousand eight hundred and eight*, but a Tax or duty may be imposed on such Importation, not exceeding ten dollars for each Person." (emphasis added)

See also: Article IV, Section 2: "*No Person held to Service or Labour in one State*, under the Laws thereof, *escaping into another, shall, in Consequence of any Law or Regulation therein, be discharged from such Service or Labour, but shall be delivered up on Claim of the Party to whom such Service or Labour may be due.*" (emphasis added)

See also: Article V: "The Congress,...shall propose Amendments to this Constitution,...*Provided that no Amendment which may be made prior to the Year One thousand eight hundred and eight shall in any Manner affect the first and fourth Clauses in the Ninth Section of the first Article;...*" [Note: the fourth clause not included here refers to taxes related to the Census.](emphasis added)

All of the forgoing are instances in which the Constitution deals with the issue of slavery without actually using its proper name.

242 - John Locke, *Second Treatise of Government*, Hackett Publishing Company, Inc., P.O. Box 44937, Indianapolis, Indiana, 46244-0937, 1980, page 52.

242a - John Locke, "*Second Treatise...*," page 14.

242b - John Locke, "*Second Treatise...*," page 17.

242c - See Endnote 240: "*A History of the Modern...*," pages 286-87.

242d - See Endnote 240: "*A History of the Modern...*," page 230.

243 - See Endnote 242: John Locke, *Second Treatise...*," page x.

243a - See Endnote 242: John Locke, *Second Treatise...*," page x.

243b - See Endnote 242: John Locke, *Second Treatise...*," page x.

244 - See Endnote 215 - *The Slave Ship*, page 47.

244a - See Endnote 215 - *The Slave Ship*, page 98.

245 - See Endnote 215 - *The Slave Ship*, page 99.

246 - *Stanford Encyclopedia of Philosophy, John Locke*, page 34; http://plato.stanford.edu/entries/locke.

247 - *The Accidental Mind*, David J. Linden, The Belknap Press of Harvard University Press, Cambridge, MA 2007, page 2.

248 - See endnote 247, page 3.

248a - See endnote 247, pages 16-17.

249 - Lou Cannon, *President Reagan, The Role Of A lifetime*, Public Affairs, 250 West 57th Street, Suite 1321, New York, NY 10107, 1991, pages 71-7, 110-13, 751. Cannon's description of Reagan as the 'Great Communicator' touches on how a consummate politician works these neuro-cultural foundations, shaping them into a specific form relevant to contemporary circumstances. In these pages he describes how Reagan liked to claim that all he did was act as spokesperson for the nation's values - as if he unearthed them as ready-to-deliver speeches out of a secret library. But that ignores the reality that he also acknowledged the importance of constant repetition in gaining acceptance for his message. He spent years shaping, delivering and then repeating his own political agenda so that it would sink into the public

consciousness. His success was based on years of refining and repeating this same basic message until it resonated powerfully with his audiences. In fact, it was referred to as *The Speech* just as one would refer to a well-crafted tool. In short, he was a skilled artisan and presenter of his own unique version of reality. He was a master propagandist.

249a - See endnotes 216 and 216a.

249b - See endnote 217, page 329.

250 - http//millercenter.org/president/gwbush/essays/biography/4.

251 - See endnote 220.

252 - See endnote 220. The barely average ranking should be used advisedly. U.S. rankings in reading and science appear to be well within the limits of average, but in mathematics our scores tend toward below-average.

253 - See endnotes 231, 232 and 234.

254 - "U.S. charter school supporters convene today;" @ Christopher Magan, *Pioneer Press*, 6/19/2012, page 5A; also see endnote 234: "FACT CHECK: Romney Off..."

255 - See endnote 230.

256 - See endnote 220.

257 - See endnote 220.

258 - See endnote 220.

259 - "National Assessment of Educational Progress (NAEP); Achievement Gaps: How Black and White Students in Public Schools Perform in Mathematics and Reading on the National Assessment of Educational Progress," page 1; http://nces.ed.gov/nationsreportcard/pubs/ studies/ 2009455.asp.

260 - See endnote 222: OECD 2011, *Lessons From Pisa For The United States*, page 26.

261 - "Best Schools In The World," Robert G. Kaiser (*Washington Post*), *Pioneer Press*, 6/12/05, page 13A.

262 - See endnote 261.

263 - See endnote 220.

264 - See endnote 261.

265 - See endnote 261.

266 - See endnote 222: *OECD 2011, Lessons From Pisa For The United States,* page 28.

267 - *The Region,* "Business Cycles and Long-Term Growth: Lessons From Minnesota," @ Terry J Fitzgerald, June 2003, page 2 (page numbers based on digital format); www.time.com/time/archive.

268 - See endnote 267, page 6.

269 - See endnote 267, page 7.

270 - See endnote 267, page 7.

271 - See endnote 267, pages 8-9.

272 - *TIME* Archive, "Minnesota: A State That Works," 8/13/1973, page 8 (page numbers based on digital format).

273 - MINNPOST, "'Spendy Wendy' and the 1970 gubernatorial election," @ Iric Nathanson, 10/27/2010, page 3.

274 - See endnote 273, page 4.

275 - Bureau of Economic Analysis: Regional Economic Accounts - BEARFACTS 1969-1979 - Minnesota: Per Capita Personal Income; www.bea.gov/bea/regional/bearfacts/stateaction.cfm; and BEARFACTS 1993-2003 - Minnesota: PCPI; www.gov/bea/regional/bearfacts/stateaction.cfm.

276 - "New Formulas for Revenue Sharing in Minnesota," *Citizens League Report*, William J. Hempel, Chair, September 1, 1970, page 31.

277 - See endnote 228.

278 - See endnote 227, page 29.

279 - See endnote 278.

280 - See endnote 231.

281 - See endnote 12: *The New Industrial State*, pages 69, 71-82.

282 - *Alexander Hamilton*, Broadus Mitchell, Barnes & Noble, Inc., New York, 1999, page 219.

283 - See endnote 227, page 30.

284 - See endnote 227, page 30.

285 - The previously cited work by David J. Linden, *The Accidental Mind*, provides important insights into our predisposition for these automatic mental formulations. They will be discussed later in the essay.

286 - The point here is that an important tactic of Goebbels propaganda machine was repetition. Repetition of the 'big lie' was essential to its acceptance. There is not a great deal of difference between that and the importance for today's political candidates to 'stay on message' - especially when that message is a carefully contrived slice of reality.

287 - See endnote 118.

288 - *The Little Book of Scientific Principles*, Surendra Verma, Metro Books (by arrangement with New Holland Publishers), 122 Fifth Avenue, New York, NY 10011, 2005, page 40.

289 - See endnotes 19 and 20. No doubt the reader has noticed that the size of GDP has shifted from fourteen to fifteen trillion dollars at different stages of our discussion. This shift reflects the chronological focus of the discussion: whether that be on the period 2008-09 or 2011-12.

289a - See endnote 19. See also "Table B-4. Percent changes in real gross domestic product, 1959-2008," *Economic Report of the President, 2009.*

289b - While the face value of the stimulus does not appear to be that much less than the gross GDP shortfall, these numbers pale in comparison with the wealth destruction of $51.7 trillion, as detailed on pages 5, 46-47. Nor do these GDP contractions accurately reflect the long-term systemic handicap imposed on the economy by the foreclosure crisis as detailed in the Credit Suisse analysis of 3/12/2007 (as discussed on pages 40-42). In short, the GDP contraction of April 2008-March 2009 does not come close to describing the enormous damage done to the economy during the Great Recession. This explains why reputable economists were calling for increased stimulus as the initial recovery failed to accelerate beyond a slow, but steady pace.

290 - See endnote 20.

291 - See endnote 20.

292 - See endnote 64.

293 - See endnote 64a.

294 - "The Job Impact of the American Recovery and Reinvestment Plan", January 9, 2009, Christina Romer, Chair Designate CEA, and Jared Bernstein, Office of the Vice President-elect;whitehouse.gov.

295 - See endnotes 19 and 20.

296 - See endnote 294.

297 - GDP data is collected on an annual basis - not fiscal.

298 - See endnotes 19 and 20.

299 - "Economic Report of the President 2012;" Table B-4. Percent changes in real gross domestic product, 1963-2011.

300 - See endnote 5.

301 - See endnote 227, page 30.

302 - See endnote 25, page 47.

303 - "Global forecast deflates market;" (Associated Press) *Pioneer Press*, 6/23/09, page 11A.

304 - See endnote 303.

305 - Comcast.net - "Ring in the new year? The party's over for automakers;" 1/11/09.

306 - "Is GM Worth Saving?" @ Bill Saporito, *Time*, 11/14/2008, page 35.

307 - "White House Open to Using Bailout Money to Aid Detroit," nytimes.com, 12/13/2008.

308 - "Bush Approves 17.4 Billion Auto Bailout," nytimes.com 12/20/2008.

309 - See endnote 306; see also: "Japanese automakers say their fate is tied to that of the Big 3;" @ Yuri Kageyama (Associated Press), *Pioneer Press*, 12/16/2008, page 17A; "Big 3 failure would signal disaster for auto suppliers;" @ Bill Vlasic and Leslie Wayne (*New York Times*), TwinCities.com(*Pioneer Press*), 12/12/2008.

310 - "Let Detroit Go Bankrupt;" @ Mitt Romney, www.nytimes.com/ 2008/ 11/19/opinion. To be fair, the headline was written by *The New York Times*. However, as his lead paragraph shows, it did not distort the gist of Romney's op/ed piece: "If General Motors, Ford and Chrysler get the bailout that their chief executives asked for on Tuesday, you can kiss the American automotive industry goodbye. It won't go overnight, but its demise will be virtually guaranteed." See also: "Having Opposed Auto Bailout, Romney Now Takes Credit for Rebound;" @ Ashley Parker, http://thecaucus.blogs.nytimes.com /2012/05/08/having-opposed-auto...

311 - See endnote 309; see also endnote 308: Bush warned that: "In the midst of a financial crisis and a recession, allowing the U.S. auto industry to collapse is not a responsible course of action."

312 - See endnote 299.

313 - See endnote 299.

314 - See endnote 307.

315 - See endnote 309: "Japanese automakers say..." and "Big 3 failure would signal..."

316 - See endnote 309, "Big 3 failure would signal..."

317 - See endnote 309, "Big 3 failure would signal..."

318 - "GM admits it's close to Ch. 11; Auditors raise questions about firm's viability;" @ Tom Krisher (Associated Press), *Pioneer Press*, 3/6/2009, page 1C.

319 - "Tough all over" (Associated Press), *Pioneer Press*, 12/23/2008, page 15A.

320 -"Hitting Bottom?" @ Tom Krisher (Associated Press), *Pioneer Press*, 4/2/09, page 1C.

321 - "GM chief is forced out; more aid for automakers; Obama to unveil plan today; short-term help will require GM, Chrysler restructuring;" @ Ken Thomas (Associated Press), *Pioneer Press*, 3/30/2009, page 1A.

322 - "Obama takes the wheel, but this road has no map; President enters uncharted territory in hopes of reviving GM, Chrysler;" @ David E. Sanger (*New York Times*), *Pioneer Press*, 3/31/2009, page 1A.

323 - See endnote 321.

324 - See endnote 322.

325 - See endnote 310.

326 - See endnote 309: "Japanese automakers say..." and "Big 3 failure would signal..."

327 - "Romney takes debate to Obama over economy, health care," @ Tim Cohen, 10/4/12; www.cnn.com/2012/10/03/politics/debate.

328 - "Romney Maintains Economic Edge Heading Into Debates," @ Jeffrey M. Jones, 10/03/12; www.gallup.com/poll/157826/romney-maintains...; see also endnotes 11 and 118.

329 - Supply-side economics actually has three basic iterations. The first is the traditional one put forward by its originator, Jean Baptiste Say, who stated that supply creates its own demand. Nearly 150 years later supply-side economics took on its more expansive iterations: that lowering tax rates can offset - either completely or partially - losses in tax revenue by stimulating economic growth.

330 - "How Supply-Side Economics Trickled Down," @ Bruce Bartlett, 04/06/2007; www.nytimes.com/2007/04/06/opinion/06Bartlett.

331 -"The Supply-Siders Respond," @ Robert D. Hershey Jr.; www.nytimes.com/1981/11/16/business /the-supply-siders-respond.

332 "A Political Comeback: Supply-Side Economics," @ Louis Uchitelle, 03/26/2008; www.nytimes.com/ 2008/03/26/business/26supply.

333 - See endnote 330.

334 - See endnote 330.

335 - "Brazil Is World's Ethanol Superpower," @ Alan Clendenning, www.cbsnews.com/stories /2006/03/13/tech/printable1394254; see also: "In Brazil, The Driving Is Sweeter," @ Trish Regan, www.cbsnews.com/stories/ 2006/03/29/eveningnews/printable1454612.

336 - See endnote 335: "In Brazil, The Driving Is...; " See also: "Brazil forecasts record ethanol output," *Pioneer Press*, 5/5/2007, Page 2C.

337 - The price of oil reached a record high of $147.27 on July 11, 2008. See: "Oil prices keep declining, reflecting drop in demand," (Associated Press) *Pioneer Press*, 7/26/2008, page 2C; "$113-barrel oil a three-month low," @ Madlen Read (Associated Press), *Pioneer Press*, 8/13/2008, page 3C.

338 - Commuting costs were not widely linked to the collapse of housing values, probably because they were not the prime mover of the housing bubble. However, comparatively cheap oil was associated with the rise of the housing boom. It did facilitate the expansion of housing developments beyond the suburbs into the exurbs. Rising oil prices, combined with lenient fuel efficiency standards and heavy marketing of inefficient sport utility vehicles, eventually helped pull the rug out from under the shaky foundations of these exurban developments. In turn this created a glut of unsold properties, undercutting those upward spiraling increases in housing prices on which the housing balloon depended. Edward Lotterman was one of the few observers to make this connection - even well before the major surge in oil prices in the spring and summer of 2008: "Home values linked to commuting costs," @ Edward Lotterman, *Pioneer Press*, 1/3/2008, page 1C.

339 - See endnote 336: "Brazil forecasts record..."

340 - www.thisnation.com/library/sotu/1987rr.html.

341 - See endnote 330.

342 - "Back in Business; Supply-Side Economists Regain Influence Under Bush," @ David Leonhardt, 4/10/2001; www.nytimes.com/2001/04/10/business/back-in-business...

343 - www.taxpolicycenter.org/taxtopics/romney-plan; this is a detailed analysis taking into consideration all nine tax proposals of the Romney plan and clearly stating the assumptions underlying their conclusions.

344 - *The New York Times Almanac 2011*, ed. @ John W. Wright, Penguin Group, 375 Hudson Street, New York, NY 10014, 2010, page 163. Non-defense discretionary spending for 2010 was $694.1B, the one year share of a $4.8T tax cut would be $480B ($480B/694.1B = 69%).

345 - See endnotes 11, 118 and 328.

346 - See endnote 343.

347 - See endnote 330.

348 - See endnote 332.

349 - See endnote 342.

350 - See endnote 342.

351 - "Why Obama Must Go," @ Niall Ferguson, *Newsweek*, August 27, 2012, pages 21-25.

352 - See endnote 351, page 22.

353 - See endnote 19.

354 - See endnote 20.

355 - See endnote 351, page 22.

356 - Economic Report(s) of the President 2009 (and 2010), Table(s) B-36. Unemployment by sex and age, 1960-2008 (and 1962-2009)

357 - See endnote 356. See also "Economic Report of the President 2011, Table B-36. Unemployment by sex and age, 1964-2010."

358 - "Compromise stimulus plan falls short of its main targets," @ Kevin G. Hall (McClatchy Newspapers), *Pioneer Press*, 2/13/2009, page 1A.

359 - "Obama has low numbers, but Bush's were lower," @ Floyd Norris (*New York Times*), *Pioneer Press*, 9/15/2012, page 11A.

360 - See endnote 351, page 25.

361 - See endnote 351, page 25.

362 - See endnote 351, pages 22, 24.

363 - See endnote 351, page 24.

364 - "Boehner drops 'go big' tactic to reduce debt," @ Paul Kane and Lori Montgomery (*Washington Post*), *Pioneer Press*, 7/10/2011, page 4A. See also: "Conservative ire threatens Boehner plan," @ Charles Babington (Associated Press), *Pioneer Press*, 7/27/2011, page 4A.

365 - See endnote 363.

366 - See endnote 351, page 25.

367 - See endnote 196; page 157.

368 - See endnote 9: *The Wealth of Nations*, pages 382-83.

368a - See endnote 368.

369 - www.usatoday.com/tech/science/2005-10-10-evolution-debate-centerpiece (this poll was a cooperative effort of USA Today, CNN and Gallup Poll).

370 - "Poll: Majority Reject Evolution;" www.cbsnews.com/stories/2005/10/22/opinion/polls.

371 - *Interpretations of Poetry and Religion*, George Santayana, Harper Torchbooks, Harper and Brothers, New York, NY 1957, pages 91-2.

372 - See endnote 371, page 98; see also page 108, wherein Santayana links Christianity's moral significance, along with its two thousand year history, to

Darwinian theory: "In Darwinian language, moral significance has been a spontaneous variation of superstition, and this variation has insured its survival as a religion." Needless-to-say, this adds a fascinating wrinkle to our earlier discussion of the hypothetical neuro-cultural foundations of humanity's more deeply held belief systems.

373 - See endnote 371, page 116.

374 - See endnote 74, page 339.

375 - *A History Of The Modern World,* R.R. Palmer and Joel Colton, Alfred A. Knopf, Inc., New York, 1961, page 104.

376 - "G.E.'s Strategies Let It Avoid Taxes Altogether," @ David Kocieniewski, 3/24/2011; www.nytimes.com/2011/03/25/business/ economy. See also: "What The Top Companies Pay In Taxes," @ Christopher Helman, *Forbes,* 4/3/2011; www.forbes.com/2011/04/13/ge-exxon-walmart-apple-business-washington-corporate. "The truth about GE's tax bill," @ Allan Sloan (*Fortune*) and Jeff Garth (*ProPublica*), 4/4/2011; http://features.blogs.fortune.cnn.com/2011/04/04/the-truth-about-ges-tax-bill. The first two sources present conflicting views, while the latter presents a middle road. The upshot, though, is that tax avoidance is a highly competitive pursuit in the murky waters of global commerce and the halls of Congress.

377 - "Trends in Federal Tax Revenues and Rates," Congressional Budget Office, 12/2/2010, page 1; www.cbo.gov/publications/ 21938.

378 - "Are Taxes in the U.S. High or Low?" Bruce Bartlett, *The New York Times,* 5/31/2011; economix.blogs.nytimes.com/20

INDEX

within auto industry, support for bailout by competitor companies: pages 174, 178; Republican opposition to auto bailout: pages 177-78; strategic importance of auto industry: pages 177-78.

Bachmann, Michele: pages 60-64, 178, 211, 214.

Bear Stearns: pages 47, 106.

Brazil; as a leader in research and development of sugar-based ethanol: pages 182-83, 239.

Bretton Woods Agreement: pages 54-60.

Brzezinski, Zbigniew: page 23.

Buffet, Warren: pages 4, 101-02, 112-13, 118-19; his experience with financial derivatives: pages 102-03, 112-13, 118-19.

Bush, George H.W: pages 31, 32, 34, 47, 185-86, 221; tax increases: **pages 185-86.**

Bush, George W: pages 1, 13-14, 16, 28, 30-32, 34, 38, 60, 61-63, 98, 110, 112, 154, 172, 180-81, 184, 187-88, 205, 207, 208; his flawed war strategy: pages 13-15, 205-06; tax cuts: pages 1, 180-81, 184, 224, 233, 237, 240.

Capital, fixed: pages 4, 7-9; society's fixed capital: pages 4, 7-9; 190-93, 199, 218-19; human capital as fixed capital: pages 4-12, 15-16, 142, 158-62, 189-93, 218-19.

Capital: pages 4-8, 10-12, 15-17, 20, 43-44, 46, 49-50, 76, 82-83, 96, 98-101, 111-12, 119-23, 127, 131-32, 135, 139, 144, 148, 159, 162, 177, 187, 190-93, 198-99, 201-02, 207, 213, 218, 227; capital glut: pages 43-44, 98-99; human capital: pages 4-7, 10-12, 15-16, 96, 99, 101, 135, 139, 144, 159, 162, 190, 193, 201-02; human capital as fixed capital: pages 4-12, 15-16, 142, 158-62, 189-93, 218-19; social capital: page 16.

Chamber of Commerce; support for stimulus (ARRA) act: page 187.

CHARTS: Chart 1, Gross Federal Debt @ Admin 1982-2009: page 27; Chart 2, Federal Debt As % GDP @ Admin 1982-2009: page 31; Chart 3, Gross Federal Debt @ Billions @ Admin 1946-2009: page 32; Chart 3A, Federal Debt As %

GDP @ Admin 1946-2009: page 33; Chart 4, GDP 1960-2010 Current Dollars: page 35; Chart 4A, $500 @ Compound Interest of 2%, 3%, 12%: page 36; Chart 5, Quarterly GDP % Change 2007-2011q2: page 36; Credit Suisse ARM Reset Schedule Chart: page 41; Chart 6, % Jobless 1960-2010: page 53; Chart 6a, Monthly Jobless Increase/Decrease Jul 2007-Dec 2010: page 62; Chart 7, Average Hourly Wages 1964-2009 (Current VS 1982 Constant Dollars): page 64; Chart 7A, Analysis Missing Productivity Factor Constant Dollars 1972-2009: page 65; Chart 7B, Analysis @ Missing Productivity Factor Current Dollars 1972-2009: page 67; Chart 8, Average Hourly Wages And Health Costs 1964-2008: page 70; Chart 9, Health Costs & Household Income 1967-2009: page 71; Chart 9a, Health Costs As % Household Income (Quintiles 1-3) 1967-2009: page 72; Chart 10, U.S. Income Inequality @ Quintiles 1970-2010: page 93; Chart 10a, Income Distribution @ Quintile Aggregates 1970-2010: page 94; Chart 10B, Income Distribution As % Quintile Aggregates 1970-2010: page 95; Chart 11, Public Education Expenditures (Current and Constant 1981-84 Dollars) 1920-2005: page 131.

Christianity: 145-46, 194-97; early Christian doctrine as justification for enslaving non-Christians: page 145-46, 231.

The Citizens League; "New Formulas for Revenue Sharing in Minnesota:" pages 161-62, 235; property tax as a barrier to broad-based educational achievement: pages 161-62.

Civil War: pages 87, 135-36, 152, 229.

Class: pages 3, 77, 91, 96, 184, 100, 190, 201, 220-21; Class warfare: pages 3, 77, 91, 96-7, 184, 220-21; American attitudes toward class: pages 96, 201, 220; increasing awareness of class conflict by Americans: pages 96, 201, 220.

Clinton, William: pages 16, 31, 32-34, 48, 80, 100, 186, 220; repeal of Glass-Steagall Act in 1999: page 48; tax increases and balanced budget: pages 100, 185-86.

Collateralized debt obligations (CDO): pages 42-43, 106.

Common market; the U.S. economy as the largest: page 84.

Conduits, financial: pages 42-43, 45, 81, 206.